SPOR
EXCELLENCE

WHAT MAKES A CHAMPION?

David Hemery MBE

CollinsWillow

An Imprint of HarperCollins*Publishers*

ACKNOWLEDGEMENTS

The Author is grateful to Autosport for the photograph
of Sir John Whitmore,
and to Colorsport for all other photographs
in this book.

First published in Great Britain in 1986
as *The Pursuit of Sporting Excellence*

Revised paperback edition published in 1991 by
Collins Willow
an imprint of HarperCollins Publishers
London

A CIP catalogue for this book is available
from the British Library

ISBN 0 00 218398 6

Set in Ehrhardt by Phoenix Photosetting, Chatham, Kent
Printed and bound in Great Britain by
Mackays of Chatham PLC, Chatham, Kent

CONTENTS

Sporting Excellence

INTRODUCTION

The prompt for this book came shortly after the finish of my Olympic 400m hurdles win in Mexico. A question stuck in my mind: 'Why me?' There were individuals in that race who were stronger, faster, and more experienced, added to which I was the equal slowest on paper, going into that final. There had to be factors other than physical ability which produced the end result. This thought was extended when watching Wimbledon. I saw that virtually all the players there had the physical requirements to reach the last handful but almost always the same few came through to play for the title. What was it about them?

Later as a coach I watched some individuals who were technically and physically well prepared, underachieving in competition. And others who, with seemingly insufficient physical preparation, exceeded expectations. What caused this to happen and what could be learned from those who did fulfil their potential under pressure? Those who work to bring the best out of others will know that skill and ability alone do not ensure that an individual will become a high achiever. In fact being very gifted may actually work against a performer because he or she may believe that they don't have to work to develop themselves.

In an Olympic final there is little, physically, to choose between the performers. Each one is strong, lean, supple and gifted. All have spent years getting to this point. The problem facing their minds and bodies is that only one of them can be crowned the winner.

The scene may change and the level of media attention will differ, but almost everyone who has been involved in competitive activity will be able to identify with the feelings of these finalists. Regardless of the levels of personal achievement, the sensations will be similar: anticipation and excitement mount, apprehension increases. What will my opponents do? Will I be able to perform up to my own and others' expectations?

What do successful international performers do to hold together so well under intense competitive pressure? Is it something in their background or personality? What are they thinking about? Does it come naturally or can it be learned? The bottom line question is: what makes a winner?

I decided to interview those who were recognizably the best and see what they had in common. The criteria for the interviewees was that they had been consistent winners and had proved themselves under the most intense competitive pressure. On the sport side all are, or have been, world or Olympic champions or recognized as the best in their sport in their era. They are from more than a dozen countries and twenty-four different sports. On the business side they are well recognized as having led successfully, nationally and internationally.

Almost everyone has experienced the exhilaration of success at mastering something. For most people memories linger of having mastered riding a bike. It may also have been the sweet feeling of effortlessness as a ball left the centre of the bat, the racket or the club; or perhaps it was a perfectly thrown ball or a kick or shot which landed exactly where you intended. It may be finding just the right words at the right time to make all the difference to someone. We know the feeling when it happens. Wouldn't it be great if it could happen more often? We watch, often in awe, but certainly with respect and pleasure, those who consistently produce winning performances and we admire those who effectively lead others to success.

It is too easy to say, 'Oh, they're just naturals, they were born with the genetic gifts to do it' or, 'Oh, he or she's a born leader.' We know that that's not the whole story; it cannot be. Billy Jean King provides a good illustration. She is remembered for having won more than her fair share of Wimbledon singles and doubles titles. She was neither the most powerful, nor the fastest player, nor the best server, and certainly not the biggest, but she won consistently. What was it that enabled her, and others like her, to handle that challenge and to keep control while under pressure? What does human achievement entail?

This survey demonstrated that no two people are exactly the same. However it also showed that there are many experiences, attitudes and actions which the highest achievers do have in common, and that there are ways in which talent can be best drawn out.

I found it exciting to realize that there are so many factors which are controllable and learnable by any performer. By adapting what the winners have done to the specific needs and circumstances of your own activity it will be possible to enhance your performance or that of those whom you lead.

For the last five years my work has been the development and running of courses, for coaches and businessmen, concerned with developing potential. I believe that any individual can become an achiever. That does not mean that everyone is born with the physical characteristics to become an Olympic winner, but along the lines of the parable of the talents, each of us has talent in some area. The key is to bring the best from ourselves and those whom we lead. The question one needs to ask oneself is: do I aspire to fulfil the talent I have, whether in sport, music, art, business or any other area of human endeavour? Another question, for the leader or coach, is: am I able to help others to bring out the most from themselves?

In many cases the answers are common sense. Many will recognize that they have done similar things intuitively. They have just never had it identified or expressed before. Others will recognize how they may have been inhibiting their progress or that of others through negative expectations or through trying too hard.

Many performers experience a change in their performance when they perceive that they are under pressure. They may produce a great solo effort in practice, only to have the percentage slip disastrously in competition; or they have one great performance and can never quite recapture it. It is referred to as 'choking' or 'losing one's bottle'. The importance of the upcoming event can work on the competitor's mind and tension often mounts. One wants to avoid the embarrassment of letting oneself and other people down. Our imagination can project uncomfortable or disastrous results before the competition has even started. We may begin to dread the event, expecting disaster. Either the desire to avoid the situation altogether or the over-intense pressure to succeed often leads to the performer trying too hard or not hard enough. Natural flow and ease evaporate into struggling effort. The muscles tighten and the performance predictably falls short. However, the best performers rarely crack under intense pressure or in front of large audiences; often, they actually perform better!

What makes an individual behave in a certain way is an extremely complex issue. We are born with a genetic blueprint and we are also a product of our environment and our past experiences. Added to this is a vital element. We also have the power of self-determination, which means that we are a product of our thoughts, hopes, dreams and visions of the future. Under the belief that human beings are a combination of body, mind and spirit, the questions in this survey touched on aspects of these achievers' physical, social, mental and moral development, behaviour and beliefs. Questions were asked in any area which *might* have affected their progress and performance.

Two hundred questions were whittled down to eighty-eight. Considering the length of the interview time, and the busy lives led by most of these high achievers, their generosity and cooperation was remarkable. I am most grateful and indebted to each of them for their time and the openness of their answers. For many, their diaries are so full that appointments have to be made months in advance. For example, Jackie Stewart has his life booked up six months ahead of time. He fitted me in around a couple of commitments during a flying visit to London: the last part of the interview took place while he was being driven to his next appointment. Wayne Gretsky receives hundreds of fan letters and requests every day: his press interviews are usually ten-minute slots. It was helpful that his Edmonton press liaison man had worked as an athletics correspondent when I was running. He arranged an extended interview, tied to photographs during the session. Although Stefan Edberg lives in London, the lives of international players today mean that they live out of suitcases all over the world. It was more than three months' wait to be able to catch him passing through London for a couple of days. The businessmen were no different. Overseas or domestic travel and multiple commitments meant scheduling interviews weeks and months ahead.

I met Torvill and Dean while they were performing in Australia and we set a time and date for when they were back in the UK. My US trip was on a three-week, cheap-rate, unlimited US travel ticket. One part became quite crowded. Overnight I flew back from Los Angeles where I had interviewed Arnold Palmer during his making of a Hertz commercial, on to Rod Laver in Philadelphia, then to Billy Jean King in New York, prior to flying back to Los Angeles the same day! All credit to Billy Jean: her agent had forgotten to let her know about our appointment; she arrived for a practice session at her club, and she cancelled a dinner appointment so as to honour the commitment which had been made to me.

Most of the sports performers have agents or managers who act as buffers and go-betweens. I was prepared to meet the performer any time which was mutually convenient. I could buy them a meal and send them a copy of the book on completion but that was the limit of my budget.

Introduction

Almost all agreed to be interviewed, many not even taking up the invitation to a meal.

The least time taken was thirty-five minutes by Stephen Hendry. Jonah Barrington and Gareth Edwards topped the time chart at around four hours each. The average was about an hour. It was my intention to interview each performer's coach as well as their parents. Early on, I interviewed Carl Lewis's, Steve Cram's and my own coach and parents; Mary Rand's coach and mother; and Lynn Davies's and Steve Ovett's coaches. However when interviewing Peter Snell in the US he told me that his coach was in New Zealand; and while interviewing Al Oerter on Long Island, New York, he said that his coach and Dad would be delighted to speak with me. His coach was living in Kansas and his Dad was in Florida. Thousands of miles for each interview? Unfortunately, such a luxury wasn't possible. I would also like to have included many more sports as well as a wider cross-cultural spectrum. Time and cost loomed to make an already daunting task quite impracticable.

My Australian visit was made possible when Dr John Cheffers became the director of the Australian Institute of Sport. He and Jean Roberts, the then national director of track and field, combined to locate and facilitate a number of interviews. In exchange, I ran coaching clinics across the country culminating in a week at the magnificent Institute of Sport in Canberra. My cousin Bob Hemery was the Australian team manager for the Olympics. He assisted by contacting some athletes in his Perth area, including driving me 200 miles south into the bush to interview Shane (Gould) Innes.

A few refused interviews. Golfer, Jack Nicklaus, fast bowler, Dennis Lillee, and football manager, Kenny Dalglish, were all coming out with their own books and didn't want to hurt sales potential. Boxer Marvin Hagler and tennis star Steffi Graf, in different ways, had been going through difficult times and both were media-saturated. Sir Donald Bradman has become a recluse and will see no one. John McEnroe's father refused on John's behalf saying that John never gets involved with such interviews.

Just getting to some individuals was a major task. I arranged a trip to the Soviet Union to interview sprinter Valeriy Borzov and his wife the gymnast Ludmila Tourischeva. This I confirmed before I left Britain. When my flight from Moscow to Kiev was to be badly delayed I discovered that making an internal phone call in the USSR was even more difficult than a call from outside. Also I had no home number for Valeriy. I asked if Intourist would change my flight or if I could have the number of Aeroflot. Each time I received the same response, 'It's not possible.' Finally, on arrival in Kiev, I was informed that Ludmila was away! My interview with Valeriy took place between 10 p.m. and midnight.

My initial study of sport's high achievers came out five years ago in hardback. Since then achievement development course experience with various levels of coaches, and workers in business and industry, has helped me to clarify, confirm and expand many of the findings in my original study. At the close of each chapter I have drawn conclusions from the experiences of those who have achieved and those who have helped others to do so.

This paperback edition includes several sport achievers who have reached the top in the last five years. Another new addition is a section on team-leading. I interviewed some top names from the world of business and sport, drawing comparisons and contrasts in how leaders have gone about drawing the best from their performers. As with the top sport performers, I left each interview wondering, 'How on earth am I going to do justice to all that this individual has contributed?' Their sporting or business records are often staggering and I am most grateful that they have been prepared to share their reflections on what they have done, and their analysis of what had helped them be so successful. Their shared experiences give us all insight into the pursuit of sporting and personal excellence.

Some will see this book portraying an optimistic view of human potential and the positive role of coaching in sport and management. I make no apology for that. I do have a positive view of the potential which lies within each of us. I also have experienced the reality of setbacks, the power of negative thought and our capacity for inhibiting our potential. I chose to look at what we can achieve and what steps we may take to move towards fulfilling our potential in body, mind and spirit; and to help others to do the same.

I would like to add that I believe there is great merit in looking beyond 'winning'. That has its own rewards and I do not wish to undervalue them. However I believe we will undervalue sport and human growth if we limit our vision of sport and life to winning and losing. Learning through physical endeavour can be intense and valuable. Sport provides us with a wealth of experiences from which to learn and grow.

Introduction

A lovely vision of how sport may be used and viewed came from motor racing champion Sir John Whitmore. He said 'Sport was incredibly important to me in overcoming what the lay person would call a sort of inferiority complex, largely through having a rather dominant and successful father whom I thought I'd never be able to live up to. So finding my own identity through success in sport was incredibly important. I also think that sport is a microcosm of life. In other words you go through all the emotions of starting nowhere and getting somewhere; through highs and lows; success and failure; and all this is compressed into each season and each career. And they are all things that you are going to go through in your whole life later. So one has an opportunity to run a microcosmic movie and experience those things that you experience later. I think they're just easier things to deal with later because you've experienced them before. Now because sport is compressed in terms of time, the emotions involved are very much more intense; so life after a time in sport is actually easier because you've been there before; it's familiar territory. I've never experienced an extreme of emotion in life, in terms of highs and lows, that has been new to me. I experienced all of them in the field of sport. I feel some people go through life cushioning themselves from their emotions and I think they miss something. It is the extremes of emotion that give you your deepest experiences in life, and sport did that for me.'

1
SPECIALIZATION

'Line up please! Okay, let's see what time you all take to get once around this field. Set! Go!' The natural movement of some of the runners will be apparent to anyone who has an eye for rhythm and flow; the variety of styles and forms has to be seen to be believed. Some are simply better suited to running faster than others. It does not mean that they are any better people, but their physiological blueprint enables them to start out with a physical advantage in that particular movement. All the people in this book started out with a blueprint which enabled them to compete in their sport at top level. But there is considerable difference of opinion as to how much their natural physique made them winners. Double Olympic sprint champion Valeriy Borzov said that his innate speed was the biggest single factor in his success, whereas some top sportsmen claim that the only physical advantage they have is that they were not born with a handicapped body.

The age old question as to which is more important, nature or nurture, will not be answered fully here but there is evidence to support both points of view. One cannot underestimate the substantial abilities born into these very high achievers. However, it is apparent that a great deal more than physical gifts goes into the making of a champion. To talk of physical factors, though, is slightly misleading. No physiological tests were carried out on these top sports stars. There is little point in finding the maximum oxygen uptake capacity of a yachtsman or snooker player, or to discover the hand-eye coordination of a marathon runner. All that can be said is that they all met the normal physical requirements for performing their sport well.

At what age did you start any type of competitive sport? Most performers started competitive sports while at school; generally this was between the ages of six and thirteen with the average starting age being at around nine. The ages at which the performers 'specialized' are given in their respective biographies. Taking out Barry John and J.P.R. Williams of rugby union, and Ian Botham, the all-round cricketer, who have never, in their opinion, specialized in one sport or at least not for more than a few months in any one year, the average age is still over *sixteen*. Most of those interviewed were very happy that they had not specialized until quite late on in their sporting lives. They had fun in a variety of sports and had only started to make a push when they decided that they wanted to exclude the other options in order to see just how far they could go in their chosen speciality.

Certain sports had a definite bias towards a younger starting age. Duncan Goodhew led the swimmers in at seven years old, Chris Evert the tennis players at nine years old. (Gymnasts would also fall into this early specialization category.) The majority of achievers seem to have delayed their decision until the end of school days; for some this meant they were fifteen or sixteen years old, and for others seventeen or eighteen. Those pressing the top end were squash champion Jonah Barrington and racing driver Jackie Stewart, both not starting until they were twenty-three, although it should be pointed out that Jackie won international recognition in shooting before getting behind the wheel of a car. At the extreme end is Pat O'Callaghan who decided to specialize at the age of twenty-six after he had won his second Olympic hammer title in 1932. His aim was the 1936 Games but unfortunately Ireland did not compete!

Were you always good at sport? It seems that several of these achievers were, or could have been, highly successful in other areas of sport. The rugby men Gareth Edwards and Barry John were offered trials with good football clubs, and J.P.R. Williams won junior Wimbledon when he was nineteen. With almost no exception, these achievers played a variety of sports. Olympic track athlete Peter Snell recalled that at school he played in the top rugby and cricket teams. 'I was tennis champion. I was a 12-handicap at golf. I had a good background at field hockey, and played badminton and table tennis. I did gymnastics and, when running schools steeplechase, I usually won.' Peter was a winner in International Superstars. Marathon runner Joan Benoit Samuelson was a state skier, and ice hockey scoring star Wayne Gretzky was the Ontario schools champion at eleven years old in 800m, 1500m and cross-country. Heather McKay, multiple world squash champion, started out as the local tennis champion and a member of the local softball team, and was twice named to the All-Australian hockey team; and she became world racketball champion following her exceptional squash career.

Specialization

Obviously these are extreme examples. However, most of those in the study were above average in all the sports in which they participated. Many who are now at the top in individual sports enjoyed team sport at a reasonably high level. Track athletes Carl Lewis, Lynn Davies, Daley Thompson, Seb Coe, Steve Cram and Steve Ovett were all good at soccer. The list could be very much more extensive, pointing out the variety of sports in which every one has competed, but the main point of interest is that there was opportunity for a diversity of sports. One hopes that the trend in Great Britain and the United States to allow sport and physical education to receive less time and funding will not result in a loss of opportunity for the young; not just for sport's sake, but for reasons of personal growth and as an educational tool.

A definite pattern emerged in the development phase of sport in the lives of these high achievers. The first step was that they were introduced to sport as fun and that it was enjoyed for its own sake. Often the games were created to suit the environment. For example, Gareth Edwards talked of using a local lane for his own England v West Indies cricket match, where the placement of the ball over walls and past certain trees had special scoring significance. Lynn Davies and his friends had challenges as to who could jump the stream furthest down the valley where it gradually became wider. The games usually had a competitive element whether they were soccer, basketball or whatever, but they were informal teams and the children enjoyed themselves so much that they would stay out until darkness forced them home. The second step in their development was the introduction of fundamental skills. Quite often these fundamentals were introduced by a parent or a school teacher, but it was done in a clear-cut manner without pressure. The basics of good sound technique were invaluable because, under pressure, people tend to revert to what is their own natural, fundamental way of doing things.

The third and final step was the introduction of 'pushing'. More will be said about this later, but in almost all cases, the push did not come from the parents; it came from within the individual and in several cases it was assisted by a coach after the individual had made the commitment.

Summary of learning points:
- Introduce your youngsters to a variety of sports.

- They don't have to specialize too early.
- Make sure sport is enjoyable; introduce the fundamentals; let the youngsters have the final decision to push themselves. (Without these three, children will quit long before their potential is fulfilled.)

2
TRAINING AND DURABILITY

In many cases, the time spent in training did not alter significantly from the start of specialization right up to top level. Olympic swimmer Shane Innes was training seriously from the age of thirteen with nine or ten sessions per week. The aspect which changed for her and most athletes over the years was the level of intensity. The rugby players I interviewed rarely practised more than three times per week from club to international level unless they were on tour. This has changed for today's top players. Fitness has become a far greater priority of the international game. Then and now there was a gradual recognition of the requirements to make it to the top. It is like stepping stones with each performer taking the first step, and doing what was needed to reach the next one.

The total time commitment varied considerably for each sport. For a top distance runner, an hour at either end of the day may well mean covering over twenty miles, and if more miles are then thrown in, the body simply will not recover in time to do the same distance on the following day. It may seem astonishing, but often the time commitment did not change whether the individual was working, studying or playing sport full-time. Obviously there were some who endured extensive hardships such as the swimmers, who had to get up in the middle of the night to start swimming in order to get the required practice hours in before school or work. In the case of ice dance champions Torvill and Dean, it was the restriction of the available time on ice in Great Britain which inhibited the hours put in. They were limited to a maximum of six hours per week and those were either after 11 p.m. or before 6 a.m.! On these limited hours, the duo reached fourth in the world and came fifth at the Olympics. They were subsequently granted the opportunity to train overseas which enabled them to spend six hours on the ice every day. Perfect scores of 6.0, gold medals and a new standard of excellence were the ultimate result. Turning professional provided the pair with the opportunity to extend even further the creativity within their performances.

A total daily devotion to training was part of the routine for both Daley Thompson in his decathlon training, and Jonah Barrington in his squash practice. The biggest difference was that Daley made training enjoyable by fitting his programme around the available training partners who came to the track for a part of the day, to do their single event.

How often do you give 100 per cent in training? Jonah's response to this was that he gave it too often. 'Training was pretty haphazard. I didn't know about half-effort and three-quarters effort. I was putting in too many long sessions back-to-back. I called them total reduction sessions. I would start again far too close to eating, and feel ill and get a cold sweat which would disappear after forty-five minutes. I would crawl through day after day and was terribly lucky not to have more injuries. So little knowledge was available. Nobody stretched or warmed up before they played.'

More than half of those interviewed felt that they gave 100 per cent every time they went out. That effort was sometimes expressed solely in terms of mental concentration. However more often it meant that at some point, if not in the whole session, they were giving their all both physically and mentally. Heather McKay said that she would rather do one hour at 100 per cent and be finished than stay on court for an hour and a half and give only 75 per cent. The old adage 'as you train so will you compete' seems to be borne out here. Additionally, the volume of training always exceeded the competition time. After very intense training, Heather often said if she ever felt like that in a match, she would give up the sport. But once in the match, she would say to herself, 'Come on, if you are tired, the other person has to be just as tired and that is when I would push and that extra little bit of training would pay off.'

The notion that it takes hard work to improve one's standard was accepted by all the athletes. Rugby league's Peter Sterling said, 'The only thing that makes you successful is hard work as there are always going to be others with similar ability. The only thing that is going to make you more successful is the amount of work you put in.' Twice Grand Slam winner Rod Laver believed that the reason he was able to go successfully through any five-set tennis match was the intensity of his practice. He would go full out for three to four hours on court, enjoying the effort, and not just playing sets but rallying two-against-one.

Another reason for giving 100 per cent to their sport came from Ian Botham and Clive Lloyd in cricket, and Billy Beaumont in rugby union. Each felt that their role as captain demanded setting an example. Clive had turned around the thinking in the West Indies team and with it came a new determination to succeed. 'In the old days, when under pressure, we were seen to be unable to fight our way out of it. I saw that if you were physically fit, it helped you to think straighter. It meant that your mind and body were alert and that to me was the most important thing in being a top class sportsman.'

It was interesting to find that some of today's top runners do not train to 100 per cent. Sprint-king and long jumper Carl Lewis said that he would give 100 per cent on starts and jumping but not running. Middle-distance star Seb Coe would give it his all in conditioning sessions, but again, not in running. The same was echoed by world 1500m champion Steve Cram. Steve Ovett, 800m Olympic champion, world marathon champion Rob de Castella and Ed Moses, Olympic 400m hurdles champion, said that they hardly ever gave 100 per cent in their training sessions. Peter Snell, another Olympic middle-distance winner, pointed out that it was not always appropriate: with multiple repetitions and steady long hard runs, the work load could be enormous and it was important not to get to a state of complete depletion with the resulting risk of injury or sickness.

There were several exceptions to this track rule. Herb Elliott, unbeaten over a mile, pushed himself to the limit on four to six days each week. Joan Benoit Samuelson pushes herself to the limit on one of her two daily sessions. Long jumper Lynn Davies was one of the majority who replied 'most of the time'. Obviously, those who did not push themselves to 100 per cent in training did not see this factor as being necessary. Steve Ovett's view was that consistency was better than quality. On a long run, feeling a bit tired, there would be the option to stay on the flat or go up a hill. He would go up the hill, 'and it would hurt but it wouldn't be 100 per cent flat out. You have to endure a bit of pain in training for our sport. It's not the name of the game, but to a certain extent it's an acceptance of pain. It doesn't have to be severe, it can be gradual.' This is not masochism where one is seeking pain, rather it is an understanding that it is productive pain. The body is being positively modified in its strength and efficiency.

How much do you think that your training intensity made a difference to your level of success? The words differed but the answer was virtually unanimous. 'All the difference'; 'totally'; 'enormously'; 'terribly'; 'vital'; 'tremendously important'; 'it was the root of everything'. It is worth noting here that the body, mind and spirit are an integrated whole. By intensity they were usually referring to pushing themselves physically, but that comes from mental toughness. Lynn Davies pointed out that the mind has a significant part in setting sights and tolerating the level of training and stress. He recalled the story of the small woman who lifted the side of a car when her child was trapped underneath. That is a perfect example of an emergency creating a personal alignment of thought (absolute clarity of what must be done), feeling (total enthusiasm to do it) and will (complete commitment and intention to act) all put into one single action. Many of our limits are self-imposed. We are neither single-minded nor absolutely clear of our action plan, our enthusiasm for doing the work is not 100 per cent and our commitment can waver. Is it unexpected that we don't create our best? It is worth asking ourselves, what would we have to do to be more clear, more enthusiastic and more committed?

Duncan Goodhew believes that an athlete is only as good as his worst day. Two to three days each week he would not be feeling up to par and those were the days that he would push himself. 'I found that 95 per cent of the time it was psychological. I would get in and forty-five minutes or an hour later, I was knocking out amazing times. I was doing broken competition distance, with five seconds' rest every 50m. I would come in with uncontrollable shakes and still maintain the times on each 50m. My body was actually shuddering with the strain and I used to take it to that point two to three times each week.'

Heather McKay summed up the overall view by pointing out that to succeed, anyone would have to go out and make the commitment whether it was in sport, work, school or marriage. If you only give 40 per cent, then you cannot expect a 100 per cent return.

I talked to the performers about the type of sessions which would take them to their hands and knees, and their level of acceptable pain tolerance. Billy Beaumont's immediate response was, 'Ah! Hanging over the rail! I think you have to do that.'

Herb Elliott explained, 'In retrospect my training wasn't to improve my physical strength or stamina; those came along as a secondary result, but the primary purpose of every training session was to toughen up mentally. A training session was totally useless until it started to hurt. That was the point when it started to be worthwhile.' Steeplechaser Mark Rowland said that at practices Steve Ovett often quotes the line, 'It's only pain!' Track athletes usually laugh at the apparent absurdity of voluntarily pushing themselves into that area. Many performers back off from the experience long before they have to.

Some top performers prefer not to use the term pain; they would rather see it more as a willingness to push oneself and that being both a mental and a physical exercise. Sometimes a coach will attempt to deflect an athlete's complaints about tired legs, for example, by replying, 'Well that's fine as long as your chest is okay.' Later in the session a comment about burning lungs could bring the reply, 'How are the legs, fine?' There was an instance of this sort of approach in a session I had with my coach Billy Smith when I was studying in Boston. My legs were painfully tired and I told Billy that they hurt. Billy put his hand on his own leg and said, 'I can't feel a thing, let's get on with the next repetition.' For this sort of remark to work a high degree of mutual trust and respect must exist. The remark would be heartless if the coach didn't know the performer. My reaction was firstly to question how bad my legs really felt. Secondly I accepted his challenge, inwardly saying 'I'll show him I can run even with dead legs.' Others could need more reassurance and a different approach. The coach–athlete relationship under intensity is finely tuned.

Usually the performer's complaints when under stress are an attempt to share the discomfort. Coaches must find a way of acknowledging that they've heard, without giving an easy out. Often the performer is not looking for that; they actually want reassurance or the added push. However caution is needed here as the coach must not hold or push the performer to a training task which will lead to sickness, injury or depression. A high degree of empathy, awareness and intuition are required.

Gareth Edwards pointed out that in a physical game like rugby, a player may be carrying an injury or may have been hit and be dazed, feeling physically and emotionally drained. This is the time when you have to be emotionally stronger-willed, to maintain and hang on when it's hurting. One key is not to be afraid of pain. Many top performers will simply acknowledge that the pain exists and put their attention on the area, experiencing the discomfort, and recognizing that it is quite bearable. One useful tool is to rate the discomfort on a one-to-ten scale. In that way the increase or decrease can be monitored. It is certainly more bearable when it's quantified, than it is when a performer simply repeats that it hurts. Ian Botham believes that one can or cannot deal with pain, but being able to cope with it distinguishes the top sportsman from the good sportsman.

In many cases, it was the blood, sweat and tears given by these top achievers which made them individual record breakers; they chose to make such efforts and it was done once they had reached maturity. Peter Snell reckoned that a top athlete could only push hard at the international level for about six years. It would be a waste if a youngster was encouraged to push like this and left sport with a feeling of distaste rather than a sense of accomplishment.

Sir John Whitmore said, 'I didn't consciously choose to endure pain. I just did whatever it took to achieve and I realized afterwards that I'd shredded myself sometimes. I'd just been so focused I didn't feel the pain. I once got out of a car and saw that I'd ripped the hands out of my gloves and my hands were bleeding, and I hadn't felt that at the time.' The combination of psychological and physical pain came during a race in which the car John was driving had a fault in the construction of the fuel cells, which caused them to split under the strain of the racing. 'For four hours of this twelve-hour race I was sitting in a pool of petrol, which is extremely painful. You only have to be sitting in petrol for ten minutes and your skin starts to peel off. The discomfort was brought to my attention particularly, by a similar car to mine going off in front of me, in the race. It appeared to be quite a minor accident but the car exploded and I realized that the reason it had exploded was that the car was a tub full of petrol and I was in a similar position. So I realized that a fairly minor accident in my condition would have created that kind of problem. It did affect me for about a lap.' On further questioning John said that the petrol burns meant that he was not able to sit down for several days!

In spite of the need for intensity, it must be remembered that these performers are enjoying what they are doing. It is their choice to push themselves. A memorable line which illustrates the level of enjoyment attached to his sport participation came from four-time Olympic discus winner Al Oerter who sees training as an integral part of his life. 'I make sure that I work out every day. Anything else good that happens, that's gravy.'

Until what age can one stay at the top? Young Tour de France cyclists are being pushed exceptionally hard while still in their teens and at a crucial stage in bone development. Concern about this and equivalent practices in other high-stress sports has been expressed by many medical practitioners, either in endurance, such as ultra long-distance running; or intensity, such as weight-lifting; or hyper-extension, as in back extension in gymnastics. A number of serious and permanent injuries have occurred in each area. Information on the implications of health and injury prevention can be acquired from the British National Coaching Foundation. The question of the natural process of the ageing of the body was raised by soccer captain Bryan Robson. He said that he had always had the will to train hard and was a glutton for punishment. He had never been one to pack it in when it started to hurt. Most of these performers were prepared to stick it out and, in a sense, discover that the discomfort was not quite as bad as they had first feared or thought, or at least that it was quite possible to learn how to cope with it. Bryan went on to relate that at the end of a practice session when they were quite tired, they sometimes had a timed run, twice around the field. He would try to see if he could beat the times he had done when younger. When others pointed out that as you get older the legs go, Bryan enjoyed proving that with age one can improve strength and endurance.

One of the classic examples of durability is Al Oerter who was challenging for another Olympic discus place in 1984, having won the first of his four successive Olympic titles in 1956. At fifty years old, Reg Harris came out of retirement and won yet another world sprint cycle title. Billie Jean King said that she was still not sure whether it was because women's tennis standards were not that high, allowing her to be ranked sixth at thirty-seven, or whether she should reassess the fact that one still can play well longer than was thought possible a few years ago. It is probably the latter. The peak of our physical achievements seems to be related quite substantially to environmental and social factors, such as getting a job and starting a family. With greater sponsorship of amateur and professional sportsmen and sportswomen, it will be interesting to see whether top performances are maintained into what previously would have been considered 'old' for a top class performer. Certainly in track and field athletics, the world records established by Jamila Kratochvilova in 400m and 800m at thirty-one, and the marathon world best by Carlos Lopes at thirty-eight, suggest that the college and university representatives of the last generation were several years short of their ultimate best performances. It underlines the need to allow youngsters to enjoy a variety of sports for as long as possible, having the fundamentals of several sports given them when young with continuing opportunities to play and compete after school days.

Summary of learning points:

- Top performers have a gradual step-by-step approach to increased training intensity.
- As you train so will you compete. You need to practise the way you intend to perform in competition.
- There is no substitute for hard work.
- Intensity is needed during at least part of training and, obviously, during competition.
- Personal alignment of thought, feeling, and will, into action, produces individual peak performance.
- Commitment to consistency of practice is vital.
- Pain tolerance is the choice of the performer. Experiencing it and grading its intensity on a 1–10 scale can benefit in several ways.
- Prime performance may be sustained to a far greater age than was believed in the recent past.
- Our limitations are often self-imposed.

3
FITNESS AND DIET

Another area which has changed considerably during the last decade is the awareness that what you eat can seriously affect performance. Seven of those interviewed were now on a high carbohydrate diet with no red meat.

Quite surprisingly, most said that they never gave their diet much thought, it was just 'Mum's home cooking'. When asked if they thought it was a balanced diet, they said yes. In most cases it included meat and/or fish and/or poultry, green vegetables and potatoes, and fruit. Several of the track athletes claimed to be junk food addicts. Daley Thompson said that he gave up so much in so many other areas that he could not face giving up his McDonald's diet, which he really enjoys. Similarly, Steve Cram is addicted to fish and chips.

Many laymen are now aware of the difficulty the body has in digesting meat. For those in endurance events which last for a couple of hours, pasta and other high carbohydrate foods were the preferred pre-competition diet. This provides glycogen, the body's glucose, which is readily available as energy for the muscles.

There has been a general move away from the commercial interest areas of high fat, high sugar, high salt, and low fibre, back to fresh fruit, fresh vegetables and no red meat. This is the enlightened view but it was surprising just how many referred to the fact that, as training increased, so did their apparent need for chocolate or similar sugary items. Obviously there is a need for a fast-burning energy source and the quick fix of chocolate or sugary items was a popular remedy. The main problem with this solution is that it can produce a roller-coaster effect as the blood sugar level rises quickly then drops, with resulting craving for another sugar fix! Carbohydrates break down more slowly in the body, providing a more constant source of glycogen.

Thirty years ago, Herb Elliott was in the media's spotlight for living on nuts and raisins. In fact, he was on a balanced diet, his breakfast was a mixture of nuts, raisins and rolled oats, which today is commonly known as muesli!

Not many performers were taking multi-vitamins pills, but one person who did say he occasionally took them was Lester Piggott. As a large-framed jockey, he had to limit himself to one main meal a day. He did not go very long without food but never ate much. When I asked him whether his sport had forced him to lead an imbalanced life, he replied, 'Well, it has really, yes. The biggest thing is not eating; I've had to be careful for so long.' I did some mental arithmetic and realized for just how long: Lester had not allowed himself to eat a proper meal for thirty-four years. That was five years ago and Lester is now back as successful as ever, not only demonstrating that premature ageing is in the mind, but extending his years of self-control. Although Lester is an extreme case, Ed Moses believes that we all eat far too much food and, on several occasions, he has continued training hard while fasting.

How did these top performers 'read' their bodies? This question was attempting to ascertain whether performers could sense when they had become depleted and notice that they should back down a little to retain health. Pushing when drained will usually result in sickness and/or injury. One or two gave it no thought, Billy Beaumont saying, 'I'm not bothered, I just get stuck in.' Another five per cent felt that their assessment was better further on in their careers. Another couple did not feel they were very good at assessing themselves, Duncan Goodhew saying that he found it difficult, while J.P.R. Williams thought he competed too often, 'The day after an international I'd be out playing flat out in a full game, in a different position, but that's just me.'

All the rest said that they could read their bodies very well. Steve Ovett said, 'I didn't in L.A. [during the 1984 Olympics], but normally I do perfectly. It's part of the tools of the trade, of being honest with yourself and respecting your body.' Snooker champion Steve Davis referred to his high degree of sensitivity. 'I do a lot of practice on my own and I can detect a fault in myself quicker that way. I'm one of the few players who can detect a fault without having someone to tell them.' The same ability is held by his successor as world champion, Stephen Hendry. This underlines the fact that a high degree of body awareness will enhance performance. Sir John Whitmore says the same from what he takes in through the car seat. 'Your whole body is used as an instrument of feedback of what the car is doing.'

Tennis player John Newcombe gave an illustration of body awareness during a Wimbledon final against Stan Smith in 1971. 'I won the first set and it was four all in the second, when I dived for a ball at the net, landed on my gut and blew the wind right out of myself. We went on to five all, then he beat me 7–5. At 4–2 to him in the third, I suddenly realized that my energy level was very low. My first thought was panic. Then I realized that after the fall, I hadn't spent any time recovering, so I thought to myself, "I've got about ten minutes before I've lost this set so I've got about ten minutes to get myself back again." So I just spent ten minutes trying to get inside myself, taking deep breaths and relaxing and summoning the adrenalin to go again. I lost the third set 6–2. I didn't lose a point on my serve in the fourth until I was serving for the set.' John went on to win in the fifth and final set. He said, 'It's funny hearing the other guy's story. Stan thought at two sets to one, he lost concentration because he started thinking of his victory speech, while on my side of the net I'd recharged my batteries and came out in the fourth changed up a gear and had another gear ready for the fifth set when we got into it.' Many a champion knows that a game is never lost until the last point is decided, the last ball bowled or pitched, or the final whistle blown.

Being in tune with one's body is vital to remaining healthy. Bobby Charlton noted, 'If I ate too much pre-match or if I hadn't slept well on the night before or maybe gone to bed an hour later than I should have done, I could sense it.' One of the most difficult aspects to judge for both the performer and the coach is when a stress-induced injury starts hurting. It is very difficult to distinguish the normal aches and pains associated with improving the condition of your body from the pain which might be signalling potential damage to the body's structure. Often it seems that the right thing to do is to press ahead and the discomfort disappears during the training session. However, Mary Decker Slaney is an example of an athlete who was not correctly diagnosed and the result was years of pain. She was continually told that she had shin splints, but in later years a bone scan showed that she had had a series of stress fractures. Most paediatricians are now strongly advocating that children are not introduced to either heavy weightlifting or long-distance running until they are fully mature and the bones have stopped growing.

Another aspect of reading one's body involves a sense of its position in space. Certainly some people have a more advanced sense than others. Gareth Edwards, for example, could simply see someone doing back somersaults and, with little practice, could duplicate the action. My personal illustration is mixed: I found myself completely disorientated while attempting to tumble-turn in a pool yet when hurdling, there were times that I was so aware of my movements, I felt as though I was outside of myself, able to see the action and simultaneously felt and corrected every slight imbalance. Jayne Torvill and Christopher Dean have increased their body awareness through ballet classes and by skating in an area surrounded by mirrors. The visual picture enabled them to define a mood in bodily art form. Billie Jean King took this one stage further than physical awareness; she felt that self-awareness was probably the most important thing in fulfilling yourself because then you can set proper goals. 'Champions have an unbelievable level of self-awareness. The talent is conception. Some are born with talent and either don't do anything with it or don't even recognize it, but those who develop their potential, they are really talented.'

What is your reaction to sickness and injury? Ginny Leng displayed the type of determination which exemplifies the spirit of a champion. Before Montreal in 1976 she had a fall and the horse fell on her. Her left arm was broken in 23 places. There was talk of amputation. The arm was saved but she was told she'd never be able to bend it again and she'd never have feeling in her hand. 'I was in a big ward and there were so many people there who were desperate, I thought, right, I'm going to do this, and I forced my arm straighter every day. I just forced it mentally and physically. And two months later I had a tingling in my fingers.' Ginny's left hand is always a bit colder than the right and she can't turn her wrist out beyond the vertical but can fully extend her arm and added, 'I honestly think that if I'd have been a secretary or a housewife, I never would have done it; if I wasn't riding and didn't have a goal to go to. I wanted to go back riding. The surgeon couldn't believe it.'

Joan Benoit Samuelson typifies the response of many other top performers who have an injury. She said that injuries were frustrating but when she recovered from them, she felt stronger and hungrier than ever for success. As I shared an office with Joan while coaching at Boston University I know a little more of the awesome determination and courage which she exemplifies. Those who follow track athletics will know that only seventeen days before the US Olympic marathon trials, Joan underwent surgery on her knee. The next day she was swimming and 'pedalling' the exercise bike with her arms! She progressed to using her legs and twelve days before the qualifying race, started easy running. She won that trial and Athletics West coach Bob Sevene said he thought she was probably the toughest athlete he had ever known. The emotional effort of running while unfit and competing on willpower alone was similarly demonstrated by Daley Thompson when he won the decathlon at the World Championships in 1983. In both cases the effort left the performer physically and emotionally spent. However both won their speciality event in Los Angeles in 1984.

Several of the top achievers have had the good fortune of not being injured, but those who were often competed with it if they could, or else worked around the problem. There seems to be a quality of not giving in to a negative happening. It's just seen as an obstacle to overcome or a challenge to be accepted. There are no, 'Poor me!' attitudes. If they do have negative thoughts they catch themselves immediately and turn their mind to what they can control; the best they can do with where they are.

Ian Botham was dismissive of what could have been seen as a major problem, commenting that at times he continued to play with 'the odd broken finger'. Pat O'Callaghan had a late case of measles at twenty-one. He still went ahead and competed in a contest of throwing a weight over a bar for height. 'I could see two bars when I was throwing the weight into the air, but that was over in a week!' To an extent, playing on in a somewhat battered condition is all part of the battle in games such as rugby union, rugby league and horse racing. Barry John was very badly injured in a motorbike crash in his mid-teens. During his international playing career, he would go to the hospital for back therapy and when he saw what some of the children were coping with, he said it put his forthcoming match into perspective. 'The therapy was more in the mind. I could say to the youngsters, "I'll kick a goal for you."'

Both Lester Piggott and Peter Scudamore take injury for granted. Lester: 'Well, we all get injured, that's inevitable.' Peter: 'You can't become a jockey and not get hurt.' This acceptance of injury might sound as if it is treated more as an inconvenience than anything else. However Peter did say, 'I'm now petrified of getting hurt, because it costs you your living.' The injury itself is seen as a frustrating interruption of plans. There is certainly a worry, even concern, about whether it will be possible to make a comeback and to be as good, if not better, than before. The intention to try is never questioned.

Naturally with some forms of illness or injury, it is unwise to try to come back into sport too quickly. Nevertheless, the feeling was that most could not wait to get back and start again. Billie Jean King had five knee operations which not only shortened her playing career but forced her to set targets such as learning how to walk again, rather than an unrealistic immediate goal of winning another Wimbledon.

Most sports performers don't believe they're the ones who will get hurt and have to end their careers prematurely. The ones who have had injuries which might have put them out or actually have finished their careers realize how little it takes and how much they have lived only in sport. They pass on an important message to the healthy – develop interests beyond sport. Your sport may be the top priority but there must be life after sport and quality preparation for life outside sport is as important as it is for top sport performance. If this cannot be considered by performers, then they've lost their perspective of sport being a part of, and a preparation for, a larger life.

Unlike workers who are prepared for retirement in their sixties, most sport performers are unprepared for the feeling of loss when their playing days are over. Injury is an unfortunate cause for early retirement but even those with lengthy playing careers, unless they have a masters' or veterans' level to enter, are faced with a serious personal challenge to find an activity which will come close to providing equal inner rewards. It may sound strange but the integration of mind, body and spirit in pursuit of excellence at the very top level cannot be matched in many other ways in life. There may be individual tasks which pose more specific challenges, such as advanced research or starting one's own business, but the fusion of a healthy, fully fit body, clarity of purpose, total enthusiasm for the quest, commitment to the goal and the exhilaration of executing an excellent performance is priceless. It makes the search for a healthy transition to 'life after competitive sport' essential.

Summary of learning points:

- There is a trend with athletes which parallels that among the general population: less red meat, sugar and salt, more high fibre, pasta, vegetables and fruit.
- The quantity of food consumed in the Western world is considerably more than sufficient.

- High carbohydrate intake is accepted as the most useful food before competition, especially for endurance events.
- Most top performers monitor and assess their physical wellbeing, which allows for greater control of themselves and their potential.
- Individuals with a high level of self-awareness have the option to conceptualize and goal-set their development.
- Problems such as injuries were seen as an obstacle to overcome or a challenge to be accepted. There are no 'Poor me!' attitudes.
- While injured or ill, the only question in achievers' minds is, how soon will I be able to get back?
- Trying to rush back too soon after sickness or injury can set you back.
- Performers should bear in mind that injury and sickness can easily precipitate early retirement. And regardless of that, preparation for life after sport is essential while still competing.

4
PHYSICAL ATTRIBUTES

There are well over a hundred sports, each requiring different skills. The physical attributes to do well at each are as varied as the sports themselves. Just within the sports in this study, the attribute requirements vary immensely.

Within track and field athletics, there is quite a spectrum of sizes. Marathon runners are usually quite slight and not very tall, the men generally 5ft 5in to 5ft 8in, and the women 5ft 2in to 5ft 4in. Sprinters are usually well muscled. Male sprinters vary in height from 5ft 6in to 6ft 2in, but rarely above that as it takes taller people longer to unwind from the blocks. Middle-distance runners have a similar height variance to sprinters, but their physiology and temperament differ considerably. Sprinters tend to be more highly strung, rather like racehorses. They also appear to be more extroverted. A general rule of thumb is, the further up the distance scale, the more introverted the runner, but as in all generalizations there are exceptions. Some top performers do not conform to the expected 'best fit'. Lester Piggott at 5ft 9in is very tall for a flat race jockey.

Within each human are speed and endurance fibres. The proportion of each will determine what distance is comparatively your best. The spectrum found in humans is similar to that found in nature. Sprinters, American football linesmen and throwers are capable of explosive effort. As with jet fuel, they ignite and burn up their energy sources very rapidly. After a few seconds' effort, a sprinter often needs to put his hands on his knees to recover from the rapid depletion of oxygen from his system. Middle-distance runners are the woodburners; they are exciting to watch as they flame for several minutes. At the far end of this spectrum are the coal- and coke-burning endurance athletes who glow for two hours or so. Even with a flame-thrower, one cannot hope to make coal react like jet fuel. No amount of exhorting will enable a marathon runner to change gear like an 800m runner. The system may be modified to some extent, but the general percentage of fast- and slow-twitch fibre types is born in the performer. A simple test of fibre types is achieved through the 'sargent' jump. In a room with sufficient height the performer stands beside a wall, with heels to the ground. One arm is extended above the head and with chalk dust on the fingertips, a mark is made on the wall to indicate the height reached. The stationary performer then crouches and springs straight up in the air, touching as high on the wall as possible. The endurance runners, having little explosive capacity, usually get 12in to 18in off the ground. Some exceptional sprinters, jumpers, volleyball and basketball players have sargent jumps measuring over 40in! Anything over 24in shows a good amount of fast-twitch fibre content.

The well-trained endurance event performer will have a greater cardiovascular efficiency than the average performer or the untrained individual. This means that the performer is able to breathe more efficiently by absorbing more oxygen per breath. During 1969 at Salford University, England, twenty road-racing cyclists were tested physiologically and given some mental-state variable tests. The conclusion was, quite predictably, that the more genetically-gifted and physically-conditioned performer will produce the better result. Without a fair amount of natural attributes, the competitor will not be vying for the very top. The more interesting question comes when looking at those with comparable physical ability. The Salford findings showed that during intense effort, the threshold level of discomfort varied between individual riders. What one can never know is what level of discomfort each individual is experiencing. Does the top performers' experience of pain not register as strongly as others' or is it, as seems more likely, and as the researchers believed, that the difference could be accounted for by what they called 'selective attention'. This will be referred to later when discussing 'focus of attention'. It is impossible to clearly separate physical movement from mental involvement. Whether consciously or unconsciously, all our movements come from a thought. You may shift from an uncomfortable sitting position or follow movement with your eye with no conscious thought of doing so. Equally those actions may be initiated through intended thought.

Various physical attributes can assist performance; for example, wide peripheral vision will assist those in sports where there are other performers or where the involved environment surrounds them. Large hands and long fingers help the basketball player for greater ball control. Throwers with long arms have an advantage because this allows them to exert force over a longer time on whatever is being thrown. Steve

Backley's height and length of arm will have provided a bonus to his technical skills in establishing the world javelin record. Bulk also helps performers who need solid force behind their efforts to throw further, or push in a rugby scrum. Al Oerter conforms with most top class male discus throwers and shot putters, being between 6ft 3in and 6ft 6in (1.90–2.00m) in height, and between 200 and 300lb (14–22 stone) in weight. The confining element on speed and size for both these throws is the athlete's requirement of staying within the relatively small circle. Although there are exceptions, America's professional football and basketball players are immense. Several basketball players are over 7ft (2.13m) tall and still retain extraordinary dexterity and speed.

Speed is a common factor in most physical sports. Team games require the application of speed many times over a short distance. Sean Kerly pointed out that as a forward in hockey he would never be required to run further than forty metres at any one time. In spite of their massive size, the American football linesmen or the international rugby forwards have such great power-to-weight ratios that in spite of their bulk they can exert enormous force and move quickly over short distances.

Some of the questions in this study have been geared towards physical effort. However, several sports require a greater percentage of mental effort and concentration. In the case of a yachtsman, it may take five minutes to inch past another vessel, gaining perhaps a foot each wave. A sudden burst of adrenalin and physical effort will not necessarily be helpful. The calm control of the yachtsman can be paralleled in the worlds of motor racing, equestrian events, bowls, shooting, darts and snooker. The requirement is to lower the heart rate and where possible bring down the excitement level. There is discussion later on the mental skills available to control the heart rate, adrenalin flow, etc.

Another obvious physical requirement is the need for good hand-eye coordination in ball sports. The brain calculates rapidly the speed and direction of the ball, puck or whatever is the target object; then instructions are sent to the muscles via the brain to place the body, hands or racket in the right position, and at the right time, to intercept and make perfect contact. If we did calculations to work out how this is achieved, it would fill pages. Most of us take this sort of skill for granted and simply focus our eye on the object and the subconscious mind does the rest.

Yet another variable between the different sports is the degree of body contact. In sports such as rugby, American football and ice hockey, the confrontation is highly physical, as well as mental. In some sports, there is supposed to be only a moderate level of body contact, basketball and soccer being examples. In most sports, direct physical contact is rare. Some have the opponents on the opposite side of a net as in tennis, volleyball and badminton. Many sports require competitors to share space and the performer reacts to the moves of the other competitors. In addition to the intentional contact sports, other shared space sports are squash, bowls, baseball, cricket, yachting, snooker, middle- and long-distance running, and horse and motor racing. In golf and sprint events, the competitors will usually be aware of each other but rarely impede another's progress. Swimming is probably the closest to the isolated effort which exists in sports like downhill skiing, the three-day equestrian events, shooting and archery.

How significant are left-handedness and cross-dominance? This phenomenon is being raised because there are a disproportionate number of highly successful performers who are left-handed or cross-dominant. When you consider that approximately one in ten of the population is left-handed, then this area should not be left out of the discussion.

In February 1985, Robin Brightwell of the BBC produced a Horizon programme based on the research of the recently deceased Norman Geschwind, head of the Neurology Unit at Beth Isreal Hospital in Boston and a professor at Harvard. In 1968 Geschwind had shown that the two hemispheres of the brain are physically different. The left hemisphere, sometimes referred to as the analytical side, for most people, controls language, writing and calculations. It is concerned with rational, reflective orientation; for right-handers, it controls the dominant hand. The right hemisphere is more spatial and comprehension orientated and includes more intuitive and current experiential awareness. For the left-handers, this right side of the brain controls their dominant hand. Geschwind showed a strong connection between dyslexia, handedness and language. Dyslexia occurs ten times more frequently in left-handed people. He identified that if testosterone, the male hormone, had seeped into the embryo before birth, growth of the left hemisphere slowed, allowing the right hemisphere to take control. This hormone is produced by the mother as a by-product in making female hormones. The negative result for these individuals is that they often have allergies and because of their left-eye dominance, they frequently have learning difficulties. On the other side, the advantage gained by these individuals is that they have a greater three-dimensional skill level. Several gifted individuals including Thomas Edison, Einstein and Woodrow Wilson have had great difficulty in learning to read. Recent research indicates that the distinction between the activities of the two hemispheres is not as clear-cut as originally thought, and there is some overlap. Nevertheless, as a metaphor for the two contrasting functions of the brain, the division remains a useful concept.

Within this study of sports personalities, both Jackie Stewart and Duncan Goodhew have severe dyslexia. Both have learned to compensate and have become exceptionally articulate. The advantage for the ball players, and in Jackie Stewart's case shooting and driving, is clear. The better the spatial awareness, the clearer the perspective. A few years ago tennis had several left-handed players including Martina Navratilova, John McEnroe, Jimmy Connors and Rod Laver; today Monica Seles demonstrates equal proficiency with double-handed left and right side play. Many of those interviewed were either left-handed or cross-dominant.

Rugby players Barry John and Gareth Edwards kick equally well with either foot. Soccer player Bryan Robson is left-handed, but kicks well with either foot, plays snooker left-handed and cricket right-handed. Stefan Edberg plays right-handed but used to putt left-handed. Stephen Hendry and Nick Faldo play right-handed but said that they ate left-handed.

US researcher Dr Bill Thierfelder has made the assessment that the left and right sides of the brain, although serving different primary functions, are not totally separate. His view is that a certain amount of skill transfer can be learned and should be encouraged, the object being to enhance and integrate the whole brain. For example, if a youngster is right-handed and is primarily a logical, linear-thinking person, then he or she could benefit from doing something to enhance their creativity. In the case of a ball sport performer, encouragement should be given to spend some time and effort practising with the other hand or foot. Not only will there be an increased personal awareness of what is required to perform the activity proficiently, but also a certain transfer of learning and the development of a more balanced muscular system. In several sports, the option of striking the ball with either foot or shooting with either hand provides a double threat to the opposition and enhances the player's chances of success.

Do you consider that you were early, late or average in physical development? It may have been imagined that most of these high sporting achievers matured early and gained adult size soon after puberty, but this study found that this was not the case. Nearly two-thirds of these performers were late developers! Some, like rugby league's Des Drummond and Ian Botham, said that they had achieved strength early on, but that they did not fill out and grow until after their school days. Lynn Davies represented another segment of this group. 'I was skilled at ball games but didn't start to grow until I was sixteen.' Bobby Charlton and J.P.R. Williams gave some credit to weight-training, the latter saying, 'Lynn Davies started me on weights when I was about fifteen and I grew five or six inches in one year.' By contrast, a little less than one quarter classed themselves as early developers. This meant that nearly 90 per cent of those interviewed perceived themselves to be different from their peers. One has to wonder, therefore, whether this had any subconscious effect on their need to achieve. If one is larger than average during childhood, then often there may be an added expectation of responsibility and performance; for those who are smaller than average, then there could well develop a personal need to prove oneself.

A clear illustration of successful handling of early talent development is the case of Chris Evert. Although she was good enough to embark on the circuit when she was fourteen years old, her father held her tournament play down to a minimum until she had completed high school. A section of the early developers achieved astonishing levels of performance very early on in their lives. Stefan Edberg won the European Junior Tennis Championships at fourteen and his first Grand Prix at seventeen. Shane Innes started breaking world swimming records at thirteen and only a month after her fifteenth birthday, she held every freestyle record from 100m to 1500m. Her time of 17 min 06 sec for the 1500m in 1970 would have beaten the men in both the 1960 and 1964 Olympics! Her schedule in Munich was fifteen races in eight days, four of them on one day. She came away with three golds, a silver and a bronze, all in individual events, and the media were disappointed!

Shane's career ended when she was fifteen. A similar phenomenon was Wayne Gretzky, who was so good at ice hockey that expectations and pressure from the media and supporters caused him to start again in a new environment. When he was fourteen years old, his parents moved him from his home in the west of Canada to Toronto so that he could become 'just another kid'. That move probably saved a great talent. Fans, Press, parents and coaches all have a great responsibility in the protection of young talent. Exaggerated expectations will often cause the performer disappointment, not to mention the supporters. It seems that many people involved with young talent are too often seeking the effects of a time-lapse camera in the opening of a rose. The real appreciation only comes when the flower can be seen in all its glory as it gradually blossoms.

Statistics can be misleading, especially with such a small sample in several different sports. However, it is interesting to note that three-quarters of the swimmers and half the tennis and cricket players were early developers. By contrast more than 70 per cent of the track and field athletes and all the rugby players classed themselves as late developers physically. This finding should encourage the talent scouts in sports such as football to keep their selection open, and watch for the late developers as well. Many of those who show great early talent will not be the ones who reach the top level. I hope this finding will also encourage the average youngster to maintain their interest and practice, because in the long run they could come out on top as a late developer.

The fact that so many high achievers are late developers should also underline the need to allow youngsters the alternative of specializing as late as possible. Let them have fun with sport and specialize when they discover to which sport they are best suited. This should encourage those who are not winning constantly to, as the Americans say, 'hang in there'. Examples are numerous but to name just a few, Steve Cram was fourth in the 1500m, aged fourteen, in the English Schools Athletics Championships and fifth in the 3000m at fifteen. Billy Beaumont started playing rugby for Fylde RFC in 1968, aged sixteen, playing full-back for the sixth team. He said that when he left school, he would have been quite happy to have made the first team at his local rugby club. At a higher level, Ed Moses didn't enter university with the intention of doing anything other than getting an education.

Summary of learning points:

- Different sports require different attributes.
- Top achievers have considerable natural aptitude, but there are exceptions to every size and shape rule.
- Practice with the opposite hand or foot could assist overall development – as would practice of activities which provide a balance in mental bias: analytical/convergent thinking v creative/divergent thinking.
- Many top performers were late developers. If you are under-sized when you're growing up, don't give up, keep developing your skills.

5
COURAGE AND RISK-TAKING

It is a point for debate whether courage and risk-taking are an inherent part of one's physical make-up or something that one has to adjust to psychologically. Some sports lend themselves to the vision of courage and risk-taking through their speed or physical contact. Several sports can endanger limbs and, at times, life itself. Examples of these sports are motor racing, downhill skiing, boxing, ice hockey, American football, rugby, and equestrian events.

There is also a more subtle element of courage and risk-taking that involves choices which often determine the outcome of a contest. Individuals need courage to make decisions in everyday life. For example, should you give up a secure but boring job to try and make it in your own business? In sport, a certain amount of courage is needed from the start. One's ego is, to some extent, on the line when trying out for a place on a team, competing for the first time in front of family, friends and public and within the event itself. Courage is needed to get up again after a hard knock down. Courage is required to take a risk and make a decision to go for it; to leave the pack and make a break on your own. Lasse Viren of Finland, Brendan Foster of England, Kenya's John Ngugi and Italy's Salvatore Antibo have all had the courage to risk breaking away from the leading pack with a long way still to go in major championships. There is always the risk of going too soon, fading, and being passed. The courage to accept the extra discomfort and risk the chance of fading has to outweigh the risk of failure, of not giving it a try and being beaten in a sprint finish. The only regret will be not having given it a try.

Many individuals are unwilling to accept the responsibility of becoming the front runner or becoming highest goal-scorer. Many such individuals fear being different. They may also fear public failure. The high achievers never saw such positions as a threat, only as an opportunity to challenge and to prove themselves. The difference is how each individual frames it mentally.

Do you consider that either courage or risk-taking plays any part in your sport? Almost a quarter of those interviewed saw no risk involved in their sport. Even Bryan Robson who is known for diving to head a ball at boot-kicking height said, 'No, it's just a natural part of the game.' More than three-quarters of the performers were aware of the courage and risk-taking involved in their sport, but for these high achievers it was not a source of concern; in their minds, they had already dealt with these factors. John Whitmore addressed the outsider perception: 'In motor racing, one's experience of it is that although one certainly has to produce some courage, one is not producing an abnormal amount. Motor racing is one of those sports that tend to be perceived by others outside, that you must have an enormous amount of courage, but that's what they're projecting onto it. But presumably if you had to produce massive amounts of courage, then you'd do something else which would require less of it.'

Jackie Stewart made the point that even in potentially lethal sports, courage involved self-mastery. 'Courage does play a part but risk-taking doesn't. I think there's a difference between courage and bravery. Bravery is usually a blind instinctive reaction, which is sometimes more dangerous, whereas courage is the control of fear and being able to channel and manipulate it, still with the full knowledge of the calculated risk. There has to be a very clear analytical evaluation of risk.' Ken Read is another travelling at awesome speed. He said that courage was definitely needed. 'To press yourself when travelling up to 90 m.p.h. on skis, you have to handle the risks mentally within yourself. You are exposing yourself to danger. You realize the course is safe but there are very high risks there. You have to be able to take a realistic view and deal with your emotions and channel them because they're right there on the surface. You have to know your limits, what you've trained yourself to do but you must be prepared to take risks. You have to know when it's worth taking a risk to win a race . . . In the middle of the downhill at Kitzbuhel, there's a section which they don't show on live television. It comes off the flat and is a long side-hill pitch that's very, very rough. You can hold a tuck all the way across it but it's really tough physically and mentally. You can do it but you get rattled around and it's a question of locking yourself in there and just holding it. You're coming across at 70 m.p.h. and many times you feel you've got to move an arm out to keep stable, but if you do you're losing one-tenth of a second. It took me five years running the downhill there to realize that if I came across there and just stayed locked in and could gut it out all the way across no matter what, I could win, and sure enough it was the big difference in 1980. Five guys can do it and five others will pop out of their tuck, but once you've realized that you can, you've taken the risk, you've extended your limit; you realize there's no more risk there!'

Ginny Leng knows from personal experience that every rider gets hurt. 'You've got to be gutsy in our sport. You assess the risks you take.' This view was echoed by Peter Scudamore: 'I'm taking calculated risks all the time . . . risks within limits.'

Lester Piggott's reaction was, 'Most jockeys have courage and have to take risks all the time; in every race you've got to decide whether to go between two horses or go on the inside, here or there; it's all calculated risk, especially today where you have to be so careful with all these young colts.'

Rugby union and rugby league are physically demanding contact sports. Peter Sterling: 'You have to have a bit of courage to dive on a loose ball when there are boots flying around. It's a physical sport and you just can't survive if you aren't courageous to a fair degree.' Peter continued about league, 'Our game is getting very disciplined with less and less risk-taking. The game is becoming one of controlling the football and not trying to get in the extra pass, which might be a risk. That is the point where you have to weigh up quickly whether the risk is worth it and a try could be on.'

A bad neck injury was the reason for Billy Beaumont's decision to stop playing rugby, but in spite of his awareness of the risks, he said, 'If you don't fall on the ball someone has to. As captain you have to do it because you could never ask them to do anything you wouldn't do. I'd never chicken out of anything – even if I knew I hadn't a chance, I'd give it a go.' Bill epitomized the blind overpowering element in the make-up of forwards. A more cautious, less risk-taking approach was held by Gareth Edwards, whose job it was to get the ball from the forwards to the backs. He said that he was told, 'Never be a hero for anyone. Never go down on a ball in a position that you can't get back up.' He said, 'I never forgot that but I never thought about it. It's a case of putting ability above recklessness.'

Also from the sport of rugby is J.P.R. Williams who spoke of the risks being calculated and learning how to avoid injury. 'You know what you can get away with. In a contact sport it's very important to know how to fall. Fall the wrong way and you get injured. You learn to fall as you would from a judo throw. I suffered a few injuries and was involved in tremendous collisions. I think the harder you go in the less likely you are to get injured.' Des Drummond liked to get involved in the most physical play. 'If you don't take risks you've had it. Trying to get through gaps between players, they try to knock you out of the way. More often than not they're the ones that get knocked back. A lot of wingers don't have the aggression that's needed. I want to get involved. I like tackling bigger blokes.' On the subject of racial discrimination, Des showed a special type of courage in letting his actions speak louder than words. 'There is racial discrimination until you prove yourself. From your own players, "black this and black that" and when they realize that there's a black chap there, they try to retract what they've said, but the damage is done. I never let them know how I'm feeling. If I get it from the opposition, I know that they're trying to rile me up. I just carry on my own game and show them I just keep performing and they can't say anything. I've gained a lot of respect from players because I don't get fired up . . . I used to when I was younger.'

Ice hockey is another sport renowned for violence. Wayne Gretzky said of the sport: 'It's rough. It's physical. But if you think about it when you're playing, then you're in trouble. I would say the faster you're moving and the more you're moving, the harder it is to get hit. When you're standing around thinking about it you're in trouble. There are some big boys out there!'

West Indies cricket captain Viv Richards laughed as he said, 'I do treasure my teeth a lot!' He went on to explain that he does not wear a helmet while playing cricket; it may take some courage but also a lot of focused attention to face fast bowlers sending down four bouncers in an over.

A similar view of being shot at was expressed by Sean Kerly. 'At the time of a corner, players are standing on the goal line with just a stick to protect them and the ball is coming in at 100 m.p.h.; it's just luck whether or not you'll get hit.' He went on, 'During the run of play it's not thought about until a ball is crashed past my ear and I realize I could have had a smashed face. Statistically you're going to get hurt, you're just going to hope . . .'

In non-contact sports, courage and risk-taking were still seen as part of what makes achievement. US golf legend Arnold Palmer wrote a book called *Go For Broke*. 'People used to say that I took chances and went for broke every time. I never really felt that that was the case. I always thought the winners had to play aggressively and that they had to go and get it. It's an inner thought as much as anything. But gambling and not laying up was one of the things that I was known for and I suppose it was just a natural part of my game.'

Stefan Edberg holds a similar view today. 'Playing safe and waiting for others to make mistakes, that's not my idea of playing tennis. Tennis for me is creating an opening and finishing the point myself. That's the way I feel more in control. Of course you have to mix it up. You can't go for your shots all the time but there are certain moments, there is no time to play safe, you've got to go for it, otherwise you're not going to succeed.'

Stephen Hendry: 'I tend to take risks. Not a lot now. I used to when I first turned professional through inexperience, but I'm still an attacking player. A lot of players play more percentage shots.'

Nick Faldo is in another game with angles and deciding to trust yourself and go for it. 'We play to a target and the courage is trusting your ability to go for that target when there are lakes and all sorts of things around that don't leave you much margin for error. Your courage is how close you hit it. You can always bail out in the middle but what I always want to find out from myself is, can I go for it when I want to go for it?'

Kip Keino linked courage with confidence. 'You have to have courage. Without it you will not be able to do anything. You have to have confidence.' Herb Elliott referred to the psychological barrier of fear. 'If courage is beating your own fears and your uncertainties, then there was a lot of courage.' Heather McKay pointed out that it took courage to push yourself past your previous limit, giving yourself that extra push when you thought you could not do it.

Duncan Goodhew did not consider that courage or risk-taking were a part of his competitive experience, but he thought that courage related far more to his training. 'It comes to reaching down for something you didn't know you had. My hardest sessions were done when I felt my worst.' He laughed, and said, 'It's easier to do it on the worst day; you feel lousy so you're not ruining a good day anyway!'

Summary of learning points:

- Top performers recognize that risk-taking is a part of their sporting life. Without heroics they just get on with business, doing what has to be done.

Courage and Risk-taking

- They don't dwell on the possibility of injury or failure, nor do they take unnecessarily high risks.
- Risk-taking means accepting personal responsibility to go for it, when it has to be done and when it counts.
- Courage is seen as overcoming any fear or apprehension by making a confident commitment in body and mind.

6
CHILDHOOD AND GROWING UP

There are such negative associations with class distinction that I felt some reluctance in asking the question of class background. Nevertheless, it was important to try to see whether or not class had any bearing on sporting achievement. Many journalists have referred to the athlete's need to be 'hungry' in order to win, and have implied that many have used sport to 'get out of the ghetto'. The 'hunger' part may be true, but the hunger was more likely to be to prove themselves, regardless of their social circumstances. This survey has certainly not shown that any more than a fraction were proving themselves because of their social class.

Only one came from an affluent family. Rarely do we hear of children of the very well-off climbing onto the Olympic podium. When American decathlete Bill Twomey won at the 1968 Olympics, it was considered newsworthy because he was reported to be the son of a millionaire.

Half of those interviewed classed themselves as middle-class. This type of class definition is difficult across various cultures, because class distinction is based on different factors; for example in the US it is largely based on money, whereas in Britain money is not necessarily a determining factor.

It was amusing to hear how Carl Lewis defined the poor. He is from a well-educated, professional family and in defining his middle-class status, he said, 'There were some rich folks who drove new Cadillacs and there were some poor folks who only had one car.' Only in America could a definition of 'poor' include the owning of a car!

The other half classed themselves as either poor, working-class or lower-middle class. Nevertheless, it would not be accurate to say that there was a desperate desire to 'get out of the ghetto'. The spartan conditions were accepted and in most cases it brought the community together. Gareth Edwards spoke of the typical attitude of the Welsh mining communities: 'The backing from parents was absolute. Things were tight but we never wanted for anything. The only thing you missed were the luxuries, but what you never had you never missed.'

Regardless of how they had defined their social background, it was stated that in retrospect virtually all recognized that their parents had made sacrifices in order to allow them to pursue their sporting interest. Whether it was purchasing the necessary equipment or providing the bus fares to away games, somehow the backing was found. Additionally, it was never made obvious to these future high achievers that they were placing a strain on the family resources. They may have been aware that it was being found, but they were never in any way made to feel awkward or uncomfortable.

Many of the creature comforts of today, including television, were not important to most in this study. The entertainment was often self-created and in many cases bore a striking resemblance to some future training endeavours. For Herb Elliott in Australia, the castles being captured were sand-hills. Roaming in the outback with her family was the game for Heather McKay when she was not involved in hard physical chores on her parents' farm. After school in the mining communities where Lynn Davies, Barry John and Gareth Edwards lived, they would join other village lads and play soccer until it was too dark to see the ball. There were no facilities for technical event practices, but the activities were fun and the stamina, coordination and individual flair were allowed to develop naturally.

How stable was your home and how supportive were your parents? In a study on public figures from business, politics, trade unions, etc, it was found that a high proportion of the sample chosen had some kind of trauma in their early life: death of a parent, abandonment, left in care and so on. Quite the opposite seems to be the case for sports achievers and double achievers, those who reached international level in sport and another area. This sport survey found that only a very few of these performers had either a parent die or parents who divorced. Even in the latter cases, the difficulty it caused had been less than traumatic. With the increased divorce rate throughout the western world, one has to appreciate just how fortunate this group has been. It also should encourage parents who are separating to ensure that their children are in a stable and consistent environment.

The answers throughout this section on home life and parents were remarkably alike. Virtually all these top sports performers felt that their home life was stable, secure and happy, many adding 'very' to the last of these. They also felt that their parents had been consistent in their behaviour. Crops grow better in good soil, and this seems to show that the performers benefited from this nourishing home environment.

Also, almost all said that their parents were both supportive and encouraging, but that they firmly believed that they were not pushed by their parents. Illustrations were often given as to what was meant by support and encouragement without pushing. For example, in many cases, it was the parents of these achievers who were the ones to drive team members to an away game. Where work did not interfere, one or both parents would be watching. In most cases it was the 'full-time Mum'.

Duncan Goodhew, recalling his development, well illustrated the benefit of a parent not pushing. Duncan said that he had been quite a bolshie teenager. This stemmed from the fact that as a dyslexic he had been labelled 'Dumbo' by his school mates. Added to that, at the age of eight he had fallen out of a tree and damaged a nerve in his upper lip, causing all his hair to fall out. At that time his eyebrows and eyelashes had gone as well so he was then known as 'Dumbo Lizard'. Kids can be incredibly cruel. His parents sent him to Millfield which has a dyslexia section and he was introduced to national swimming coach, Paddy Garrett. Swimming started to put his life together. Increases in competence increased his self-confidence. He recalled a visit home: 'My mother was brushing her hair, I was fifteen or sixteen and I walked in and said, "I'm giving up swimming." My mother stopped brushing her hair and then carrying on said, "Well, whatever you want to do", and that really took the wind out of my sails because I'm sure that if she had said, "Don't you dare give up now", I would actually have done the opposite.' It took Duncan about ten days to decide for himself that he wanted to swim again, but the decision was *his*. Later in this chapter much will be said about parental ambition. These achievers all feel very strongly that pushing the child will more likely result in them quitting sooner rather than later. When parents are not sure of the line between encouragement and pushing, the only way to *know* is to *ask* the child, lovingly and openly, 'Do you feel pushed or pressured by us?'

Stefan Edberg said, 'If you don't have support from your home, I think it's going to be very difficult.' Christopher Dean thought that it was important that parents were there as a sort of rock, 'to support you when you needed it'. Jayne Torvill remarked, 'They can advise you but they don't push you. There's quite a difference.'

Support can come in all forms. For Olympic yachtsman Rodney Pattisson, it was his father setting a trend by building him a boat suitable for children, and not setting him against adults too early. Rodney's view was that parents usually pushed the wrong guys: 'The guys with ability don't need to be pushed.'

It would be helpful at this stage to put briefly into context the findings relating an athlete's upbringing to a theory of personal development and motivation. Many will be familiar with the name of Abraham Maslow, who was a professor of psychology at Brandeis University in the United States. He was largely responsible for giving the world a more hopeful and positive view of humans through his Third Force theory. Sigmund Freud had made a huge contribution to greater understanding of human psychology; however he had been studying the sick. Maslow pointed out that if we're trying to discover how fast a human can run a mile we don't look at the sick; we must look at the best and see how we can improve upon that. One cannot discover the positive capabilities of humankind if the main source of investigation are the psychologically unwell. Maslow researched great people of history and interviewed many of the outstanding individuals of his time. One of his theories was a five stage hierarchy of human needs. He proposed that in order for human beings to fulfil their potential, they had to progress through these stages. In his view the needs at one level had to be largely fulfilled before the individual would develop or advance to the next level. It is relevant to note that this sport achievers survey endorses his theory.

The first two levels have a largely physiological basis. The first stage for the continuation of the human race is the need for air, food, water, sleep and sex. The second level is the need for safety and security. In the first two levels, the families of these achievers provided the nurture, stability, safety and security to enable them to move on to the third level, the psychological need for love and the sense of belonging. This may be fulfilled from several different sources. In addition to close family ties, performers can also gain a real sense of belonging from both a good coach–performer relationship and being part of a team or training group; and of course from outside friends. The fourth level is the need for self-esteem and the esteem of others; being able to feel that who you are and what you do are recognized as worthwhile by yourself and by others. Sport holds an unusually strong position here. The public at large follows sport in some depth in every part of the globe. If someone finishes a marathon, a personal feeling of accomplishment and recognition from others is usually established, regardless of whether the individual took just over two hours or just over ten to complete the course. Sport provides a unique opportunity in this regard and has been opened to almost everyone from tiny tots to geriatrics, whether mentally or physically handicapped, gifted or not. The recognition and interest shown by parents will go a long way towards giving the youngster the sense of self-worth which he or she needs.

The fifth and final area Maslow called the need for self-actualization; in other words, becoming what you are capable of becoming. This level has also been called self-realization and it provides an open-ended and never-ending quest. At some stage in the lives of these highest achievers, they fulfilled a part of their human potential. It should be noted that even those touching on this level will be operating, at different times, on each of the other levels. It's just a question of at which level one spends the majority of one's physical and emotional energy.

What was your relationship like with your parents? Nearly three-quarters of these top performers characterized the relationship with their parents as either close or good. The remainder were almost evenly split between being only close with their mother, having respect for their parents or being neither warm nor close, because their parents were either too busy or too old or because there was friction or strife in the family.

Several family differences can be attributed to the way in which the offspring were treated. They were certainly not all treated the same. Some went away to school which made any meaningful relationship difficult. For Valeriy Borzov, it was a case of being selected for a sports school. In the Soviet Union, the choice is left to the child and his parents to decide, but it is rarely refused as it is seen as a privilege and an opportunity, just as a scholarship offer is seen a few years later at American colleges. The biggest difference seems to be that the State and those who organize the different schools provide the care and socialization. Family support and encouragement was 'nothing special', said Borzov. The family is not the most influential factor. One of the reasons for this is that up until recently there has been full employment for over thirty years in the Soviet Union: either university or technical training with a guaranteed job to follow. The result is that children are dropped off at school at 7.30 a.m. and picked up at 6.30 p.m. from the age of three; in fact, they can be there from the age of one. Many do not pick up their children during the week but have them live at school. At fourteen, Valeriy was selected to attend a 'special' school where he could receive specialist coaching alongside his academic lessons. 'In school the best care is given to each child, but they are not pushed.' The route was similar to that found in the West with the child being introduced to sport as fun. Later came the careful introduction of skills, and at university the intellectual understanding and serious training.

In order to reach the top level in world sport, there is a requirement for independence and self-responsibility. However, parents do provide a significant early influence as role models and guides. Three further questions were asked about aspects of the parent–child relationship which might have had bearing on the achievers' values and behaviour.

Were religious values important to your parents? More than half said yes. Several who were not religious, still had a code of living based on Christian principles but without going to church. Billy Beaumont said that the code would have been by the Ten Commandments.

Did they stress the importance of fair play and sticking to the rules? Once one moved to values upheld by the parents in terms of whether or not they had stressed fair play and keeping within the rules, the positive response was almost unanimous, saying yes, they had always been told to play fair and abide by the rules. The sentiment was so strong, in fact, that it elicited responses such as 'totally', 'very much so', 'no question', 'always', 'a very high standard of integrity' and 'no lying or cheating'. Billie Jean King had been told by her father: 'If you cheat you'll never have won. You may walk off the court and everyone else may think that you won, but you didn't win at all.'

Several performers recalled incidents where their parents had made a direct intervention to alter their behaviour. John Newcombe was playing a junior final and was losing. 'I was dropping my racket and all that and my mother was sitting at the court side, and usually said nothing during my matches. But on this occasion as I passed her, she sort of hissed, "Why don't you start playing tennis and stop feeling sorry for yourself?"

Within three paces I realized that she was right, so I started playing tennis, stopped feeling sorry for myself and won the match.'

For Arnold Palmer, it was his father. He spoke of a match when he was about sixteen years old. He had just missed a short putt: 'I wheeled and threw the putter fifty or sixty feet over a row of poplar trees. I went on to win the match with a sizeable putt on the last hole. I was elated about my success but when I got into the car, it was total silence. I expected "nice going" or "congratulations" – there was nothing. The first thing that came out of my father was said in no uncertain terms: "If I ever see you do that again, in competition or otherwise, you will not play golf and live in my house at the same time." He meant it and I knew he meant it.'

A story was related about Bjorn Borg, how early in his playing days, he had displayed a bout of bad temper on court; afterwards his parents locked his racket in a cupboard for several weeks. Lynn Davies spoke about the ethics that can come from a whole community. 'My father was very critical of bad sportsmanship. You find that coal miners generally have a tremendous code of ethics, a tremendous sense of fair play.'

Was the discipline used verbal or physical? The most direct area of parental intervention in a child's behaviour is discipline. The question was asked in order to find out whether or not there was any bias in the form of that early discipline. For two-thirds it was entirely verbal. Several emphasized the fact with statements such as, 'Oh, we were never hit!'; 'I can never remember being hit'; and 'We were just told why it was wrong.' A further one-fifth said that they received both verbal and physical punishment. Comments varied from, 'We got what we deserved' to 'Both, but no beatings, just a short clip'. Very few said that it was primarily physical with about the same number saying that they received neither physical punishment nor verbal berating. This was either because they were away at boarding school, or that expectations within the family were such that it was unnecessary.

It was interesting to see how the different forms of discipline seemed to affect the relationship with their parents. As the total number interviewed was not large, it would be wrong to draw too firm a conclusion; however, the following analysis does give a great deal of food for thought. For those who had been verbally disciplined, virtually all had a good relationship with their parents. For those who were both physically and verbally disciplined, just over half were close to their parents, another quarter had respect for them and the rest were not close to their parents.

Three-quarters of those who received primarily physical discipline said that they were not close or they had strife with their parents! Parents who still believe in 'spare the rod and spoil the child' may establish control, but in these achievers' cases, it did not result in a good or close relationship. It appears that parents who were prepared to take the time to communicate with asking, listening and discussing, at least in this group, produced closer relationships. That certainly has been my own experience as a child and as a parent.

These top achievers were then asked which attributes would best characterize their parents, and which of the attributes they had taken from their parents had helped their sporting performance. The attributes listed give us a reasonable insight into the qualities needed to reach further towards our potential. They are as follows: diligence, fairness, hardness, control, discipline, conscientiousness, dedication, sincerity, courage, honesty, integrity, enthusiasm, pride, reserve, diplomacy, humour, determination, humility, and last but not least, patience. To this list could be added positiveness in vision and ambition, for without a challenging and positive view of where we would like to get to and a drive to get there we will not be establishing new heights of personal achievement.

In several cases, both parents were seen as very similar types. Other performers felt that the combination of both their parents provided a balance. Where one was intense the other was controlled, and many felt that they had taken the best from each parent. Both Steve Davis and J.P.R. Williams referred to taking their love for sport from their fathers and the mental toughness and hardness from their mothers. It would be fair to say that the parents in general were greatly valued, many achievers saying that they could not have wished for better parents.

Behavioural guidelines from parents, not given verbally, were more than made up for by example. One attribute which was consistently agreed on was that their parents were extremely hard working. Ed Moses referred to it as 'the work ethic'. Whether it was on a farm, in the mines, driving a cab, teaching, running their own business or running a home, their dedication, effort, commitment and reliability were evident to their offspring. This diligence was an example followed by all.

Do you consider your parents to have been competitive people?
One might have expected a positive response but in fact less than half of these achievers considered their parents to have been competitive. It is interesting that this is an attribute evidently not acquired by example.

Did you feel that your parents had high expectations for you and if so in what areas? Expectations represent a less overt form of parental pushing. More than half felt that there were no high expectations expressed or felt from their parents. Almost one-third said that the pressure they felt was not related to sport, but to the importance of getting a good education. Lynn Davies, for example, was encouraged by his mother to have the option not to go down the mines. Education is seen as a strong tool for upward mobility.

The remaining performers, who constitute less than one-fifth, felt expectations in all areas. Ken Read said, 'There was expectation for each of us in the family to realize our potential in everything.' Billie Jean King: 'Every area. I once came home with a school report showing all As and one A− and my Dad asked why there was one A−! I said "Daaad!" and he said, "Oh, I was only wondering what it was for."' For both Heather McKay and J.P.R. Williams, the sport expectation was tennis, which was not the sport of their ultimate success. But with them, as with Al Oerter and Peter Snell, reference was also made to the importance of scholastic achievement.

With the parents who did have high expectations, there was no mistaking the belief expressed in their offspring. Steve Cram, in his interview, which incidentally was prior to his multiple world records in 1985, said that he thought his parents at times tended to over-estimate what he could do. Perhaps now he will have to agree with them!

The parents of these achievers may not have been deceiving themselves in expressing their belief and faith in the youngsters who they knew could reach the very top if they fulfilled their potential. A problem arises with parents who are working with a child who doesn't have the talent or personal ambition to make the top. Often, neither parent nor child understands the number of levels which there are to climb and consequently sets unrealistic or unattainable targets. The answer to this is to retain the dream but to share a discussion and, with the child's input, jointly decide on short term, challenging but attainable goals. If over-ambitious parents set the targets for the child, rather than letting the child lead the process, very easily the youngster can start to feel insecure or inadequate; he or she cannot match up to the parents' expectations. The key is to ask the youngster what they want to go for. The parent's role is to help and support a realistic and enjoyable next step. The parent must give support and encouragement. Most often, the goal-setting is either done by the individual performer or in concert with the coach. Nick Faldo's parents provide a good example. 'They didn't say, like a lot of fathers today, "Come on, get in there and start hitting golf balls and hopefully you'll wind up like Nick Faldo." They were always encouraging. If I said I wanted to try tennis, they'd say, "Oh, there's a pro down at ICI [where his father worked] who's giving lessons." And they would always put me into that sort of thing. I never had a father who said, "Oh, I was all right, I could knock it up, I could do this and do that, I'll show you what to do son!" I joined Welwyn Wheelers – a cycling club – and had qualified coaching in athletics, swimming, everything.' Note that the interest was first expressed by Nick. Parents have to wait for the flower to open, not force it open. They may ask if there's any interest, but they must wait and listen, and when it's appropriate, be willing to provide the opportunity.

All too often parents can be over-ambitious on their children's behalf. John Newcombe had an early problem with his father. 'If I'd won, it would be a really nice ride home. If I hadn't, by the time we got ten minutes from the house, we'd be having an argument. Finally, I said to my mother, if he didn't cut it out he just couldn't come to matches and if he insisted on coming I wouldn't play . . . so he cut it out and it was fine.' This statement makes one wonder how many youngsters have stopped playing because their parents have become too involved, demanding victory. Their children's success in many cases has become an extension of their own ambitions, perhaps linked to feelings of frustration at their own lack of achievement.

Only Lester Piggott said that he was pushed by his father, but added that he thought he needed to be. Lester was trained by his father and started riding for him at the age of fourteen. 'I think that for anyone to be good at anything they need some help and they've got to be pushed a bit. Nobody's a natural really. They've got it there but they've still got to be put right at the beginning.' Lester felt that he was lucky to have a father who shared an interest. As with Seb Coe and Steve Davis, each was coached by his father. Seb remarked that he was the one who pushed himself and that there had been occasions when both his parents had told him to back off.

Billie Jean King's parents went out of their way to get her to tournaments but did not ask, 'Did you win or lose?' but rather 'Are you happy playing? Are you sure this is what you want to do?' One might well have expected that Shane Innes was pushed by her parents to produce such fantastic times whilst still so young, but not so. 'My parents were always very supportive and encouraging, never pushing. My Dad would sometimes turn off the alarm clock so I wouldn't go swimming in the morning because he thought I was too tired to go.' In fact there was conflict between her parents and her coach because they believed that Shane was too young to be doing so much training. They felt she was being worn out and might get tired of it mentally, so they were trying to hold her back. Most other parents also showed their concern. Three-Day Eventer Lucinda Green's parents told her to give up riding if she did not enjoy it. Ginny Leng felt strongly about the pushy parent. 'If people are going to be good, they're going to be good, and I find it somewhat distressing when youngsters are pushed, being told "You will win!" I think that's detrimental. I also think that by just hyping them up, telling them they're marvellous without any criticism, then they'll be a wreck in life; they won't have a realistic view of life. Enjoy being a star for as long as it lasts, but just bear in mind you're not going to be there very long, necessarily. And people have short memories.'

I believe that parents, coaches and the performers themselves need to retain the view that peak performance in sport is achieved relatively young. Chances are that the performer will have forty years after their top playing days are over. Also careers can be ended prematurely through injury. How many young aspiring performers are encouraged to prepare well during their peak performance days, for the time after-wards? What could they be doing to prepare themselves for the equivalent to work retirement? Sport may be the number one priority but it need not be the only priority.

Many of the achievers shared disturbing stories about parents who had demonstrated over-ambition. Here are a few illustrations from three continents. In little athletics in Australia, a young lad of eight, running in a national championships, was passed in the last few yards of a quarter-mile race. At the finish, he fell to the track exhausted, crying because he had lost the race. His father came over and whacked him about the head, shouting at him for losing. I related this story to an Australian coach who said that he had watched a similar scene where a girl was told to swim her last repetition in 60 seconds and she finished, obviously in distress, having swum it in 62 seconds. Before she was even told her time, her mother slapped her across the face, saying that she could have tried harder! Ed Moses talked about those parents involved with their children's track athletics practice in the United States. 'I've seen six, seven, eight, nine year olds doing five or six back-to-back 400m. I'm against pushing. The person is usually going to motivate themselves if they're going to be a champion, even with a good coach. The worst thing I'm aware of is that some parents are putting their kids onto anabolic steroids!' Apart from the illegality within the sport, that shows a criminal disregard for the normal and healthy development of their children. Arnold Palmer commented, 'I've seen pushy parents in every sport and the results are generally bad. The kids that are pressured to play sport usually get sick of it and are disgusted with it for that reason. They decide to do something else.'

When Gareth Edwards was at a New Zealand school which boasted of having trained some of the greatest All Blacks players, the headmaster pointed out a boy who he believed could have been the best of the lot but had stopped playing. Gareth went and spoke to the lad who said that he had started playing competitive rugby at the age of five and so by seventeen, he had already played intensive rugby for twelve years and had had enough. Gareth's opinion is that, 'Currently in Great Britain, we have many do-gooders in mini-rugby, and too often the only things being taught are how to stop the opponents and how to set up certain moves. They neglect the basic skills – how to pass and how to kick.' Billy Beaumont saw mini-rugby as being all right in most aspects such as teaching children the rules of the game and how to enjoy themselves. 'But don't get them organized into competition at the age of eight because you're taking the whole fun aspect out of the game. You see little lads crying because they've lost the game . . . so what?'

Heather McKay in Canada said, 'Part of the problem with sport today is that the parents want the kids to be what they weren't and are trying to live through them. There's a difference between encouraging and standing behind versus pushing, and when the kid gets old enough to make a choice, they give it away because they've been pushed so hard.'

The obsession with winning as well as pushing children at such a young age has not only forced youngsters to drop out of sport, but in an extreme example in tennis has produced a resentment towards a father to the point of being willing to kill him! There is nothing wrong with introducing children to sport at an early age, but the whole affair has to be kept light-hearted and made to be fun. The important aspects to be stressed here are taking part, making an honest effort and being pleased with the feeling of movement; the thrill of scoring if you can; the gaining of knowledge about how to play; experimenting with different styles and techniques; discovering that with practice one gets better; and hopefully one is encouraged and recognized for effort and improvement even if one is still in last place. This is where it helps to keep a note of performances. No matter how slowly one runs or how few points are scored, if it is possible to measure improvement, then it is a marvellous source of reward. Apart from the thrill of success, sport provides an incredible learning experience and opportunity.

Wayne Gretzky felt he was shown the difference between being pushed and having a responsibility. 'I wasn't forced into any sport but I had agreed to play for a local baseball team and half-way through the season, I wanted to quit. My Dad said, "You finish the year, then you can quit." '

This now prompts the question as to whether or not the sport played by the parents influenced their child's choice. On the basis of the current study, it seems to have had little bearing. In exactly half the cases, only the father played any sport. It should be noted that several of those interviewed had parents who lived in an era when sporting opportunities for women were far less open than they are today. Nevertheless in a few families, only the mother played. In about one-third of the homes both parents played some form of sport. Rather surprising is the fact that in more than 10 per cent of cases, neither parent had participated at all. Even more amazing is that more than two-thirds of the achievers succeeded in a sport not played by either of their parents.

Within the group who did follow in their parents' footsteps, one-third of them had both parents involved in the same sport. They were Billie Jean King and Chris Evert from tennis, Carl Lewis in athletics, David Bryant in bowls, Clive Lloyd in cricket and Lester Piggott from horse racing. The remaining two-thirds had fathers who had played the same sport and in several cases, the father was a very significant figure for these achievers. Arnold Palmer's father was a golf professional. 'I'd watch my father and I suppose I admired him and what he did.' Peter Scudamore's father Michael won the Gold Cup in 1957 and the Grand National in 1959. 'That was always a great influence on me.' Peter added an amusing story about his mother being totally against him riding, dreading him getting hurt. When asked why it was okay for her husband but not her son, she replied, 'I always felt Michael knew what he was doing'! Peter added, 'Parents often don't see that their children have grown up.'

Were you competitive with your siblings? More than half of those in this survey said that they were not in a competitive situation with their siblings. Two who referred to their relationship as close and non-competitive were males who had sisters both older and younger than themselves. John Newcombe was the second child of three; Peter Sterling was third child of four, the other three being sisters. In several instances, the lack of competitiveness was attributed to the fact that there was too great an age gap between them. Three years was often the break-even point. Any greater age difference and the individuals often referred to their brothers and/or sisters as much older or much younger.

The rest who did have brothers or sisters said that their relationship was competitive and the majority of these were born about two years apart. Many referred to fighting, particularly between the years of nine and fourteen but becoming closer later on. This is a familiar pattern in many families.

The position in the family was varied: 8.5 per cent were only children; 29.6 per cent were first born; 42.3 per cent second; 15.5 per cent third; 2.8 per cent fourth and 1.4 per cent eighth.

The findings in this section raise more questions than answers. It is logical that the first child has the most attention from parents and they are the ones to whom the parents look to set an example. The eldest child often takes some responsibility for the younger siblings.

Previous studies on business achievers have indicated that the largest proportion of those who reached the top in that sphere were the first born. This is not the case for sports achievers. A survey of competitors at the Mexico Olympics 1968 showed nearly 60 per cent were second born. However, in the follow up study at the Munich Games in 1972 there was a more normal distribution. I do wonder why, similar to the Mexico survey, there is a disproportionate number of second born sporting achievers in our sample group. No explanation is readily apparent.

Summary of learning points:

- Sufficiency is the name of the economic game. That was what these achievers experienced, accepted and valued.
- Parents can support their youngster's development by providing a happy, stable and secure home environment.
- Parents are role models, so we must behave the way we want our children to behave. These achievers believed that good standards, fair play and working hard were lived values and passed on from home.
- If parents want to retain friendship and mutual respect their discipline needs to be verbal rather than physical.
- Over-ambitious parents will tend to kill the interest and enthusiasm in their children.
- Balanced parents will ensure that their children enjoy their sport, supporting and encouraging their children's interests without imposing on them or pushing them.
- Apart from the thrill of success, sport provides an incredible learning experience and opportunity.

7
PERSONAL ATTRIBUTES

As all these achievers have been performing in front of huge audiences and watched by millions on TV, one might be forgiven for assuming that they are all extroverts. In fact, the opposite seems to be true. A remarkably distinguishing feature is that nearly 90 per cent of these sports achievers classed themselves as introverts. In my parallel study on double achievers, those who reached international level in their sport and had gone on to achieve notably in another field, the main difference between this group and the highest achievers in sport was that the double achievers were on the whole extroverts. The requirements for success in business certainly differ from sport because, at least in some areas, there is a need for an outgoing personality in unfamiliar social surroundings.

Reference is often made to the loneliness of the long-distance runner, and when one comes to think about the number of hours of single-minded effort and inward reflection required to reach the top in many sports, it is not surprising to find that the vast majority of these athletes started as introverts. Steve Davis said that he did not mind either being alone or with just a few people practising because he would rather have been there than at a party.

Obviously, many of these achievers have been thrust into the public eye and have had to adapt. Barry John put it that he was a 'trained' extrovert. Billie Jean King referred to it as an 'adopted front'. Steve Cram, John Whitmore and several others said that sport was the tool which had brought them out. Some said that in their youth they had been painfully shy. The general consensus was that their sport had helped them to become more outgoing, and had assisted in the promotion of self-confidence.

As was mentioned in the Third Force theory, sport can assist greatly in allowing an individual's needs to be fulfilled. Jackie Stewart, as well as Duncan Goodhew, suffers from dyslexia. Their sense of belonging and self-confidence were increased through sport. Their achievements allowed them and others to realize that they had a special ability. Both have compensated for the perceptual difficulty and become exceptionally articulate.

Peter Snell experienced the benefit of sport having a link across cultures. 'When my family moved, sport was a means of deriving social acceptability in any new group situation; for example, if I went away to YMCA camp, I would have immediate acceptability on the basis of my athletic skills, being able to play cricket, being able to run reasonably well, and so on. So I learned at an early stage that there was value in being physically competent.'

Do you consider that you were either assertive or aggressive off the field of play? A certain degree of assertiveness and aggressiveness is obviously needed on the field. To test the distinction between the two, individuals were given an illustration of assertiveness: they were asked whether they would send food back in a restaurant if it was not cooked properly. On this basis, over one-third considered that they were neither aggressive nor assertive off the field of play. Bryan Robson said that he was happy to give instructions and take command on the field, but off the field he was quite the opposite. He added, 'I walk away from people in pubs or restaurants who are making uncalled-for remarks, trying to set me up for a fight.'

Just over half of those interviewed said that they were definitely not aggressive but were assertive. Nick Faldo said that he would send the food back, then laughing added, 'Especially if I was paying!' Rodney Pattisson said that he stood up for his own rights and the rights of others. 'If someone makes a questionable move in a yachting race, many will say, "Who cares?", but I will get a ruling on principle.' Duncan Goodhew and Steve Cram pointed out that they had become more assertive since winning. Kip Keino added, 'Getting aggressive doesn't help anything.'

Aggression towards another is not limited towards other humans. A couple of these achievers felt strongly about cruelty to animals. Ginny Leng said that she and her family have chosen not to use any drugs, even the legally used anti-inflammatory type like Bute. She said that they chose to run them without drugs because they felt, if they can't do the job naturally, then they shouldn't be doing it.

Other top performers gave their own words to define their assertiveness. For example, Herb Elliott said that he was persistent; Billie Jean King referred to her actions as 'manipulative' and Peter Sterling said, 'I'm not a follower.'

Just under 10 per cent felt that they were at times both assertive and aggressive. Daley Thompson said 'I can be both but I don't like to be.' Carl Lewis added a serious but rather light-hearted note, saying that he was extremely aggressive when shopping!

It is recognized that in most sports there is a need for an assertive and/or aggressive action. Steve Ovett sees the track as a place where you take the rough with the smooth and you give as good as you get. If that means an exchange of elbows, so be it. Having said that, Steve does not see himself as an aggressive person.

Many of these achievers did not perceive their actions as aggressive against others, rather that they were directing the energy inwards. In some individuals, this produced a creative tension which was a vital source of usable energy. There is a philosophy behind this. One can climb the ladder of success by putting others down. It is an aggressive action if you step on someone else in order to win or take the next step up the ladder. On the other hand, it is possible to see a race as two or more people, or teams, going in pursuit of the same goal and the efforts of one enhance the efforts of the other. In this light, each person's best effort raises the standard of the whole. This is cooperation in competition. All those who agree to play within the rules are cooperating in order to have fair competition. Individual or collective assertiveness and competitiveness may be looked at as constructive rather than destructive behaviour. Sport is providing an opportunity for the development of ideal qualities or the opposite. The choice belongs to each individual. The pursuit of excellence may be individually and collectively elevating.

Earlier in this chapter, there was reference to the large percentage of introverts found in this study coupled with the fact that they were at home in their sporting environment. In this bounded area, assertiveness, and in some situations aggressiveness, can be acceptable behaviour. For the shy person, it is a perfect arena through which to channel these instincts. Nevertheless, sport will survive in a healthy state only if assertive and aggressive behaviour is coupled with the ideals outlined in the paragraph above. The philosophy must be understood by players, coaches, media and fans alike. The aim may be winning but it cannot be at all costs. There must be respect for others as well as ourselves; respect for their efforts whether that results in a win or not. Kip Keino referred to the fact that he would not look down on someone who came fourth or fifth, because he knew how hard each person in the competition had worked just to get into the race.

Do you consider that, emotionally, you were an early, late or average developer? It is refreshing that at forty-eight years old, Al Oerter continues to say most things with a laugh. He followed his statement about being a late physical developer by saying, 'Emotionally I'm just coming together!' Nearly 60 per cent felt that they were late developers emotionally, while a quarter thought they were early and one-fifth said that they thought they were about average.

Certainly if every free hour out of school time is spent playing sport, the performer's social interaction will be limited. Team work may develop as might close friendships among training partners and coaches; however other social interaction could be inhibited. There are several aspects to emotional and social development and many more questions would need to be asked to gain more than this general impression of the development of these athletes.

Ian Botham answered that he thought he was naive until about the age of fifteen. Many others put their age of reaching emotional maturity as much later than average. Seb Coe said he grew up quickly between twenty and twenty-one. Certainly few, if any, were prepared for the media pressure which hit them once a real level of success had been achieved. Television interviews are the norm now for those achieving international success. Looking back I find it hard to believe that it never crossed my mind that I would have to make after dinner speeches if I won. I was so shy the thought might well have dampened my enthusiasm. It took several years before I felt comfortable in public speaking.

An aspect of naivety may actually help the young aspirant. If a youngster at the beginning knew the degree of difficulty and the time and work required to reach the top, he or she might well be overawed and lose heart. The old biblical saying is very relevant here: you are only tested up to the level you are able. Take one day at a time. You need to know where you're going but all you need to be focused on is the next step. Billie Jean King said that at eleven years old, she had set her sights on winning Wimbledon. Only later on did that become 'scary', when she realized the enormity of the task she had set herself. It is through a lack of inhibition and not having limits to one's aspirations, imposed personally or from outside, which can be vitally important to the level of success reached. It might be termed naive thinking or just open-mindedly asking 'Why not?', but many new techniques and future records are subsequently thereby created.

Summary of learning points:

- A performer does not have to be extroverted or outwardly agressive to reach the top.
- Introversion can help the performer who must spend hours of practice time on their own.
- Sport can assist in personal development: overcoming shyness, promoting social acceptance, self-confidence and self-esteem.
- Even though highly assertive and competitive behaviour is acceptable on the field, high priority must be given to mutual and personal respect.
- Having a certain amount of naivety concerning potential drawbacks to an aim may be helpful. You need to have a vision of where you are aiming but only need to have your focus and energy attending to the next step.

8
COACH–PERFORMER
RELATIONSHIP

Just over 10 per cent of these performers said that they never really had any coaching. Jackie Stewart and Sir John Whitmore come from a sport where there are no coaches or trainers. Few if any hammer coaches existed to help Pat O'Callaghan to his 1928 and 1932 Olympic wins. Two of today's athletes who had no significant coaches, Ed Moses and Joan Benoit Samuelson, read a lot, experimented for themselves and then later on they had advisors with whom they sounded out their ideas.

Almost 20 per cent of those interviewed had some coaching involvement from their fathers. For three men, Ian Botham, Arnold Palmer and David Bryant, their fathers were the ones who gave them the basics and apart from that, coaching was relatively minimal. Viv Richards' father introduced him to the fundamentals, and for Carl Lewis both parents were coaches. However, both had other significant coaches who assisted in their development. Carl referred to the relationship with Tom Tellez, his long jump coach. There was a marriage of personalities and a mutual respect which is essential in any good coach–performer relationship.

The introduction of the fundamentals by the father was mentioned during pre-game interviews by Superbowl quarter-backs Joe Montana and Dan Marino. Both said that their fathers had taught and stressed upon them the fundamentals of play. Joe referred to family support as well as his father's dedication, and Dan made the point that he was not pushed by his father. 'But if I wanted to do it he'd be there to do it with me.'

Four other performers' fathers had a more significant role in that they were the main coach. Lester Piggott and Steve Davis referred to the basics given to them in technique. Sebastian Coe and Chris Evert were taken to the lift-off point by their fathers, after which they could cope for themselves but with their parent still retaining an advisory role. Seb's father was not involved in athletics at all; he had cycled, but the main aspect he brought to the task was a clear logical brain. He applied his scientific and engineering training to the study of middle-distance running. To an extent, the success he has had with Seb is testament to this naive yet fresh approach. Peter Coe was not weighed down with tradition in his thinking. Seb said, 'I've got a great debt of gratitude for the amount of time and intellectual effort that my father applied.'

A little over one-third of the achievers said that they had had more than one significant coach, many saying that different coaches assisted them as and when it was required. Duncan Goodhew said, 'It's like a piece of string that makes the distance; you cut one bit out and it's not going to make the distance.'

Perhaps one would have thought that a significant coach–performer relationship could only take place with one type of coach for each person; however, experience shows that that is not the case. Another one-third of the performers had more than one coach and several of them demonstrated that they could relate with and be stimulated by different types of personalities and coaching styles. My own experience was of a gentle, patient, technical hurdles coach working in cooperation with intuitive genius who was determined enough to hold me to the agreed session, no matter how difficult it was. From British coach Fred Housden I gleaned the intellectual understanding of the mechanics of my event. From US coach Billy Smith I learned the meaning of work. He had the ability the best coaches need. He could read me and suggest the ideal workout for the day, which fitted my energy and enthusiasm level with our long-term aim. Duncan Goodhew experienced three very different coaches. 'Paddy Garrett of Millfield School was a friend with a sarcastic sense of humour which cut to the bone and was an effective way of dealing with teenagers. He played me like a salmon. Don Easterling at North Carolina State University had a financial and contractual hold over me. We used to have head-to-head confrontations as we were both extremely hot-headed; we were conflicting characters. And lastly Dave Haller, the British Olympic coach, was really a quiet person with a "save it" type of attitude. His unique quality was being able to reduce the workload to make an athlete peak in competition. He knew what to say and when to say it, and during that pre-competition period, he was exceptional at bringing confidence into his swimmers.'

Forty per cent of these achievers experienced a deep or intensely significant coach–performer relationship which was non-family based.

It is in this group where sometimes the name of the coach becomes as famous as that of the achievers. Here are some who have become legendary: Herb Elliott and Percy Cerutty; Peter Snell and Arthur Lydiard; Roger Bannister and Franz Stampfl; Welsh rugby and Carwyn James; Peter Sterling and Australian rugby league with Jack Gibson; Nick Faldo and David Leadbetter.

Is it important for a coach to cultivate a particular style? Most people would advise that no one should try to be what they are not. However everyone has a choice as to how they interact with others. The quality of that interaction really determines whether the coach–performer relationship is a success or not. Having said that, the individual personalities vary and there are horses for courses. Olympic long jump champion Mary Rand said, 'There's someone for everyone. John le Masurier was quiet and that suited me.' As soon as possible the coach and performer should see whether they have a decent rapport and can work well together before committing themselves to a long and potentially disastrous relationship.

There are several types of coaching styles. A number have been given labels, which may be helpful as a model, but it should be understood that there are mixtures of each in every individual. It seems that most of the coaches had the capacity to be uncompromising at a certain level. They would not allow the gifted athlete to consider laziness as an option and most of them are from a generation where authority was not questioned. In some cases, their discipline produced an unnerving quality; if athletes stepped out of line, they would face great displeasure and that could jeopardize the relationship. It seems that the mature athletes who worked with these authoritarian coaches chose to adhere to the strict regime because they knew that it was the best way for them to fulfil their own ambitions and dreams. Al Oerter referred to his high school coach as authoritarian. Jonah Barrington spoke of Nasrullah Khan as very authoritarian. 'He had an aura about him . . . an air of considerable authority.' Peter Snell referred to Arthur Lydiard as 'an evangelist, dogmatic and a great motivator'. Herb Elliott spoke of Percy Cerutty as inspirational but also that his way was uncompromising. Lynn Davies spoke of the late Ron Pickering as quite authoritarian, quite dogmatic, but he also pointed out there are many aspects to each coach. Lynn also referred to Ron as 'very enthusiastic, a very good teacher, communicator, and motivator of people and a very strong outgoing personality that I responded to.' Peter Sterling spoke of the exceptional rugby league coaching record of Jack Gibson. He also referred to the fact that he was an authoritarian and a good teacher. 'He spoke slowly and the words were carefully chosen.' He went on, 'He was very good at reading the game, the opponents and us but the best thing that I could possibly say about him was that he was more interested in you off the paddock than on. I think he must have a good feeling for psychology because he believes that if you're happy, then you'll come through; if you're having trouble at home, it'll affect your game.'

In most cases, the performers reflected that their coaches had concern for them off the field: they were not just interested in the results produced but had a concern for the achievers as individuals. This can be termed a 'humanistic' approach. It seems that this additional element is the binding ingredient which enabled the authoritarian approach on the field to be accepted by the performer. Even though there was the appearance of heartlessness and intolerance in the authoritarian treatment on the practice field, out of the training context there was a genuine friendship and respect on both sides.

For a coach–performer relationship to be successful, there has to be a matching of several different aspects, including aims, respect, commitment and communication.

One difficulty in deciding the aims is that the coach and performer may not know how far each is capable, or indeed prepared to go. Nevertheless, for each individual, whether a beginner or potential world champion, the aim must be personal improvement. The goal setting must be challenging and realistic, positive, measurable, time phased and agreed. Obviously, the aims of the coach and athlete must coincide. If the coach would like the performer to become a champion and the performer is only interested in having some fun, then their relationship is probably not going to work. Likewise if the performer wants to reach his or her full potential and the coach does not share that interest, then there is bound to be disappointment in the relationship.

Why is respect important? Without mutual respect it is difficult to have confidence in the other person's efforts, and performance is tied closely to confidence. Asking how much mutual respect exists will test the level of faith in each other and the strength of the relationship. Respect may be generated in many ways – respect for ability, knowledge or achievement – but most important of all is the respect for the individual. A personal illustration of commitment increasing respect occurred when I was a student at Boston University. I usually met Billy Smith at 3 p.m. but on this particular day a blizzard had started at noon. I went to the door of the parking area at 3 p.m. not really expecting to see Billy, but instead bumped into him on his way in. I asked whether I should do some weight training or have a day off. He pushed the door open against the wind and driving snow, and said, 'Out there's the road to Mexico!' I thought he was joking but he clearly wasn't! As I did a series of 800m runs, Billy just stood there with his coat collar up and his back to the wind and driving snow. I hoped that my efforts would raise his respect for me and certainly his presence during the session in those conditions raised mine for him. He had been willing to go through it with me. It is that sort of mutual endeavour, under intense conditions, which strengthens the coach–performer relationship.

Must there be a consistent commitment by both coach and athlete? At the introductory level, over-intensity should be absent but the need for consistency is still vital. This is the time when the basics are repeated, in an enjoyable manner, so that the correct form can become second nature.

When the performers make their decision to commit themselves to the pursuit of excellence, then there is a requirement of time and effort needed from both athlete and coach. Gareth Edwards spoke of Bill Samuel as 'a man who cared and gave me time'. Few young athletes give much thought to the time, commitment and effort required by the coach. Their thoughts are often very self-centred and to an extent they have to be, but it is only in retrospect that the wealth of knowledge which has been given can be fully appreciated.

Without knowledge and understanding a performer can very easily be injured or burnt out, never to fulfil his or her promise. Initially the coach holds most of the cards, but as each performer is different the coach must involve the performer by asking them questions. How much do they know? What do they like to do? What do they consider are their strengths and what needs working on? Also although the coach may know the mechanical ingredients, firstly the way they are put together can produce very different results; and secondly the training regime which has worked for one individual will not work exactly the same way with someone else because the structure, chemistry and mentality of each individual is different. This difference provides a challenge of creativity, for coach and athlete, to put the best package together for each person. In sports where the performer starts very young such as in gymnastics and swimming the coach has added responsibility.

Ideally coaches are working to help the performer to grow. That means assisting and encouraging the performer gradually to take more responsibility for their learning and what is done. This must be gradual and progressive. It is the role of the coach to assist their growth to independence. The performer then chooses to have the coach as an advisor and friend rather than be in a perpetual 'child' role. An example of an evolved relationship is where Steve Cram was given the basics by Jimmy Hedley but determined his own track sessions from the age of eighteen. 'Jimmy's role has changed to being supportive, a motivator. It goes beyond a coach–athlete relationship. He's a friend of the family and another sort of father figure.' If coaches think about it, they will recognize that once the competition is under way, the performer is 100 per cent responsible for their actions. If the coach has been taking 100 per cent responsibility up to that point, have they really prepared the performer as well as they might? Ideally the venture and the learning are a shared responsibility.

Initially the youngster needs guidance and the coach's knowledge and experience are invaluable. However it should be noted that more than 90 per cent of our actions are performed unconsciously. We taught ourselves the highly complex tasks of learning to walk, to talk, to ride a bike and to catch a ball, by experience. The key ingredient was that we paid attention to what was going on, became more aware and endeavoured to focus on what we discovered was appropriate. It has been my experience in the last five years that the best way of helping the performer to discover their most appropriate focus is by asking them questions which raise their awareness of what is happening. Their discovery creates ownership and retention. It also raises their self-esteem and confidence.

No doubt it also helps for coaches to be widely read in their field, and if this is coupled with experience and feeling then the coach is well equipped. Elliott referred to Cerutty as 'inspirational'. 'He put together a nice blend of enthusiasm, confidence and intellect. He had a broad base of reading and knowledge on which to base his arguments and his directions, so that you felt there was some weight in them, and his own personal life experience added to this and so the whole blend of his knowledge and experience gave enormous believability and credibility.'

Is it necessary to have played the sport in order to coach it well?

Experience must be gained from somewhere. For the coach to have had personal experience of the sport is, without question, helpful, but it has been shown that it is not essential. Seb Coe's father demonstrated that a study of the sport and a knowledge of the individual are the key ingredients. The performers themselves can give the coach an appreciation of the elements they require. The coach will also better appreciate what the performer needs and have a clearer perception of the reaction to the demands being placed on the performer if there is dialogue.

The description given by Heather McKay of what she was taught by each of her coaches would lead us to believe that it would be difficult, if not impossible in some sports, to teach without experience. Heather said that she was taught stroke play by Vin Napier. 'He was a teacher and perfectionist on strokes and footwork technique.' Keith Walker followed on from Napier and of him she said, 'He taught me how to get the relationship of wall angle, height, pace and spacial awareness – I started to think at twenty-two!' The assistance from Kevin Parker came next. 'He helped tactically by teaching me the best choice of shots.'

Ron Pickering, whose sudden death in February 1991 was a great loss to the athletics community, gained some help from his wife Jean, a former European long jump champion, when coaching Lynn Davies. Ron had a physical education background and apart from his coaching experience, saw many athletes as he travelled in his capacity as England's team coach. He pointed out the significance of exposing the athlete to experience. 'I was absolutely convinced Lynn had to rub shoulders with the Americans, and over there, Ralph Boston beat him by a foot. [Lynn beat Ralph by less than two inches in the Olympics.] I think he was the first British athlete to go into the American trials. We had to raise the money to sponsor that.'

Is it helpful for the coach to set an example by attempting to lead and demonstrate? The problem here is one of ability. At some point in the coach's career, he or she may have been very competent. However, if they have not continued to practise their skills, then the demonstration may be less than helpful. In most cases, there is a happy medium where certain skills can be demonstrated by the coach, for example how to hold the equipment, or what the finishing position should be for an effective follow-through. Alternatively the coach could ask the performer to take a few throws, for example letting the hand be at different angles, and ask them to notice the relationship of the feeling and what happens to the object being thrown. The performers may have more natural talent but in several instances they said, 'I was never asked to do anything that my coach hadn't attempted first.' It is no longer rare to have the coach participating, albeit at a reduced level. One man who retained his intensity of effort alongside his athletes was Percy Cerutty, and a photograph from Portsea circled the globe showing Percy, then in his sixties, leading a group up the dunes. Herb Elliott recalled how on the morning of one of his races, Cerutty came back from a run and said to Herb, 'You may run faster today but you'll never run harder!' Percy lived out his example.

Communication can break down. If a performer is not completely open and does not tell the coach that he has a slight injury, the coach will not know that he needs to modify the training. On the other hand, if the coach fails to give clear instructions, then the athlete may start to practise an incorrect motion or do too much or too little training.

All the rugby union men spoke of the ability of Carwyn James to communicate effectively. He was cited as having the special ability to deal with different types of people in varying ways. This is a very unusual gift and makes them ideally suited for coaching teams. J.P.R. Williams referred to Carwyn as someone who was able to treat everyone individually. 'Coaches today tend to treat the forwards and backs the same in training and it tends to make everyone average. Carwyn was not strict, instead he used gentle persuasion, but his force of personality was like a breath of fresh air. A lot of coaches place so much importance on winning; you don't need that, you need some positive coaching and you need to be relaxed to play a normal game. He would say, "It's okay to be nervous but try to be above the atmosphere. Get out there and express yourselves."' Barry John commented on Carwyn's attitude. 'He was in search of excellence and he got the best out of each one of us. It was man management. He had total authority, a counsellor, he would ask, cajole, talk, invite thoughts. He'd probably made up his mind anyway but he'd ask you and that made you feel important.'

Elliott said that he and Percy had a tremendous rapport. 'We had a happy knack of being able to understand one another after about two words of a sentence. Percy might take half an hour to explain to a person something he was trying to get at, but within a couple of sentences, I would know exactly what he was talking about – there was a sort of empathy.'

No matter how widely read and experienced a coach may be, if he cannot communicate effectively then his knowledge is worth very little. Communication is possibly the most important of all areas. It is an essential requirement for any effective relationship. Many is the time when a highly intelligent teacher or professor is criticized for being a poor teacher because of a failure to communicate effectively with his or her students.

I have been co-leading a coaching communication course for the last five years. Having had interchange with more than five hundred coaches and athletes from local, regional, national and international level from forty or more sports it is my belief that in sport, business, education and even parenting, the inclusion or increase of questions alongside the traditional talking route is an essential evolution. The two elements which the coach's questions are trying to generate in the performer are increased awareness and responsibility. As these increase, performance improves. The most fundamental goal setting question is, 'What do you want?' Discovering comes from awareness in their current experience, through 'What are you sensing?' The coach follows the performer's interest, giving guidelines and input when appropriate or desired for explanation or demonstration. This process is performer-centred. A course teaching the skill of effective questioning is administrated by the UK National Coaching Foundation.

Motivation is not an easy term to define as it can be initiated from so many sources. In practical terms, the coach may not need to have a very good understanding of the athlete's underlying motives. What he must be able to do, however, is attach importance to the athlete's drive and desire to demonstrate to himself and others that he has a talent which he is trying to fulfil. The coach does need an appreciation of the importance of psychology.

Exactly how the coach motivates is variable. It is really a misinterpretation that the coach motivates the performer. A good coach brings out the best from the performer. Jonah Barrington said of his coach, 'He was the catalyst in regard to my own ambitions.' Top performers are usually very well motivated; all that is needed is for the coach to touch the stimulus which challenges and inspires him to reach for the height of their ability. Peter Sterling put it well when he said, 'If you look at the film *Rocky* and get all hyped-up before going on the field, it's going to be belted out of you in the first tackle. If you're not self-motivated, you're not going to make it.' Many athletes could not readily identify any action or word which was said or done by the coach in order to motivate them. There was just a mutual understanding that they were travelling down a road together and they both knew that the aim was to become the best. A few coaches are able to inspire by example, others may do so through words and for some it may simply be their presence. Often the coach is there prior to competition, simply expressing faith in the performer's physical and mental preparation. What is important is that both coach and athlete desire the performer's attainment to reach another higher level. Ideally the performer has the inner motivation and the coach's ambitions for the athlete are on an even higher level than his own. John Whitmore cited his Ford team manager Alan Mann. 'His personal ego didn't interfere with how he got the job done. He had no great ego needs to be seen as the great team manager himself. He was just getting the job done, so 100 per cent of his focus was on the right thing, rather than 50 per cent of his focus on being seen to do the job right. He had more faith in me than I did and that helped me build up my own faith in myself.' That is a genuinely motivating action. Conversely if the coach does not have faith in the performers or team, that will come through to them at some level, and could create a self-fulfilling prophecy.

It is very rare when a coach has the knowledge and ability to inspire in the manner of Percy Cerutty. Herb Elliott eloquently summed it up: 'Percy wasn't standing there with a horsewhip flogging you up and down the sand-hills. His motivation would come in an indirect way. He seemed to sense what your own appetites and ambitions were. He would put the plate in front of you, he wouldn't shove it down your throat. You'd choose your own direction. An example would be a winter's night at Portsea, sitting around the fire and he'd start to talk about Beethoven, Jesus, St Francis, Leonardo da Vinci, anybody that he'd studied who was a great person, not in a sense of a passing thing like winning a gold medal or winning an Australian championship or anything like that, but in the sense of a person who is still spoken about hundreds or thousands of years after they've died. Somehow or other he would excite a sense in me and I think in many others that each of us has our own greatness, we are all totally unique and we always will be, so that we have a tremendous opportunity for being great in our own sort of way. By talking about other people being great, he'd touch your own sense of yourself and freshen up your ambitions and almost challenge you in a way, though without saying it, not to waste your own greatness and that would sort of fire you up. He just had that ability – he did it with knowledge and careful planning, I think, of how he would speak but he never ever said, "Don't waste your greatness." He just let you make up your own conclusions so that the path you chose appeared to be self-chosen.'

Could you have reached the level you did without a coach? The question was asked to see whether those performers who did have coaches felt their ultimate level of success would have been possible without that relationship and help. The question is hypothetical and Steve Davis gave the honest reply, 'Who knows?' About 10 per cent of the performers were not sure and usually said that it would have been a lot more difficult. For example, Al Oerter replied: 'It would have been very difficult. I probably would have wound up in sport in some way because of my size and strength, but I don't know if I would have been able to enjoy a sport as long as I have done. I would probably have been in baseball or football and have been long retired by now.'

Jayne Torvill and Christopher Dean also said that it was a difficult question to answer. Christopher is the creative one who puts the pro-gramme ideas forward and then they work on it together. Betty Callaway and Courtney Jones are advisors and friends and their opinion is valued on the choice of music and ultimate performance.

Nearly 20 per cent felt that it might have made some difference but that they probably could have reached the top in their sport without significant coaching assistance, Lester Piggott saying that he thought it just would have taken longer. Several of the team sport players, such as Bryan Robson and Gareth Edwards, said that they were able to develop their individual skills but needed the coach to develop the team situation. The remaining two-thirds believed that they would not have reached the level they did without the assistance of their coach and they usually cited at least one good reason. Of course, many reasons have already been covered concerning the coach–performer relationship. Nevertheless, further insights were given into why their relationships were valued.

Ken Read said that there was no way he would have reached the top without his coach Scott Henderson. 'He'd work and work at something until he thought we had it and then he'd shift to the next thing.' This step-by-step approach requires a great deal of patience on the part of the coach but is invaluable for the performer because under pressure, humans revert to what is second nature. If the fundamentals are sound and have been repeated correctly enough times to have become second nature, then the form will not give way in the most important tests.

Bobby Charlton was another who said that he did not think he could have reached his ultimate level without his coaches Jimmy Murphy, Bert Wooley and Sir Matt Busby. Of Jimmy Murphy, Bobby said, 'I never went on the field without thinking of him. I supposed he brainwashed me but, just as you learn to ride a bike, it becomes second nature. Anything from a professional point of view that I did as second nature was something that Jimmy Murphy taught me; whether it was marking, doing a one-two with someone and getting a return pass, or whether it was a shot on goal, there was always something there that Jimmy Murphy had worked on with me.'

The fact that a coach can become a part of an athlete's thinking was mentioned by Steve Ovett several years ago. In recent years, Steve has had a close friendship with Matt Paterson who has also given him advice, but in the early days Steve was introduced to the sport by Harry Wilson. When Steve was only eighteen, he said that he could hear Harry yelling at him, even though Harry was not physically present. It was an experience which I had personally encountered in my time with Billy Smith. While training alone, there would come a point of tiredness where the need and temptation were to slow down, but the acquired conscience from my coach was strong enough for me to feel his eyes on me and hear his voice encouraging me not to ease up until the end of the session. The expectations and will of my coach somehow had become ingrained and merged with my own will and self-expectations.

For Nick Faldo the 100 per cent trust is in David Leadbetter. 'He's a brilliant man. He's really studied it and works a lot with video and understands it.' The communication is two-way. Even though Nick is the best in the world he is still willing and eager to learn more. 'David said that I was his best listener. The most intense person he's ever coached. I'm always wanting to know more and take it all in. I like to know why everything's doing what it's doing.'

Being in the right place at the right time was considered to be important in the fortunes of these athletes. Lynn Davies said, 'I'm pretty convinced that if Ron [Pickering] had not come to Wales as national athletics coach, I would not have continued in the sport.'

Another important aspect taught by the coach was making the performer think like a winner. Those achievers who win do not waste their time thinking of the reasons why it might not be possible to achieve a goal; they do not give such negative thoughts the time of day. The focus is on the ways of achieving the next step. Billie Jean King said that she was given practical suggestions as well as a role model by a Wimbledon winner. 'Over a period of three months, Alice Marble taught me how to think like a winner, yet she was nice. I knew what it was to be around a champion and how a champion thinks. The first thing she said was, "You get too close." She talked about the face of the racket in relation to the ball. I devoured her scrap books.'

As mentioned earlier, one of the greatest gifts a coach can give is a sense of belief in the performer. Frank Brennan worked with Billie Jean on strategy and focusing. 'At fifteen, he told me, "You're going to win Wimbledon one day."' Finally for Billie Jean, Lew Hoad helped to put everything together. 'I gave up my job at twenty-one and made the commitment to be number one. He changed my serve, forehand and strategy. It consolidated my game. It was a tough period, ranked number four in the world, and during one game I served thirty-five double faults. People questioned why I was changing and I said, "Because I want to be the best."'

Knowledge both of the physical and psychological may be gained in conjunction with academic and scientific research or it may be simply the application of common sense. When Valeriy Borzov was asked if he could have reached his potential without his coaches, he gave a firm answer of no. Valeriy had been taught the basics by his school coach and then he had learned about the workings of the body and mind from a professor at his sport institute who worked with him for twelve years, from 1966 to 1978.

Less sophisticated but equally helpful was the role of Pat Burgess as described by Lucinda Green. 'There have been masses of people who I've put my trust in and have been the cornerstone on which to build, but the person who has seen me through the longest and has been the most helpful of all is Pat Burgess. She is no world trainer of any sort, she just trains in a back field over tin cans and poles but has this wonderful quality of common sense which so many people lose when they start learning techniques, and an ability to know what a horse is thinking and feeling, and to see why a rider isn't getting on and why that horse isn't going. She's a really gifted person.'

Before closing this chapter on the coach–athlete relationship, it is worth asking the question: What does the coach get out of all this? In many cases they will get as much, if not more, from the experience as the achiever. It is a very true saying that in giving, one receives. In fact both parties do give and when each knows that the other is devoting their best effort, mutual respect and allegiance are gained, and a closeness is established. Trust is also established when the performer knows that the coach is not trying to exploit him or her by 'living off' their success, either financially or through self-glorification.

All of the coaches referred to the value they placed on their personal relationships with their performers. This is quite possibly the most important element in the long term. The mutual effort towards a common goal brings a closeness and sharing and thus enhances communication. This makes the process valuable in itself, regardless of the outcome. All the better if it results in a winning performance, but if there is an intrinsic worth in the endeavour, then both parties gain and grow by the experience. There are several factors which contribute to making the relationship valuable. The situation evolves over a considerable length of time during which there is a sharing of the spectrum of emotions: joys and sorrows, frustration, despair, humour, hope and elation. The goal is shared and the endeavour is mutual. In the close coach–performer relationship, the coach can become totally consumed with the performer, and their projected aspirations become one and the same.

In many cases, the gifted performer will inspire a coach to learn more about the sport or event, bringing about a mutual learning experience; indeed the coach will often learn more through working with a gifted performer than working with one of lesser ability. A young performer who has the necessary ingredients to go to the top kindles an enthusiasm in the coach and an eagerness to work with a would-be achiever. The coach's role then is to work the performer but also to preserve the performer's enthusiasm. My coach Billy Smith said, 'If the athlete is force-fed then the enthusiasm can be chipped away. You can parallel enthusiasm with motivation. When the enthusiasm is at its highest, the performance will be the best. It almost overrules physical logic, too. Enthusiasm is the key.'

My other coach, Fred Housden, intentionally took on athletes of all abilities because he wanted to broaden his own learning experience in how to teach at all levels.

Tom Tellez has coached Carl Lewis since 1980. He saw the necessary ingredients as going beyond pure physical talent. 'There are other kids who have just as much ability. He's got a lot of ability but I think there are other athletes who have had or do have right now as much ability, but I attribute his success to his parents, his home life and his stability. I think they created a sense that there are no limitations to what you can do if you want to. The Lewis children were brought up with that idea. Anything is yours if you want it and are prepared to work for it.' Later he added, 'I think our personalities kind of hit. I'm not a dogmatic kind of coach, I tend to work with the athletes. I don't like to overwork kids. They have to be self-motivated. I work on mechanics. You prepare the athlete mentally by preparing him physically.' He then spoke of what he gets from it all. 'You plan something . . . you conceive of a model . . . we've built this model and he is the model and he's doing everything well . . . that's the thrill I get out of it.'

I asked Billy Smith when he started goal setting the Olympic 400m hurdles for me. He replied, 'Oh, first or second day.' His wife added, 'I was in hospital having given birth to our first daughter, Susan, and he came in and said, "There's a kid named David Hemery who showed up at camp today. He needs work. He really needs work, but he's got great technique, he's going to be good, I'm telling you, really good." I said, "How good?" It was almost like he was afraid, he kept saying, "I don't know, I just know he's going to be really good" and he sat there rubbing his forehead, he was just so excited.' One reason for a coach being nervous before the relationship starts is that 'with opportunity comes responsibility' and Billy said that he did not want to mess it up.

John le Masurier was big enough to be self-critical of his taking too much responsibility up to 1960. He said, 'I think I nursed Mary [Rand] too much in competitions in this country. It's a great temptation to go out and see where the foot comes on the board in the run-ups prior to competition. It was a lesson we learned from. It was better after Rome to say, "Right, you're on your own. Go out and do it and I'll watch you from afar. I'll talk to you beforehand and I'll talk to you afterwards." She had to learn to do it herself and be self-supporting.' For John, one aspect which meant a lot to him was the friendships which he had with his athletes. 'Mary and my wife would have long chats on the phone. I think it's very helpful if the people you're coaching are individuals you want in your home. Mary, Vic Matthews, Sue Platt, we were one big happy family really, and I think that was an advantage.' For Ron Pickering, 'The great joy days were the training days. The competition days were always the stress days.' Ron worked out in the weightroom with Lynn where there was an element of mutual challenge. Ron said, 'It took three years before he could out-lift me – and it took another year before he could beat me at everything.' Ron used his verbal dexterity and wit to goad Lynn to the next level of effort. For example, Lynn would be asked to demonstrate for some assembled coaches and Ron would climb all over him verbally. 'He and I knew it was humour but the crowd didn't and he would get such sympathy from them. I can remember the phrases, "Yes, 25ft 4in [7.72m] – that's grade three for clerical workers in Outer Mongolia! Do you think these people have travelled 150 miles to see a grade three performance of that sort? Don't you think they deserve to see you at your very best? I mean I've seen you on a cold day do things and really, to waste their time . . ." And the banter would go on. Lynn was asked by someone at the front, "How do you feel about that?" To which Lynn replied, "I love it. It brings out the best performance in me and he knows it." I was constantly challenging him, attempting to put him under competitive conditions.'

Unlike John le Masurier, Ron told Lynn that he was on his own prior to the big meeting against the Soviet Union. It was, however, the first time that Ron had had a long-distance perspective of his athlete. From 75m away, he saw errors in movement which he had missed by always being right beside the take-off board. The new visual perspective altered the game plan for the future. It caused a complete rethink of their approach to the event. Ron said that over time, their relationship changed. 'Far less authoritarian, far more man to man, far more intimate, because we were talking about minor adjustments and philosophical discussions, we were not talking about command-response situations. My new role for the developed athlete was to be his eyes when he needed them and to be much more subordinate. My value to him was to use the experience of life rather than my experience as a coach and that is where our friendship developed in that I would expect him to come to me about money problems or marriage, and that was far more important than to create simply a practical and correct environment from which he could develop athletically. The environment became more important than the event and I think that happens in all cases.' Ron also referred to the coach's home as being a place where the athletes came as friends and that they would talk to his wife about things that were troubling them which they would not have shared with him. He thought that this was because of the coach–athlete rapport, which is based on high expectations of one another.

At times it can be a thankless task and as has been said already, the athletes are at times very egocentric. The strength of the experience is in mutual learning, where both sides recognize and appreciate that the other is giving of their best.

Enthusiasm is generated in the coach because the performer with all the necessary elements for world achievement does not come along every day. A line from *Chariots of Fire* spoken by coach Massubini says it all: 'You can't put in what God left out.' In many cases, a performer may have the head but not the body, the heart but not the coach, the body but not the will, so when a good coach meets a willing performer with sufficient mind, heart, body and will to get to the top, it is understandable why this recognition would lift the spirits, and the experienced coach will see the potential and try to realize it.

Summary of learning points:

- Ideally a coach should be sensitive to the needs and energy level of the performer.
- Many good coaches are uncompromising on the field, but genuinely care about the wellbeing of the performer off the field.
- For a coach–performer relationship to work there must be shared aims, commitment, respect and communication.
- A coach can gain knowledge and understanding through personal participation and reading but often the most value of all will come from asking the performer about their experiences.
- The coach asking questions which increase the performer's awareness and generate more responsibility in them will help these performers to grow and get the most from themselves.
- A coach should appreciate the differences between performers and treat them according to their needs.
- A coach acts to stimulate the interest which is already in the performer.

Coach–Performer Relationship

- Maintaining the performer's enthusiasm is the most important element for the coach.
- A coach's reward is often more from the high quality relationships than the successes. The mutual endeavour to develop excellence brings its own satisfaction.

9

TEAM LEADERSHIP AND MANAGEMENT:

INVOLVING THE PERFORMERS

How do the most effective leaders and managers communicate and relate with their teams? This chapter is different from the others in that a deliberate attempt has been made to compare sport with an area outside; in this case business management. As leaders in sport or business the aim is identical – to bring the best out of ourselves and the individuals whom we lead.

The following people were interviewed: Neil Benson – senior partner in Lewis Golden & Co., chartered accountants, non-executive chairman of Moss Bros and of Godfrey Davis; Sir Michael Edwards – chairman of Charter Consolidated and several others, ex-chairman of British Leyland; David Evans – chairman and chief executive of the Grass Roots Group; Sir John Harvey Jones MBE – ex-chairman of ICI, chairman of *The Economist*, vice-chairman of Grand Metropolitan, and many other roles; Billy Beaumont MBE – director of Blackledge (family firm), ex-captain of England rugby union team; Sue Campbell MBE – director of the National Coaching Foundation, regional netball and athletics coach; Ron Dennis – owner and director of McLaren International (world champion team); Richard Noble OBE – team leader and driver of Thrust II holding world land speed record; Peter Shilton MBE – former England goalkeeper (world record 125 caps); Graham Taylor – ex-manager of Watford and Aston Villa, current manager of England football team; David Whitaker OBE – ex-international player, coach of Great Britain's Olympic gold hockey team.

From the calibre of these contributors, and the insights which they shared from their experience, this chapter and the next could easily have made a book in themselves. In these two chapters, learning points are included after the answers to individual questions.

Leaders have choices as to how they relate with their teams. At one extreme the leader can be an irresponsible dictator and at the other he or she may take no responsibility, the team doing as they wish. In the spectrum in between there are many options but to identify just four, 'telling' and 'selling' ideas, plans, and action are 'leader-centred'; and two more, 'sharing' and 'empowering', are 'performer-centred'. More and more leaders and managers are recognizing the value and benefits of being skilled in each of these four options, rather than being stuck predominantly in our traditional 'telling' mode. What really struck me in this group was the predominance of performer-centred thinking or, at the very least, evidence of an evolution in that direction.

The quality of any leader, coach or manager's communication will hugely affect their team's commitment and performance. All the above people have been highly successful in their leadership roles. All have related well with their performers.

The questions I asked centred around *how* these individuals lead others. The unexplored side which obviously counts for a great deal are the qualities which these individuals possess. Several were recognized as leaders from early days, as school monitors, prefects, head of school, team captains, president of the student union, leader of army outward-bound training, etc. They all have a presence which cannot be ignored – an inner drive, a quiet or not so quiet determination, a positiveness, and energy and enthusiasm which would carry many with them. However, there are many determined, assertive, articulate individuals who are shunned. These leaders were not, so how did these individuals lead?

How would you describe your leadership style? The majority of these superior leaders involved their performers as part of their leadership process.

Sir John Harvey Jones said, 'My leadership style is highly participative.' He described why and then how he helps people grow through questioning. 'We are always more comfortable telling people what to do. Because after all we have the job we have because we did their job and did it well, but the difference in business (in sport there may be a longer time slot) is that what did work two years ago won't work today, because everything's changing at such a rate. The problem is to persuade industrial leaders that they're out of date. We are always more comfortable doing what we did before than what we ought to do now, and so there's a built-in preference – also you feel better. The guy you've just told thinks he feels better because you've taken his problem away. You feel better because you feel you've taken his problem away. You feel better because you feel you've grown or shown you're really smart, and actually what you've done is failed both ways. You've failed to help the guy develop and you're taking a big risk in the decision because you are applying yesterday's solution to today's problem.' He went on to say how he would handle the situation. 'I'm fanatical about delegation and I'm fanatical about not allowing people to delegate their problems upwards. So even though I think I can say yes or no or resolve a problem, I won't.' He explained that when someone came to him with a problem he always asked them what solution they had thought of first. The chances were that, since they were in touch with current practices, their idea would work. He would usually encourage them to go ahead, aware that the responsibility was his, as the manager. 'You always have to push credit down and take blame up.' Consistent with his belief that with rapid change all solutions must be reviewed in light of each new situation, Sir John went on to say, 'The trouble is that people try to systematize it. People love programmes. But we are all different at different times. You can have broad principles, but judgements are made the whole time – how hard to go, how soft to go, how supportive to be. I think that there is a lot more interest in *enabling leadership*.'

This parallels sport so well. Performers cannot be expected to follow a linear progressive programme, nor one written in stone. Each day and almost at every instant the effective coach and manager needs to monitor and assess each performer in light of their current situation, asking them questions for two purposes: first, to raise the performer's self-awareness as to where he or she is physically, mentally and emotionally – something the coach is well-placed to understand; second, to enable the performer to make his or her own choice for the next step. The advantage of the questioning process here is that the performer will gradually learn to self-monitor, and self-question, which means they can continue their development when you, the coach or manager, are not around.

Sir John mentioned another aspect of leadership. 'I believe the role of the leader is to set the long-term goal of the strategic direction in which you're going. And I don't care where, as long as I'm moving forward instead of backwards. If the direction everyone else wants is not where I thought we should go, I'll go . . . once the thing's rolling, you can change direction anyway. I may see that they were right or they may realize it isn't the right place to be and head towards my preferred course, or we may both come to realize that we'd rather be in a third alternative. In industry (and I suspect with any team) you can only move with the hearts and minds. And you don't get the hearts and minds by just beating people about the bloody ears. You get it by involving them, endless debate and discussion and then giving them their head and showing that you trust them.'

Richard Noble confirmed this last point when he said, 'It's got to be very participative. The thing's only going to work if you're leading them in the direction they want to go. So my leadership style is very free, to have them doing their own thing, within the boundaries set out and agreed as their responsibility. The leader's role is far more as a chairman than a dictator.'

The responses from many more of these leaders were that their style had gone through an evolutionary process. They had become less authoritarian and more participative.

Sue Campbell said, 'Management of other people is the crux of what the NCF is about, and I've thought a great deal about the style with which I manage, and I've changed that quite a bit over the years, from being quite authoritarian, and "You will do it this way", to a working-together partnership, with me guiding rather than telling. My style now is more like a coaching style than a leadership style. I use those skills I used in sport coaching to manage and lead people. It's a bit more in line with your questioning style, trying to lead by giving people responsibility and then guiding them to use that effectively. But you must be aware that if you manage in that way, people will make mistakes, as they do when they're sport performers, but part of the learning process are those mistakes and you have to guide them through that, and support them. It's neither an autocratic nor a *laissez-faire* style, it's more democratic and like coaching.'

Ron Dennis said, 'It has been, in the past, more autocratic than it is now. I think the formula for success is constantly changing. Over the last few years the company has grown four or five times bigger, and it's not humanly possible to communicate effectively all the way down to the grass roots of the company. So you have to put into position, and this is part of our growing, an effective management structure to not only coordinate the human resources of the company but also provide the conduit through which the *esprit de corps* and the motivational messages are passed.' He explained that a more complex managerial structure is needed as a company expands to foster inner motivation and free spirit among the team; autocracy won't work in the way it would for a military body. He went on: 'My own role in the history of McLaren I want to see as a positive chapter, but I don't want to see McLaren finish on my retirement or death, and I think it's the role of all management to leave behind a structure that can allow the company to move forward and to grow – but more importantly to leave behind them the values that have served the company well, which come from your own ideas and ambitions.'

David Whitaker said, 'I think what's really needed in a good leader is the ability to use the style which is most appropriate to the situation – to have the flexibility to alter your style subtly, so that you help the people you're coaching achieve their highest standards. My personal style has evolved. It's a style that might be called more performer-centred or more democratic, but one has to be able to be more autocratic at times. This predominantly democratic style has evolved because of my experiences as a performer. I wasn't asked many questions and my input was not particularly valued, even though I was the person at the sharp end.' The feeling that his contributions would not have been appreciated made him determined to do things differently once he was in the coaching role. This was reinforced when he noticed how the enthusiasm and motivation of youngsters is so often blunted instead of developed; and then, observing his own children, he noted how they learned by experience. 'A number of things came together at the same time, so I began to experiment with a more open style of coaching. And I think the real basis of it was that I believe that most of the answers to team difficulties, whether they be team integration, technical or tactical, are actually wrapped up in the performer, rather than wrapped up in the coach. I think the coach has the vision and real quality coaches know quite a lot of the answers to problems, but to actually get the performers to verbalize or illustrate the solution then firstly they must be *their* solutions to *their* problems, which is absolutely essential and far more powerful because it promotes their intrinsic motivation. They find their own solutions rather than have them imposed on them, however well, by the coach.'

David Evans was another who said that his style had changed across the years: 'I would describe myself initially as a Plantagenet leader, leading from the front before the gates of Honfleur or whatever; not a general at the back saying "It's time we went over the top." I've always tended to be with the troops. I've always led by example. They say that success is born out of perspiration and I've never been afraid to perspire . . . In the last ten years I've not assumed all the responsibility. I've become, in a sense, less selfish and encouraged others to lead their parts. I get people involved in decisions and I tend to work by consensus rather than vote-taking and as time goes on you adjust the style to meet the needs of the organization. Being a coach for a sports team you're always looking for the interplay and when you run a company, large or small, you've got lots of different interplays every hour, every day. Your management style, your chairmanship style, your leadership style will reflect the nature of the organization in part.'

Billy Beaumont: 'I've been working with a local junior squad and last year I spent quite a bit of time telling them what to do, and by the end of the year I think they were getting a bit cheesed off. This coming year I'll be involving them more. If they feel more ownership they'll enjoy it more. It was something I did without realizing it when I was captaining the British rugby team. I liked to involve performers and be involved in decisions and goals. I never put people in an untenable position. It's man management; different people react differently. Also if you're prepared to give . . . you're leading by example.'

Neil Benson: 'I believe in having good individual personal relation-ships. I'm as far removed from confrontation as possible. I think it's as close to being the old-fashioned notion of popularity as makes no difference. I want people to follow because they're either enjoying me or enjoying what they're doing and if in doubt they will follow on the basis of personality; and if I slip up I have enough brownie points to take them through on personality. It includes a lot of smiling, a lot of laughing and a lot of keeping people up, as it were. It's not dour.' Enthusiasm, however generated, is just as vital to performance levels in the work place as it is in the sports arena.

Graham Taylor used a player's reflections of his honest approach to identify another requirement of leadership. 'The best thing that was ever said to me, which I took as a tremendous compliment, came from a professional player at Watford who said to me, "There's one thing about working with you, if you get it wrong, I'm confident that you've got it honestly wrong." By the very nature of the job, there's a great deal of insecurity and suspicion. Managers have to make decisions in terms of team selection and someone's left out of the side who played well the previous game, but because there's a new situation, a different selection is made. Often a variety of reasons are given to that player, which he knows aren't truthful. It's far better to say to the fellow, "Look, I know that you did well last week, and you did everything that I wanted, and I really do believe that we have to select this side, which means there's no room for you." Also, I'd like to think, I'm enthusiastic and positive. I've never ever sent a side out that, inside myself, I've thought wouldn't win. Another consideration with professional footballers is that their peaks and rewards come very early in their lives, and it's a problem to maintain a balance about everything. The system promotes and pushes them and can chew them up and spit them out. So the manager has to take great responsibility and has to have a caring side. In a club situation I'd be very interested and involved in the players' welfare off the pitch.' Graham said that although there is the boss-employee relationship, he is looking to develop trust. And he added that with the England team, he aims to keep them as relaxed as possible, so that they don't go over the top by the time of the game. In times of pressure, or following some poor results, he aims to project belief, confidence, positiveness, and control of the situation. There are some parallels here with high-flying young executives needing to maintain perspective and balance in their lives, while the company leader needs to maintain composure and positiveness, focusing on what can be controlled during difficult economic times.

Peter Shilton said that on the field he led by example and respect, by putting 100 per cent in training and trying very hard during the games. During the game, 'a lot think it's criticism but it's not. I'm well known for talking to players on the pitch – directing and organizing. I'm trying to help them, and that doesn't mean being nice all the time. It's instructional, positional play, being able to explain to them. I'm the eyes in the back of their heads. Sometimes I'll see players starting to play as singles and that's not as good as a team collectively. If they've done well I'll encourage them and say "well done". If I see people giving it away a bit I'll scream and shout and they respond. Over the years I may have overdone it at times but they know I'm only doing it for the benefit of the team.' And off the pitch Peter leads by sharing his concerns with management. 'I've always chosen to work with managers I respect – someone whom I can trust, who's honest and someone I can talk to. That's two-way, and it's not about agreeing with each other all the time.

Disagreements show that each of you has your own thoughts. It's on the basis of being a man. Some managers bear grudges because they can't take criticism and that's not being honest with themselves.'

Sir Michael Edwardes began with his belief that top people in industry don't lack intelligence, but 'worry about making mistakes as opposed to going for success'. He named *courage, boldness* and, more than anything else, *lack of pettiness* as the main criteria for effective leadership. He liked the attitude of ex-cricket captain Tony Greig. 'How many times have the MCC ended up in a draw because of lack of boldness? Tony Greig wouldn't have done that. He'd have said, "Come on fellows, let's bloody go for it" and the result is that morale would have been higher, and with boldness you can actually accomplish things. On the occasions when we showed real boldness during the strikes at BL, when people said, "If you do this there'll be an all out-strike" and we said, "Well there's no other answer, we've got to do it", we never got the strikes.'

Sir Michael described leadership as bringing about change and management as managing existing situations and people. 'A manager is someone who administers a thing in a very orderly way; a civil servant tends to be a good manager, whereas Churchill was a leader. The chap who has got a bit of each in him is a very valuable commodity.'

Equating coaching and leadership Sir John Harvey Jones defined leadership as enabling ordinary people to achieve extraordinary things. He defined management as the art of getting things done or achieving a pre-determined aim, through the willing collaboration of people. He immediately followed this by saying 'I think the process is exactly the same because just as in business, as I understand it, the task of the coach is partly, of course, to work on the physical aspects, but primarily it is to create the state of mind where the man believes he can do it. I'm absolutely clear that you can't do things you don't believe you can do and if you do believe you can do things then you've got a sporting chance you can actually do them.' This statement ties in exactly with one of the main theses in this book: 'The Mind is Key.' Sir John echoed Sir Michael's thoughts on boldness: 'The problem is that people set themselves unduly low aspirations and the task of the leader is continually to ratchet up their belief in themselves and increase the size of their aspiration.'

Sir John compared chairmanship skills to Leonard Bernstein conducting a symphony orchestra, making sure everyone is heard – 'realizing that the chap on the left is actually jumping up and down inside although he's not actually saying anything. A chairman can make a lot of dissent safe and equally can do a lot by pushing things the other way, saying, "Oh you do all surprise me because I thought you were all really pissed off with the personnel policy," etc. Chairmanship is a combination of preparation and great flexibility. As chairman I will never allow silence to imply assent. I don't take votes at the end of a meeting, I go round and I say, "Now I want to hear from each of you where you are and why." They all have to actually say where they are.'

Summary of learning points:

- The quality of communication between leader and performer hugely affects performance.
- Telling is easy because it's familiar, but old solutions tend to be used and the person being told doesn't develop.
- Solutions aren't written in stone – each person and situation needs monitoring, assessing and enabling.
- Questions, which increase the performer's awareness of their experience, create change and provide the performer with recognition of choice, thereby motivating and empowering.
- Leaders share their vision, goal and strategic direction.
- Democratic leaders discuss and as necessary modify and agree the goals, then give responsibility for specific areas. They appreciate that learning involves making mistakes.
- Forward movement in any direction is preferable to inertia. This can only be achieved with the hearts and minds of the team.
- Dictatorship doesn't access inner-generated potential.
- Completely cutting off performer input demotivates.
- Allowing performers to verbalize and illustrate their own solution to problems promotes their intrinsic motivation.
- The most able leaders have flexible styles.
- Leaders must model what they expect from their workforce.
- Enthusiasm is as important to performance in the work place as it is in the sports arena.
- Performers value a leader's honesty.
- Leaders need to care about life balance in their young high-flyers.
- Going for success as a leader means courage, boldness and not being petty.

- Coaching people in management or sport is helping to develop a state of mind where the performer believes he or she can do it.
- Most people set their aspirations too low.
- Silence in a team does not imply assent. Able leaders involve their performers in dialogue.

Do you think about and plan how you lead others? A couple said that they let their intuition or instinct guide them – they just stayed present with each situation as it unfolded. Neil Benson said, 'I pride myself on it being instinctive.' The majority did plan how they led others and quite often that was done in conjunction with the performers.

Peter Shilton saw the biggest thing in management as personality, and then illustrated the need to be fully present in the moment. 'Management is about sensing the right moment to make a comment, when to take the heat out of a situation.'

Graham Taylor said, 'I don't sit down and think how I'll lead this player or that player. It's almost an assumption. I've been leading teams since my mid-twenties and held responsible positions from school days. I believe one of the failures of football is how they appoint people. Good players may not have leadership qualities, and there's no real apprenticeship.'

David Whitaker was in the majority saying, 'Oh, an enormous amount of planning goes into all coaching and leading, I think it's essential. But the plan is an outline, a framework; the actual detail of how you help people to perform at very high levels is developed in conjunction with the performers. It's a dialogue. You plan but you must have flexibility within that plan, otherwise you'll finish up imposing your needs on the situation rather than the performer's needs, and if you forget about the performers then I don't think you're truly coaching.'

Billy Beaumont said that at first he did have a complete plan for the day, but also he sought advice from the other performers in the team, on which he acted later.

Richard Noble observed that input from the responsible team leaders modifies original plans and that 'the project doesn't really start to run until it's lost your original standpoint. In other words it has its own identity rather than your identity. It starts with the leader's objective, then there's discussion around that. It has to have a shared vision. I had a clear objective but didn't plan how I led the team.' Richard brought into the team top people in their field and they then held full responsibility for each of those areas. Richard then acted more as a chairman leader.

Ron Dennis said, 'Of course, achieving success in motor sport, which is a very complex sport, taking in commercial as well as sporting aspects, necessitates the need for a clear strategy. Apart from recognizing the goal, which is relatively easy, there is the need to communicate the strategy to all the people participating in the team effort. And a Grand Prix team is seen by most as those at the Grand Prix circuit, but that's the tip of the iceberg.'

Sir John admitted that he was not a detail man; he needs a 'sweeper-upper'. However in this area he plans very carefully: 'I'm a great believer in Process Planning which is an industrial technical term for planning the way in which you do work, rather than planning the actual task. One of the problems in industry is that we are all very achievement and task oriented – we like to get stuck in, doing the job, and we don't spend a lot of time planning and working out *how* we are going to actually get the commitment and hearts and minds of our team members.' He pointed out that all sorts of things are crucial to the process – the way in which the meeting is set up, the type of furniture and its arrangement, the meals served, the general atmosphere. He prefers to be informal and relaxed, in shirtsleeves, with people free to get up and pour themselves a cup of coffee. He believes industrial leadership is not receptive to openness and discussion of issues in a real way: 'Brits are very, very bad communicators, and mostly in Britain people communicate by what they don't say rather than what they do bloody say. So you have to be able to read the people and change the atmosphere. I'm a great believer in friction. Unless you are actually discussing things that really worry you, where the discussion actually gets a bit heated, you're almost certainly not in the right bloody subject. Dancing over issues and rubber stamping! There's too much to be done, the thing's too serious, to ponce around having a board meeting spending a whole bloody day where we don't decide anything differently to what was on the agenda when we first came in.'

Hearing these words I couldn't help but reflect on my experience of many amateur sports governing body meetings. So often there are reports on what has been done and assignment of who will report on advances at the next meeting. Serious issues concerning the performers' needs, the need for organizational restructure, the awkward problem of politically motivated members or power struggles, are rarely if ever raised. A key question in sport and business is, whom is all this for? Is the performer serving the sport and business or is it the other way round? And if it is the former, what positive energy could be released, in either area, if the performer's development came first in priority organizational planning?

Summary of learning points:

- Successful non-planning leaders stay in the moment with their performers, taking each situation as it evolves.
- Democratic leaders who have a plan use it as a guide.
- Task and achievement orientation should not exclude focus on the process.
- Process Planning focuses on *how* to create real dialogue and openness, or whatever will make the meeting worthwhile.
- A great amount of positive energy could be released if we put performers' development at the top of our priority organizational planning.

Do you involve performers in their own goal-setting and problem-solving? David Whitaker made this one of the cornerstones of development of the Great Britain team in their four years between the Los Angeles Olympics and their win in Seoul. Their learning to become problem-solvers through a questioning process allowed him to stand back and benefit from a broader perspective so he could make decisions on long-term issues and complex problems. The performers, initially, were reluctant to adopt this approach because they hadn't experienced that form of learning. There tended to be a series of monologues instead of a dialogue or discussion. 'But once they became open and honest, genuinely understanding the problems and needs of each other, they all came together, because they all wanted to get to the same place in the end, they all wanted to achieve a high standard.'

Ron Dennis answered affirmatively. 'I have my own style. I think one of the functions of management is to see weaknesses in people and provide the support and guidance for change, either improving on them or compensating for them. Also, if you see people with character traits that are not productive in a team environment, then you don't put them in, but, correctly positioned elsewhere in the organization they can contribute a great deal because of their expertise.' Ron Dennis doesn't like to lose staff, interpreting it as a failure on his part, rather than theirs, and tries to find them another position within the company – or even outside.

Graham Taylor made the point that different situations and circumstances will determine how much he involves performers. During a half time he is usually the only one talking. 'I don't want anything said that might confuse the situation. I might bring in an assistant manager, a coach, or I may pick a player and say "What do you think?" but in seven to eight minutes you can't involve twelve or thirteen people. In team talks during the week, I'll ask for contributions, again as long as I don't see any confusion coming out of it. I like them to be clear that we're clear. Among eighteen players, certain groups dominate, the strong voices in the changing room, and a manager has to be careful to enable others to contribute. There may be six weeks between internationals. I'm keeping regular contact by going around to the clubs, meeting one, two or three players at a time; they have far more to say in a small group like that. Before the upcoming England–Ireland international I phoned all the players mid-week and said, "I know what's your most important next game and that's your [league] game on Saturday, but the moment that whistle blows at twenty to five, I want you thinking about a successful international. Just think of it as another First Division fixture and they have home advantage." ' He then clearly outlined the travel arrangements. He found that some don't want to be involved, preferring the manager to take the responsibility and give orders. 'Even so, I think they like to think they've been taken into conversation, been asked, "What do you think?" ' The point about some performers not wanting to take responsibility confirms Bobby Charlton's view that many players are so looked after in professional football that they don't learn to take responsibility for themselves. Players should check how much they are limiting their potential to grow.

When a problem arose for Richard Noble's team he would discuss it with whoever held responsibility for that area, and find out what was needed. 'People knew what had to be achieved, so discussion related to that overall objective. The main thing is you've got to catch it quickly.'

David Evans said, 'There's a dilemma from a business perspective. It's a debate I've had with some very senior members of British industry and commerce. Is it top down, bottom up or somewhere in between?

Now, if you're running a business there are goals you'll be driven by: shareholder goals, investment goals, and so on. And that in itself produces an economic model for your business. And that means parcelling out responsibility for those economic goals. But clearly there is potential for upward and downward goal setting. Goal setting in a supra sense, of the company, has to be done partly by one man, there has to be a guiding light, that's my view. But that doesn't mean to say that he should determine every single ingredient that will make the proposition successful. Unless you involve everybody else who have differing skills and differing responsibilities it won't succeed. And to draw the analogy from *Animal Farm*, you can't be Boxer the horse dragging all the other animals along with you. They have to be willing participants in the exercise. I've held a belief, from as far back as I can remember, that there's the capacity to do better in everybody. We look at constantly developing everybody. Their role is debated with them in the first place. There is a key-task quarterly assessment. At the end of the day it's the individual that succeeds because of his or her motivation.'

Billy Beaumont was recognized as a player's player. He led by example but did not railroad the team. To this question his immediate response was, 'You have to. To get the best out of your team members you try to involve them and be open with them. I try to. I try to help them assess their strengths and weaknesses and try to point them in the right direction. You have to find out what they want out of it. Some want to be number one. Some will only perform with a kick up the backside. Others respond to a pat on the back.'

Billy shared a story about Bill Shankly. After a couple of bad games, he had gathered his team and asked the least experienced player what was going wrong. Some leaders seem to think they're supposed to have all the answers all the time and that it's a sign of weakness to admit that they don't always know. Bill had demonstrated two things: honesty with himself and the humility to publicly admit he needed and wanted input. By sharing the problem with the team he demonstrated that he valued them and was open to their opinions, right down to the least experienced man – who may, after all, have a mind less clouded by past experience and therefore see more clearly what's going on.

Neil Benson said, 'I think it's absolutely vital. But having said that, I have a broader picture and on occasion there's an element of manipulation which has to take place. A part is listening to what the individual has to say about the problem and how it needs solving, and then if I felt I had to lead them in a certain direction, I would like to convince them it was their idea, in order to help them implement it.'

Sir Michael: 'First of all you involve the other people in the strategy. That strategy is agreed between you, *so they own it along with you.*'

Sue Campbell was no different on involvement: 'Our staff meetings and our policy meetings are very much a team effort. I have opinions and so do my staff. The only time I would go against the majority vote is if I thought financially it was taking us into a difficult place. Certainly, in terms of individuals, I involve them in a lot of joint goal setting, mapping out their own course. We discuss what the problem is, I throw questions, trying to get them to articulate the way they want to go. We agree on that, and they go away and do it.'

Sir John said that he likes to use the illustration of Jackie Charlton. 'He goes in with a team and doesn't change a man. And I think that's a key thing. I don't go for leaders who come in and clear out everyone who is there, move in five superstars of their own and then get on with it, because I think that is immensely disruptive to the people who are there. The leaders I admire are those who take the people who are there – the bunch who consider themselves to be Fourth Division – and just build them up and build their confidence in themselves and build their competence as well.'

Sir John went on to say how he involves and stretches performers in their goal setting, by insisting they can do better. The trick is to set them a slightly higher target, something achievable, and, if necessary, pull a few strings behind the scenes to help them – making sure they get the credit. 'Then the following year, when you sit down with them, you say, "All that bloody fuss, look, you walked it. Now, come on now, we've got to do better than that this year." And if we're in front, I compare us with how far in front we are of the next best and the following year the same thing again. Then if you're successful, doing a Jackie Charlton, you may have to change one, or at the most two, people in the senior management. You know you've won when they come to you and say, "This is what we're going to do this year", and you think, "Shit, they'll never make it!" And they do it.'

Summary of learning points:

- Teaching and empowering performers to become problem-solvers helps them grow and also releases the coach/leader to review and reflect on other issues and opportunities.

- Ownership comes out of discussion, not imposition.
- Initially performers may shrink from taking personal responsibility. But acknowledging one's potential is exciting and empowering.
- Meeting in small groups enables greater communication.
- After a 'guiding light' has set an overall objective, there should be involved goal-setting at all levels.
- The capacity to do better is in everyone. Each person must find their goal within.
- Open questions to performers help them to clarify where they want to go.
- Willingness to admit ignorance is healthy for the leader and the team.
- Goals which stretch the performer make their achievement more personally rewarding. It's really vital that the performers feel it's their success.

Did you try to establish common goals? Most frequently the leader had a vision, a suggested target goal, or had sketched out a first draft, whether for a corporate or a sporting team, saying, 'This is what I think we're trying to achieve. Do we all agree with this?' After this vision had been shared democracy came in and discussions took place.

David Whitaker articulated well the reason for, and value of, establishing common goals. He said, 'If the performers are not party to them I don't see how they can be fully committed to them when you're not there. Anyone will work when the boss is looking over them but the most crucial time is when you're not there and I reckon 95 per cent of their time the boss isn't there. And what's the use of people really working for only 5 per cent of the time? And if they discussed, established and agreed upon their goals the chances are that they would have those at the forefront of their minds while they were training.' David also pointed out that the leader's enthusiasm can provide a type of contagious momentum.

Sir Michael: 'If a leader can't get consensus, he needs to move on. Leaders don't find it easy to step down, which I think is an ego thing.' He gave illustration of his means of achieving consensus. 'Let's say the results for one year were not good enough. I would sketch out a more demanding budget for the next year and send it down the line. I would say "This is what we're trying to achieve. Do we all agree?" And there would be a debate. First they buy the objectives, then you agree with them *how* you get to that objective, and everyone's got to give a little bit to get there – cut capital, increase effort, cut numbers – and by the time that's done, and it's done in a democratic, involved way, then you say, "OK, maybe we're not going to get there but we're going to have a really good go at it." And it's as simple as that.' Sir Michael made reference to an exception. He said that all his life he had made the big decisions by consensus. At BL only one of the eleven in the working party thought that Land Rover and Jaguar should remain separate entities, and he sided with him. 'I said, "I apologise that you should be the people to suffer from an autocratic decision but I carry the can if this lot fails and I'm not going along with a wishy-washy compromise; we're going to do it like this." And by being straight-up about it, by admitting that it was not a desirable way to do it, by looking at all the weakness in doing it against their wishes, they accepted that and we went ahead with it. So there are occasions . . .'

Sue Campbell: 'It's like a mini-contract. We get to a position where we all have the same understanding and expectations. No one is left saying, "Well I thought you were going to do something different from that." It's a bit like setting the rules of the game. And if everyone understands the objectives you're working towards, there are ways in which you can support each other very positively.'

For both Richard Noble and Graham Taylor, the setting of a common goal was easy; for the former it was the breaking of the world land speed record, for the latter it is victory in the European Nations Championships.

Summary of learning points:

- If team members are not party to establishing a common goal how can the leader be sure of their commitment when he or she isn't there?
- If a leader cannot get consensus he or she may need to step down.
- Each performer needs to be clear about the extent of their responsibility.
- Common aims promote mutual support.

10
TEAM LEADERSHIP AND MANAGEMENT:

DEVELOPING TEAM SPIRIT

What did you do to establish commitment, mutual trust, mutual respect, enthusiasm and cooperation? Graham Taylor said, 'You must have a true belief in the players. You can't have a fake or insincere belief and hope to encourage these qualities.'

Peter Shilton said, 'If you're self-confident you can overcome a lot of things. Confidence has to do with positive thinking.' He also mentioned the importance of courage.

Billy Beaumont gave illustration of how he would instill each of these qualities. 'Confidence by making them feel important – giving them responsibility, although some don't want to take it; enthusiasm through agreeing common goals, and through getting good results with limited resources.' To gain commitment and trust: 'All contribute to the team, and I let them know they're needed and exactly what they mean to every other member of the team. Mutual respect comes from honesty, application and training. If you're not fully pulling your weight when sprinting with the team you're letting the side down.'

A large physical presence does carry impact with many. Neil Benson said, 'It helps to be six foot and big.' There is no logic for this but it has largely been a fact that size gives an initial impression of a commanding person. However, as Neil Benson went on to point out, 'All the mistakes I've made about individuals have been because I've been fooled by a big impressive guy. It's a shock when he turns out to be a little shit!' Taking this very small sample of excellent leaders, the variety of body types was considerable – small, medium and large were all represented.

Neil Benson underlined that qualities are often instilled by modelling and mirroring – engendering enthusiasm by being enthusiastic, getting commitment by demonstrating commitment, etc. Trusting means letting go, and it's what you have to do to gain trust.

Regardless of the capability of any individual, self-confidence is required to move towards excellence.

David Evans spent much of his time on this part of the question. He said, 'On a personal level, my confidence-building technique has been to find them an avenue in which they could succeed with a bit of effort. Taking a simple example, in our earliest days I did most of our new business presentations, and I would take someone by the hand to where we were going to do the presentation, then give them a specific but fairly broad role in that. And we'd point out afterwards where they may have erred but would generally clap them on the back and make them feel good about the way they did the job. So it is done gradually, one step at a time. It's not a case of here's a confidence booster, let me inject some into your blood stream. It's building blocks, every day, in every way, giving people just that little bit of extra, that makes them feel, "I can do that." If someone's best 100m is 18 seconds, there's no point in talking to him about the world record, but he could take off a second and in so doing would achieve something important for himself. It's the same thing in business.' Like Neil Benson, he mentioned the infectious and imitable nature of enthusiasm, trust and commitment.

Richard Noble said, 'These are all elements of a good team and they're all interdependent. If one person isn't "performing" that can break down all those elements in the team. There's less commitment; trust, enthusiasm, etc. So success at the top level depends on having a homogeneous team with the very highest quality people you can possibly get. Plus, of course, their ability to *self-motivate*. Given these elements you're creating an atmosphere in which this team can actually operate. What happens in a relatively unstructured operation like this is that these people find that they can actually impose a limit of their identity on the project. They can actually influence it, their views are taken into account.' He went on to say that the job satisfaction was such that people worked harder than normal on the Thrust project, despite the poor pay, and only those with 100 per cent commitment stayed. 'And I felt very much in the last year when we were running at Black Rock desert, that if anything major happened to that car, like blowing the engine or smashing, the team would solemnly get down and rebuild it. There was nothing we couldn't do. It was a wonderful feeling, a really wonderful feeling.'

Sue Campbell said, 'This may sound like a rather arrogant thing to say, but people say that I model it.' There is no doubt that Sue is enthusiastic and committed. She encourages the commitment of her staff by explaining the reasons and beliefs behind her enthusiasm, sharing her vision and making them part of it. She said, 'I'm a great believer in ownership, and I believe that everybody here feels they *own* a part of the NCF. Even the two part-time secretaries have a piece of work which they own, which they lead, and if they want any of us to attend a meeting on this topic, then they call it. That doesn't necessarily make each person possessive about their bit but they do feel proud about it. You respect that everyone has a valid role to play and that respect gets reflected back.' In talking about re-establishing contact with her staff after being away she demonstrated her awareness and sensitivity. 'I tend to be out quite a bit but as soon as I get back I tend to walk the job. I go and talk to everybody. It may not be more than a couple of minutes but I can pick up an atmosphere in that time, and I'll usually dig around a bit and see what's going on.'

David Whitaker started from the standpoint that the most important person for the individual is himself or herself. 'So if the coach puts the performer at the centre of the learning and development process, you've acknowledged that they exist and are important. That inevitably develops their self-esteem and once they have that then the possibility of moving them towards cooperation is so much greater. Then they begin to say, "What can I offer the other players?" Giving a little bit more to each other and giving up a little bit of what they wanted is the start of greater commitment, trust, and cooperation in the team.'

Ron Dennis sees that self-responsibility is a vital ingredient. 'I think you've left one element off that list and I'd put it at the top, and that is *personal discipline*. If you don't have the ability to discipline yourself, then you don't have the foundation to build your own career, at whatever level it is. And if your team members have personal discipline, it allows you, as a manager, to build on it. It is reflected in commitment and loyalty. All of those qualities can have firm roots in the pre-requisite personal discipline. Let's say I'm an athlete; I'm going to train, I'm going to control my diet. And when I go to bed at night, I'm the only person who can really evaluate whether I have done what I feel is necessary to achieve my goal, be it a four-minute mile or whatever. And therefore it all goes back to self-evaluation and personal discipline. If you start with that foundation then all of these things come far, far easier – motivation, responsibility, self-respect, credibility and confidence.'

Sir Michael: 'I come back to pettiness. You won't get commitment, you won't get trust, none of these things will you get if you're petty. Secondly if you don't give credit where it's due but try to take the kudos yourself, you won't get commitment, you won't get trust. I would compliment the people concerned and say they'd done a great job. I never, ever, took public credit for these things that we did. I think a lot of demotivation at the leadership level comes from people who are insecure themselves and in a sense they push down the other guy as a way of boosting themselves. I've found the best way to boost myself in business leadership is to compliment the other guy. If you push the other guy down a foot you might move up an inch, and what happens? The company loses eleven inches.'

I picked up Sir John's use of the word 'trust' in his response to the first question in the previous chapter and asked him, 'How do you show them that?' He replied, 'Oh, that's easy, isn't it? You have to stamp on any lack of trust that you may have. You know as well as I do that you show lack of trust every time you check what someone is doing.'

Summary of learning points:

- To encourage ideal team qualities, a leader must truly believe in the potential in the team.
- Commitment and trust can come out of performers believing they're needed and wanted.
- A leader truly demonstrates trust and belief by 'letting go'.
- Don't judge a book by its cover.
- If leaders model and mirror the qualities wanted they can help to promote them.
- There is an interdependence. If a team member lets things slip in any area, the slide is felt in the whole team.
- Putting the performer at the centre enhances his or her self-esteem, so proving a base for cooperation.
- Personal discipline and self-motivation are pre-requisites for fulfilling individual and team potential.
- Pettiness will lower morale and reduce commitment.
- The leader taking credit for others' efforts reduces trust and lessens the leader.
- If you push another down to get yourself up, both of you lose stature.
- Trust means not repeatedly checking up on what the performer is doing.

What do you do to acknowledge improvement and show that you value team members? David Evans believes a requirement of managers, on a daily basis, is to walk amongst the staff, talking with them – to recognize their needs and acknowledge them as individuals. 'Improvement is acknowledged in the proven, time trusted manner of a good pat on the back. It's also acknowledged in the structural sense by their salary, their position in the system. And it's driven by the key tasking processes and we assess everyone quarterly. Mr de Bono said, "I've discovered that men will die for ribbons." Because for the most part people lead very humdrum and boring lives in their business careers. I'm very tactile, I don't have any qualms about putting my arm around a man or a woman and saying, "That's a terrific job" – a corporate cuddle and occasionally a corporate wag of the finger. It's got to be a combination obviously.'

David Whitaker recognized the need for caution in what can be a delicate situation in a team. 'While you must value individuals, you have to be careful not to overvalue someone to the detriment of another. You can fall into the trap of valuing over-highly a goal-scorer or a goal-saver and the media tend to do this. And I believe it's important to recognize their particular gifts but they're being given that opportunity because of what the rest of the team is doing.

Praise should be public as well as private. If a player was valued in the team but did not very often get public recognition, and it was deserved, then it would be very appropriate to make that a public recognition within the team.'

In answer to the question 'How do you let your players know you value them?', Graham Taylor just gave the simple answer: 'By telling them.'

As a team captain, Billy Beaumont wanted the team to know that he was proud of them even when they lost. 'Nobody likes to lose but there's no harm in it. You have to be able to look the team in the eyes and honestly say we couldn't have done more.'

Sue Campbell chose a similar perspective: 'I think I recognize people most in times of adversity, when they're going through a difficult time.' She also mentioned her team rallying to her defence and aid during difficult times, which demonstrates the closeness, mutual support and cooperation within her team.

Richard Noble said, 'With group dynamics, what is absolutely essential is that everybody knows when something successful has been achieved.' Richard would let everybody know informally. His projects maintained funding and support through high public awareness, and he would see that the people who had actually achieved the success had it publicly attributed to them.

Neil Benson said that his way of valuing performance was showing greater intimacy. He said, 'I'm a bit old-fashioned so it took a long time for me to call people into the office by their first names. If you were a subordinate and I normally called you "Mr Hemery" and something went really well and I said, "That was great David", that would be a real reward. I think it may be cynical, but I regard that as currency and use it appropriately. It's obviously very important also to say "That's terrific" when it's genuine.'

Ron Dennis said, 'Of course there are financial incentives. Everyone's on a bonus, proportional to the company's success.' I asked what he would do if the team had done a great job. He said, 'I think it's wrong to praise them immediately after having achieved it. It has no value. It's like saying, "You've done a good job, here's a sweet." I think it's much better to let perhaps an hour or two go past, then come back and say, "We were under a lot of pressure then, everybody did a really good job." Occasionally I'll set a bit of a challenge, like, "Can that be done in half an hour?" They say, "We'll give it a shot" and I say, "OK, beers are on me if you're able to achieve it." Nine times out of ten beers are on me anyway, so it's basically a humorous incentive.'

Sir John said, 'Praise should be public and recrimination should be private. Praise is usually verbal but I sometimes write to say "thank you". I'm a great believer in reward systems which are immediate rather than systematized. If I hear of anyone at any level doing something that I think is bloody good I just write a little note, something like, "Just to say thank you very much indeed for the outstanding job you did on the M4 crash", then when I get back to my office I have my secretary send a case of wine with my card inside.' Three objectives are achieved: the worker is boosted in his wife's eyes, he will tell his mates, and he'll recall the gesture on twelve occasions. 'If you added that amount of money to his pay, he wouldn't notice it. People don't work for more money, they work for recognition. I don't like cutting a guy's rise. If you really don't think the guy's done a good job you don't give him any rise.'

Sir Michael: 'There is more damage done in this country by

meanness, not rewarding people enough.' He was an exception in this group in his attitude to social relations with performers in his team. 'I almost entirely avoid social relationships with these fellows. I sent flowers to all the wives at Christmas to acknowledge the rough times they were having.' Most of Sir Michael's acknowledgements would be through the wife: 'I might have occasion to drop a note to a wife to say, "I'm sorry you've seen nothing of him for the past two weeks but he really has done a fantastic job." '

Summary of learning points:

- Performers need personal appreciation, acknowledgement and recognition beyond pay.
- If team unity is to be maintained, praising individuals has to be done with great care and sensitivity.
- Simplicity works – tell them you appreciate them.
- Effort needs to be valued and appreciated in times of loss.
- All praise must be genuine.
- Too much praise devalues its impact.
- Praise should be public, recrimination private.

Any comment on the development of awareness and responsibility within your team? In sport, and I suspect in all areas of life, the best performers are highly aware within their areas of expertise and they take full responsibility for themselves and their advancement.

Graham Taylor said, 'I can do it now and again but I use other people because, as a football manager, you have so much authority and power over those people, they will not always relax enough to come out to you. I have had in a psychologist and a chaplain, which has helped me to manage situations in a better way, and that's the whole purpose of it all. You can't expect the boss man to do everything himself; and to expect a player to take every problem to the man who can actually drop him, who can affect his position, status and family life, is asking a bit too much.' Graham Taylor saw no shame in delegating this sort of authority but considered it to be a professional approach to the matter. Football is a notoriously insular profession but he believed his successes at Watford, on and off the pitch, were testimony to the efficacy of his style. He believed in having people help him manage. 'Losing the ability to share the decision-making means you also lose the ability to share the success.'

David Whitaker said two key principles, awareness and responsibility, were the foundation of his developmental training. His questioning style was intended to make the performers find their own ways around problems, rather than provide them with pat solutions. 'They did have set moves and some additional solutions provided by me as the coach and in the developmental phase we would debate what were the preferred solutions to various problems. Then in the game they had the responsibility to decide at each moment their best option.'

Ron Dennis agreed that awareness and responsibility were absolutely key. Ron mentioned the growing pains in the company and also how, when things are going well, everyone accepts credit, and in failure, everyone points to the top. I suggested that his transition from an autocratic style of management to a more involving style might temporarily accentuate this – it does take time for shared accountability to be fully understood and accepted.

Sir Michael: 'When you're leading a team of any sort, you want each person to feel a high level of ownership [in their area] . . . and they've got to feel an ownership of the whole as well, a communal ownership. If you start taking ownership away from them you end up with nobody owning the problem.' (Sir Michael identified this as Gorbachev's problem.)

Sir John sits down with everyone at least once a year and asks what sort of training *they* think is needed. 'I'm a great believer in lots of little courses. I don't believe in sending someone to Harvard and getting back a pre-stamped, ready-made Harvardian model, because I want our own model, wherever I am. And the models are different.'

Sue Campbell said, 'I do encourage some sort of social interaction out of the office. I also try to give people a clear responsibility and then encourage them to involve others in the work that they do.'

Summary of learning points:
- Top performers have high awareness within their field, and take responsibility for their choices.
- The most effective way of increasing these two elements is through questioning.
- Awareness can be developed to recognize the cues to problems and to find various solutions.
- If ownership (i.e. responsibility for decisions) is taken away, it ends up with nobody owning the problem!

- It takes time for performers used to autocracy to fully understand and accept responsibility.
- Some leaders find that the power of their position can inhibit openness. Others that open discussion is easily possible.

What do you do to resolve conflict and the problems of internal politics?

CONFLICT WITH MANAGEMENT The qualities of truth, honesty and courage are the protective place for Graham Taylor. He pointed out one of the awkward conflicts he faces every game. He has to pick eleven from twenty-two. 'Back in their clubs they're number one on the list, and every time they're not selected for England they experience some form of rejection.' They might start to believe they are not good enough or not rated, or they might suspect favouritism. On returning to their clubs their manager supports them, giving the impression that if *he* were the England manager he would have picked them. Graham Taylor understands this and has done it himself as a club manager. But he still expects there to be mutual commitment between himself and the players. 'And if for any reason you can't keep your promise, you *must* tell them why you've had to change your mind and been unable to keep the word you gave them three or four months before. That gets trust.'

Richard Noble had crashed Thrust II in a display at Greenham Common and thereby destroyed about six months' work by the team. He said, 'It was through not recognizing one's limits.' The difficult part was the fact that he was the team leader and as driver also had the executive role. 'And by falling down on that it effectively destroyed my position as a leader. And I'm grateful to Ken Norris for getting the whole team together, and we sat down and discussed the whole thing openly and thoroughly, and everybody decided that they would be happy to continue with the team and with my driving, which was a wonderful vote of confidence.' Richard took full responsibility for the failure, which required total honesty and a lot of courage. I believe that the team's vote of confidence would have been largely due to Richard being big enough to admit weakness. 'I think it comes back to leadership. If you're being absolutely truthful and honest, being willing to take the tough decision rather than take the easy way out, it breeds a tremendous following amongst the organization. It was a real pleasure to work with a team like that. It was a wonderful, wonderful experience.' I'm sure it worked both ways.

David Evans said, 'I very rarely lose my temper. I've never seen any value in it. Conflict is handled by debate, discussion, discourse.'

David Whitaker said that he would openly discuss the conflict with the performer in private, and see how the situation could be taken forward. It would be extremely positive to share certain issues openly with the team. Some issues simply disappeared when aired and discussed in this way.

Sir Michael reinforced his boldness theme: 'In rugby you see it again and again – the side that doesn't sling the ball out, that holds the ball, and the fly half that runs back into the forwards the whole damn time. That's bad leadership. It doesn't take a genius for the captain to say to the guy, "You do that again and you're not in the team next time round", but English people are very diffident about telling people to do something.'

Sue Campbell said that she treated conflict with an employee as if it was with an athlete who wasn't prepared to do the training that had been agreed for that session. Through discussion a fair compromise might be reached.

DIFFERENCE OF OPINION WITHIN THE TEAM Sue Campbell: 'I tend to act more like a referee than a coach. So I've tried to create an opportunity for people to discuss the conflict or issue, where the emotions have been left behind. If they start to get emotional in the conflict, I'll simply say, "Let's leave that for now. We'll come back to that when you can actually discuss it at a different level." Because once that first punch is thrown, you've got a problem.'

Richard Noble agreed: 'Somehow you've got to keep emotion out of it.'

Sir John: 'I don't believe you can make progress without an appropriate level of conflict. The most important thing is to depersonalize conflict.'

David Whitaker not only agreed but extended it into the management team: 'I think positive conflict is essential. Once you stop debating things seriously and clinically as a management team, with a bit of controlled friction, you stop performing. Without it you're not testing each other or pushing the boundaries back; you're not moving forward; it becomes too cosy.'

David Evans spoke of the value of internal competition. 'Like a good whisky, it needs to be well blended. Without competition it's flaccid, with too much it's destructive.' In the best games, there is cooperation in competition, both within each team and between the opponents, who agree to abide by the laws and the spirit of the law.

Peter Shilton was one who initiated constructive confrontation with manager and players alike. 'You can definitely learn through conflict. Players learn how to handle certain situation. You can be taught by experience, by a quiet word. The word "honesty" comes here again, and being willing to listen.'

CONFLICT THROUGH INTERNAL POLITICS   While talking of the benefits of internal cooperation v internal competition, Richard Noble said, 'The trouble with direct competition within is that while it does stimulate some people, it really demoralizes others. It can be very, very difficult.'

Peter Shilton said, 'You can't afford conflict in a team. If a cog doesn't go round, a machine can grind to a halt. A team means exactly what it says, a team, not individuals. If you want to be an individual go and play tennis or golf.'

Ron Dennis said, 'There's no place in my sport for internal competition. It's not constructive. I want everybody covering for everybody else. And I don't mind if the guy cleaning the garage comes up and tells me something that I've done [wrong]. If anyone in the team recognizes anyone else making a mistake, they can let that person know in a constructive way.'

Sue Campbell said, 'If you can identify conflict at an early stage, that's important. That demands a level of sensitivity in leaders and managers.' She added that the leader had to be in close enough communication with his or her line managers so that they were not afraid to raise a problem before it escalated into a crisis.

David Whitaker referred to the power and control issues which abound in these conflicts. 'If one performer or one group is seen to hold great sway with the management then you're setting up a power issue. You can have experienced people who have valid input on strategic issues for the team and that's best done in an open group. If it's done privately, repeat it in the open group, enabling disagreement to be voiced.' If there was internal disagreement he would talk to the people individually or together to get it sorted out. Trust, respect, and the desire to perform he saw as crucial; friendship was a bonus.

Graham Taylor is aware that some people have personality problems. 'I've sacrificed a very talented player for the good of the whole. You may win the odd game with them but you don't win long-term. Their power in the dressing room can have a bigger influence than the manager on the field. You have to get rid of them.'

Sir Michael sees the disruption caused by internal politics as a cancer. He makes it clear to those involved that he would be prepared to sack someone to eliminate it.

Sir John's attitude was similar: 'I spend a lot of time in most organizations I run killing politics. I take it head on. If somebody is making a creepy political comment, I'll say, "That's a creepy bloody comment. I don't pay creeps."' He expressed distaste for the games people play to conceal their motives. 'The danger of conflict is that if you aren't terribly careful all the energy goes inside, but without conflict you aren't going to be dealing with things that matter.' Conflict, he believes can show that people care.

Summary of learning points:

- Conflict resolution requires open discussion and debate, appreciation of other people's positions and flexibility on all sides.
- The issues need to be clarified, without emotion.
- Hard decisions must be taken with the honest reasons for the choice made plain.
- If a promise cannot be kept, the reason *must* be stated.
- Accepting full responsibility when you get it wrong, and fail, requires great honesty and courage, but will often win admiration and support.
- Positive conflict – honest, meaningful debate – is healthy, and essential for new routes to be discovered. Such conflict shows that people care and the right problems are being dealt with.
- Discussion requires clear speaking but even clearer *listening*.
- Effective team work requires mutual trust and mutual respect.
- In teams there's no room for internal politics.
- Destructive conflict needs to be nipped in the bud.
- The ideal is cooperation in competition for a place in the team, leading to a new cooperation with your team against the opposition. This requires a bigger picture than self-interest.

Do you treat different people differently? Peter Shilton said, 'When it comes to rules, it's not one rule for one and another rule for another – it doesn't matter how big a name anybody is, or how important anybody is in whatever position they have in the structure of the club or the team, everybody's treated the same. But individually you treat the personality differently. Your motivating factor is you know what turns people on or makes them respond. Some people will respond if you gee them up, criticize them to a certain degree or niggle them; they'll come out fighting. And some people respond if you put your arm around them, show them a bit of concern.'

Graham Taylor echoed this second point, putting an unusual slant on the compliment that he treats everyone the same: 'I don't. If they were all the same, we would treat them all the same. There are some slight subtle differences.' Some people don't even need to be spoken to. 'Messages are being given out all the time when you're not saying anything. And you can give some very warm ones to people without apparently saying anything to them.'

Ron Dennis said, 'Yes, you must do. It's critical. I interface with their characters. You've got to know your workforce personally. I can assess most people quite well from a distance, just by watching them work. In the team [about thirty at a Grand Prix], then, there's an opportunity to get much closer. Then, of course, there's the added complexity of us being in partnership with Honda, and a large part of the team on the engine side is Japanese, so there you've got a far bigger challenge, a cultural difference in both the literal sense and the business sense.'

Neil Benson has a great gift of delivery and is a quite outstanding after dinner speaker. He continued with the theme of enjoyment and talked about 'understanding what particular fun button an individual has and pressing it. Some people are turned on by straightforward friendliness, some by subtle humour, some by references to a hobby or foible.'

David Whitaker said, 'Favouritism is the worst thing in a team. The best leaders are firm but fair. Obviously if you're going to get the best out of people you can't treat them all the same, but you don't prostitute your principles.'

Billy Beaumont said that he did treat performers differently, 'by paying a lot of attention to them and identifying with their needs and perspectives'.

Sue Campbell compared this to the teacher's situation. At times a teacher has to treat all the children consistently, 'but then you have to adapt the style to match the needs of one particular child. In management I've found that the most important things are consistency and calmness – even when you aren't calm. I try never to go into situations when I'm angry or upset. I always give myself two deep breaths before I go in so that I'm under control, and things can be debated without emotion.'

Sir Michael said that while an extrovert could be complimented in an almost off-hand way an introvert might need more direct and explicit praise. Sir Michael would have an idea of the psychological make-up of all his employees from the five hours of tests they all have undergone.

Sir John: 'Mostly it's knowing people and watching them like hawks. I never have meetings in my office. I always walk into other people's offices. I expect to notice if somebody's off colour, usually before he does or before he tells me. Very frequently there's something you can do as well, and I say, "Nip down to the doctor" or "Take the afternoon off." I like to see people and to be seen, so I always eat in the canteen and sit with people who are there – secretaries or the drivers or whoever they might be. I like informality and dropping in on people. If I hear there's a birthday party or something going on I try to drop in.'

Summary of learning points:

- The rules must apply the same for everybody, regardless of power or position. Leaders must never be seen to be playing favourites.
- Different personalities require different handling.
- A leader's behaviour needs to be consistent and calm.
- The most skilful leaders have the flexibility to communicate as required. Humour can be effective.
- Leaders need to be able to identify with the needs and perspectives of their performers. This requires great awareness and sensitivity – a lot of paying attention!

How do you define charisma and do you recognize it in yourself?
One dictionary definition is as follows: a spiritual power given by God; personal quality or gift that enables an individual to impress and influence many of his fellows.

There is no doubt that certain people can excite a greater vision, through which the listener becomes inspired. Some paint a picture in words or actions which inspire our spirits, minds or bodies to be or do something more than exists right now.

David Whitaker saw charisma as 'the ability to excite people about a concept, belief or vision. Within the hockey arena I recognize that I have a bit. I don't know how much, but I recognize that I could motivate coaches to coach and players to play by helping them to believe they could truly perform both individually and as a team against absolutely anybody. With enthusiasm I was showing them the stepping stones, in a logical way, leading them towards the summit in a style that valued them and motivated them. It was sincere; I trusted them, I respected them and tried to illustrate my love for what we were doing and my complete belief in the fact that we could achieve it.'

Graham Taylor said, 'I've never felt it. But lately people have said, "He has presence." That can make you feel quite big-headed, if you're not steady. I never intend to dominate, I just get involved with it. Other times I'd rather withdraw, but I do know this: if I have any strength, I'm not a bad observer.'

Sue Campbell, 'I think charisma isn't necessarily to do with leadership and it's a somewhat indefinable magical personal quality which stands people out a little from the crowd. Do I have it? People around me think I have it, but, this may sound funny, I'm not sure I feel I have it. The only time I'm aware of affecting people in that sort of way is when I do public talks. And I find myself getting into the material and then it's almost like there's somebody else talking, like I'm watching me perform. And when I deliver information to a group I can feel that group slowly come into my hand, if you know what I mean, and that's the only time I'm aware of something special. And even then I don't actually feel like that is me, but something else. I'm not aware of being charismatic but certainly my staff and the people around me tell me that I am, and I don't know what that means really.'

Neil Benson also said, 'It's hard to acknowledge because I don't actually think I have it.' Charismatic people, he felt, don't have to fight to be heard, people are immediately interested in them. He suspects it may have something to do with physical presence. Our conversation at this point took an interesting turn through the problems of having a charismatic individual who misuses their gift for personal self-gratification – political, financial, sexual, etc.

While writing this I couldn't help but recall a part of the interview with David Evans who was wondering whether he truly involved people in debate at meetings or whether, and these are my words and not his, he used his considerable intellect, debating skills and charisma to sway the emotions and thoughts of the group to his intended end. At least he has the insight and conscience to look at the possibility of this unintentional manipulation. David Evans acknowledged that he had confidence in himself and saw that as an ingredient of charisma. 'But being self-confident should not overwhelm the other traits of leadership. I think people look at those individuals who they say have charisma and see, within them, an inner glow which goes beyond just the job function. They have that look that says the promise will be delivered; it isn't just flashy, they're believable. You could almost call it quasi-religious. I think charismatic people have that sense of religious fervour about them, not a fanaticism, a fervour. It may only be marginal but it's that star quality.'

Billy Beaumont believed that others were attracted to charismatic people because they are willing to be open and honest in their communication. 'They performed well and they commanded respect, mutual respect.'

Ron Dennis said, 'I suppose anybody who is a leader and who feels he has the support of those whom he's leading, must give out something, some sort of vibes, that people pick up on, that allows them to feel comfortable being led.' He recognized this quality in himself but wasn't happy with the term 'charisma'. 'It conjures up for me a rather egotistical, superstar type image; and it would be ludicrous for any human being to sit in front of me and deny that they have ego. Everybody has ego. It's a tremendous motivating force, but one you have to really be in control of, because of all the human traits it can be the easiest to trip over.' He went on to say that too many accolades can make a successful performer forget that some credit is due to the team behind them.

A similar warning came from Richard Noble. 'A leader with charisma can get out of step, reflecting his own view and not that of the group or organization or even a country. If there was any charisma in what I was doing I'd acknowledge a sheer bloody determination to succeed and to beat the system.'

Peter Shilton: 'I think that is something you're born with. It's your star quality really. I think, for example, Paul Gascoigne has charisma. He responds to an occasion. I remember an incident in Albania when he wasn't even in the team. It was a training session supposedly behind closed doors, but, being Albania, this was the highlight of their year! Half-way through the training session about 4000 filed into the ground to watch. At the end of the training session we always had shooting practice. And all of a sudden Gazza took the stage – a bit of fun and what have you. The ball was being laid off at the edge of the penalty area and he got them to a point that every time, as he ran up they'd go, 'Oooooah!' And he'd just cut them with his hand and they went quiet. He was rolling over and being funny and they were laughing. He was like a comedian on stage and he'd got these 4000 people in the palm of his hand, and we just stood there watching. It was amazing; he'd got the confidence to do that and at that time he wasn't even in the team!'

Sir Michael, 'I think people thought I had it. Certainly I had an effect on the workforce on the television. It's a helpful addition but not necessary. The charismatic chap is more likely to be extrovert, but introverts with leadership capabilities can lead very effectively. He's got to have other attributes, and both have got to have a quiet dominance. Charisma without the other attributes is a disaster.'

I was surprised at Sir John's reply: 'I don't think I have! I think it's a self-fulfilling prophecy. I think it's a very dangerous thing because unless you are very careful you begin to believe your own propaganda and if you believe your own propaganda you're in trouble.'

Summary of learning points:

- Some charismatic speakers inspire self-belief in the listener.
- Considerable caution is needed over the potential misuse of influence, and the dangers of egoism.
- This group appears to have a healthily balanced perspective. They hold the ideal combination of inspiring a following but using that to assist the progress of others.

Do you plan how you lead yourself in the same way you plan how you lead others? Neil Benson caused a smile, saying, 'I'm embarrassingly unplanned.' David Evans also said no. 'I'm not sure I would like to actually. We don't have an Olympics to run. We don't have a time scale like that. We have more of a vision about where mankind, in this case Grass Roots kind, may be in four years. I think if I planned more I'd lose some of my spontaneity. You should plan your demise – to phase yourself out.'

Peter Shilton said that he admired three goalkeepers: Gordon Banks who moved into position so early he made saves look easy; Peter Bonetti, who was very agile and would come off his line to catch the cross at its highest point; and Lev Yashin, the Soviet keeper who was 6ft 3in, very athletic and wore all black. He'd give an air or aura of invincibility before he went onto the pitch. Peter seemed to take from each of these models. 'You can, by your image, be unbeatable before you go on the pitch. I got a reputation of being very good one against one and a lot of strikers used to freeze.'

Billy Beaumont said that he was more critical of himself than anybody else.

Ron Dennis was quick to say yes, and then took Billy Beaumont's response one stage further. 'Most of the time I'm disappointed in my own performance.' He went on to explain the problems he had with fitting in work, the family and the quest for personal fitness.

Richard Noble said he always had. 'You have to, time is so precious. I prioritized and ordered each day, and also prioritized secondary action. For example, if I have three key tasks for the day and I get through the first sooner than expected, I will have decided whether it is more important to start the second task, or whether the next step on the first task is more important. And you must be absolutely ruthless in not letting it get out of hand.' He believes that physical fitness and mental fitness go hand in hand and that when fit he could cope with a much greater work load and emotional load. John Ackroyd, who was responsible for the design and build of the car, was also keen on fitness and was careful about what he ate and drank.

Sue Campbell gave a good example of self-coaching. She said, 'I think I'm pretty well organized. I work very hard but I try to have a reasonably balanced life style. I think about my level of commitment and I have little discussions with myself. I draw up little contracts with myself in the same way I do with other people – joint goal-setting with myself; for example over exercise. I do spend a little bit of time just managing me.'

David Whitaker based his framework on what he imagined the players' needs would be, but stayed flexible. 'I trusted my framework but I wasn't a slave to it; I also trusted my intuition.'

Sir Michael: 'Tremendously. But if you've got the right team around you it has the effect of disciplining you as well. I think I operated for five years way above my natural ability level because I set standards that were so high and employed people who were so bright and so good that they lifted my own game.'

Summary of learning points:

- Too much planning could kill spontaneity.
- Plan how and when to phase oneself out of leadership.
- Assuming the air of what you want to project, before entering an arena, at work or on the sports field, will affect you and the opposition.
- Time management and key task prioritizing are invaluable tools for effective self-management.
- Since the spirit, mind, body and emotions are all interconnected, a fit and healthy body promotes strength and stamina in all areas.
- All of the group are very hard working but aim for a balanced life. Work certainly has the highest priority. Self-discipline is a major feature in all of their lives.
- Surrounding oneself with a good team helps to raise one's own performance level.
- Asking oneself 'What do others need from me?' provides a useful framework.

Do you take any personal stand on ethics? Ron Dennis said, 'We care deeply about *how* we win. It's not winning at all costs. It's not what people think of you that matters, it's what you think of yourself. It's back to personal discipline, being able to stand in front of the mirror and say, "I've done nothing to be ashamed of." '

Neil Benson: 'Every situation you face has a moral or ethical aspect. You're conditioned to behave in a certain way and you don't think about it. The only problems come when it's an unusual or a pressure situation. And then you had better be a person of principle, and that applies to a company. Taking an ethical stand is a recipe for missing opportunities and being accused of cowardice, which you have to recognize as the down side. But it's important to instill as a principle in a company or a team, and it's a heavy burden because it's undefined. It's rather like the difference between the American constitution and our own. I like the fact that we have to make our own minds up as to what is constitutional. That to me is a very adult, mature way of running your life or your company. And you don't have to look through acres of case law. It's either right or it's not right.' I have to say that this is very appealing to me as I believe that, at some level, every one of us knows if we are totally comfortable with a decision or action. I believe that if we're willing to be quiet and honest our conscience will always be our guide.

Sue Campbell saw the NCF as an embodiment of her ethics. She had grown tired of the constant battles between organizations in British sport, led by people who didn't have sporting values. She believed sport had a set of values, such as fair play, team work and not resorting to retaliation, which could be transmitted to other areas of life. 'One of the nicest letters I got after being awarded the MBE said "The greatest thing you've done for the National Coaching Foundation is that you've lifted it beyond bureaucracies and beyond politics, into sport." One of the greatest problems in British sport is a rather childlike attitude: "Our organization has to be the one that does it or we're not interested." There isn't a feeling of camaraderie or working as a team to make this a better place. The decisions are made on what is right for their organization with little or no thought for what is best for British sport.'

David Whitaker said, 'I'm against performance-enhancing drugs. I couldn't select a player who I knew was taking drugs. In terms of playing the game, I'm against professional fouls but I play to the umpires rules. If it hit your foot and the umpire says it hit your stick and went in the goal, I'll accept that as part of the run of the play or the rub of the green. But I couldn't be holding somebody's shirt. I think that's an acceptance of failure. I couldn't deliberately kick the ball in the goal, or ask people to do that. I'd expect them to play honestly and openly to the laws of the game; and the interpretation of those laws is up to the umpire. So there's a marginal issue there.'

Graham Taylor said, 'It's a thin line but I see it clearly and I don't step over it. If I go into the penalty box and I can find an extra half a yard of pace to cause the defender to mistime his tackle and send me flying for a penalty, I think that's honest. I've used a deception of pace. What's not honest is just going for the dive. I want my men to know I don't want to get involved in cheating, even in the heat of the game.'

Peter Shilton was very clear. 'If you cheat at anything, I think it's a weakness and eventually it'll show up in other areas. I think there should be mutual respect between all sportsmen. It's an old-fashioned view but I think it's the right view.'

David Evans said, 'For better or for worse, because I lead by example, I have tended to work by a fairly tight ethic. I've never fiddled my expenses. I've never done all the things I'm in a position to do. In a way, a leader has to be like Caesar's wife, above reproach. Events like the Guinness affair are really demeaning to the whole superstructure of general and senior management, because there is absolutely no need for it. It's only greed. And the ethical standards you use will be matched by your staff's.'

Sir Michael made an interesting point: 'You will not get the *top* people working with you unless you have the highest standards of business integrity. If you value what you get out of corner cutting at £1000, the damage you do in demotivation of good people is minus £20,000. There may have been some weak leaders but the standard of integrity in British business is very high.'

On the subject of charisma, before I had asked anything about ethics, Sir John volunteered, 'What I admire in people is integrity and intellectual honesty, and I admire people who are honest about themselves and their motives.'

Summary of learning points:

- A genuine desire for fair play and strong ethical values was championed by all of the group.
- It matters *how* you win; victory without cheating has real value.
- Under pressure and in unusual circumstances your principles will be put to the test.
- Holding to principle may cost in short-term loss, accusations of cowardice, and the burden of responsibility.
- Leaders are responsible to themselves *and* are models for others. A slightly shady saving will cost you *far* more in the demotivation of your good people.
- If you cheat you may get away with it at the time, but there will be comeback sooner or later. This law of karma works in reverse too – you get what you give.
- Each of us has the ability to know, within, whether an action is honest. Even after mistakes one will always be able to face the mirror, and that is our most important test.

- British sporting organizations have not yet lifted their vision to the benefits of cooperation. Self-interest and power and control issues are holding back potential.

Any other comments? Coming out of the question on values Neil Benson shared an interesting thought on the valuation of people. He pointed out that nowhere in any published accounts or supporting accounts is there anything about 'the value of your people' to your business. You have records of how many and their average pay, but nothing to say that you have decided to invest in a top quality graduate recruitment programme or that specific training greatly increased the value to the company of certain individuals. One advantage to the company of doing this would be to have an important annual guide as to whether you have helped develop your 'people assets' appropriately. A second would be a more accurate valuation of a company. A simple illustration of how a company is misvalued by not including this concept is as follows: Those who worship the bottom line would value as equal two identical companies who had profits of £100,000 at £1 million. If one company decided to invest £20,000 in a new graduate each year, their bottom line profit could drop to £80,000 and that company would then, quite unreasonably, be valued at only £800,000, a lesser company than the other!

If this valuation system was used it could prompt employees to be traded like football players, with compensating transfer fees being paid by companies who buy especially gifted employees from other firms.

Sue Campbell reflected that her style of dealing with authority and others was learned from her parents. 'I learned the business of respecting others; being proud enough of yourself and feeling good enough about yourself to be able to say to anybody what you thought. That doesn't mean being rude. It means being able to express freely what you truly believe and not necessarily be afraid of the costs. I learned to make mistakes and realize that they were one of the best learning processes. My dad was a layman philosopher. If I had a problem he'd say, "Tell me about it." And I'd say "Well, Claire called me a bighead!" and he'd say, "Well, are you?" He always got me to understand, to address my own personal strengths and weaknesses, through actually questioning.' This experience helps her work to her strengths and ask for help in her weak areas. She felt many managers convince themselves that they're infallible – an unrealistic attitude.

David Whitaker respects his opponent but has no sympathy in battle. He also has great respect for his performers. 'They are putting themselves out on a limb during peak performance. It is absolutely crucial that you recognize that you're asking them to extend themselves beyond standards they've achieved before, physically, emotionally, psychologically; and as a team they are going into arenas they've never been in before. Then they're going to want to come back and do it again. They're going to stay with you.'

Richard Noble mentioned the business parallel of the professional sports people's problem – not being prepared for coming down off the heights. Even though performers need to have top priority on their project, there must be a wider context into which it fits. Otherwise they can easily wind up feeling lost.

A vital ingredient in most teams, a sense of humour, was acknowledged by Peter Shilton.

Sir John said, 'I do believe in trying to have fun and demonstrating that I have fun. I use humour to defuse conflict and also to get closer to the pain threshold, because if you can laugh you can get much closer to the pain threshold, as you have to in athletics – to increase the pain tolerance. Usually I'm laughing at myself or laughing at us as a group.' For myself, I remember laughing at our idiocy in the intensely painful, but highly effective, sand dune training sessions at Boston University.

Sir Michael Edwardes said, 'I am always very hesitant about bringing an unfit, overweight person into a team; it suggests a lack of discipline. I'm sixty and play squash three times a week and tennis once. I'm not overweight. My energy is greater than it was at fifty. I'm sure I'm fitter than my opposition and I think that's material. I wouldn't want anyone on my team who wasn't physically fit.' He spoke of drive and agreed when I equated this to the 'will to win'. Humankind has an innate drive to evolve, to improve on what has been before.

Billy Beaumont said that motivation is easy for the initial goal. The most difficult task is to keep motivated once it has been achieved, like Liverpool Football Club. He believed that confidence and cooperation were major factors.

Summary of learning points:

- Humour is vital and it can be used to defuse conflict, engender enthusiasm, increase pain tolerance, retain perspective by laughing at oneself, and tell some home truths.
- Knowing one's strengths and weaknesses leads to self-acceptance, which can increase one's potential.
- One needs to develop sufficient self-confidence, self-respect and respect for others, to be able to say honestly what one believes.
- Respect your opponents.
- Particularly respect and support your performers when they are taking steps into new territory.
- For personal balance while striving and for reintegration after the excitement of the heights, performers and leaders need to retain a view of the bigger whole.

Postscript: This chapter was a look at people management. It is an obvious point, but one worth making, that the projects the performers are undertaking make little or no difference. Sport leadership, business leadership, orchestral leadership, all leadership is largely focused on communication skills; which is primarily what we have been hearing from these highly successful leaders. I was interested and pleased to note the shift of style emphasis from predominantly authoritarian to growing and empowering through questioning. Managers and coaches who have shifted largely to this style have been achieving better bottom line results in business and better performance at major championships in sport, because the performers are more aware, appropriately focused, more self-responsible and enthusiastic. It is the area of performer development work I have been in for the past five years. The conclusion at the end of this book gives more explanation. Mentioning this is like a commercial, but I choose to look at it as sharing my belief – that we owe it to ourselves and our performers to value the development of our potential.

11
ALTERNATIVE SUPPORT

Was there any other person apart from your parents or coach who helped you to achieve your goal? It was at this point that many of the athletes who did not have a coach who had influenced them named people who were important either as a role model, advisor, teacher, partner, or someone who had given inspiration.

ROLE MODELS   Most role models will be unaware of whom they are inspiring. They are, nevertheless, an extremely significant source of aims. For children, parents and older siblings are the first and most obvious behavioural role models. However, once the individual is old enough to make a choice of a career or ambition, the impact of another role model may have just as significant an effect.

Ginny Leng said that she was inspired by Lucinda Green, Richard Meade and Mary Gordon Watson and watched videos of them for hours. 'I wanted to be like that.'

Duncan Goodhew is not at all sure whether Nigel Johnson was aware of being his mentor. A fellow student at Millfield School, Nigel was going to the Olympics, and that became Duncan's goal.

Ian Botham and Viv Richards independently cited Brian Close, during his captaincy of Somerset's cricket team. Viv said, 'I was young and raw and he was the captain. Mentally, he was a hero for me. He would get hit by a bouncer from fast bowler Wesley Hall and he wouldn't rub the spot. He'd just stand there with his chest up.' Ian's comment was, 'I always had the will to win but he certainly helped drag it out of me early on. He taught me one thing above all – that nothing is lost until the last ball is bowled. He only wanted to win and he never asked anyone to do anything he hadn't or couldn't do himself. He lived hard and played hard – a very determined man.'

Barry John also chose to follow an example set by a cricketer. When he was twelve or thirteen years old, he read about one of the most respected West Indies cricketers, Gary Sobers. Gary had decided to prepare himself so that the selectors couldn't drop him no matter what the conditions or what was required. He worked on being capable of bowling fast, slow or spin. He learned to play defensively as well as score dramatically. Barry said that from reading that, he decided to apply the same principle to his own game of rugby union. He worked on being able to kick with either foot and to prepare himself to be invaluable and indispensable no matter what the requirements or conditions.

Jackie Stewart recalled two outstanding drivers. 'Fangio was the great man of racing while Sterling Moss was the epitome of a racing driver.' He also referred to a pre-motor racing team-mate who had influenced him strongly. 'The captain of the British shooting team, Glynne Jones, a great character, had a tremendous influence on how I behaved and how I looked at serious competition and how I looked at life. He is a humorist and fun to be with but also a successful businessman.' One other strong influence was mentioned by Jackie: 'Bob McIntyre, the first motor cyclist to do 100 m.p.h. around the Isle of Man, attacked his motorcycle racing in such a profound way and it was he who started me on weight training and getting fit.'

ADVISORS   Individuals take guidance and receive support from all types of people. Rod Laver recalled that he had had little coaching. 'No one showed me how to hold a racket, but I had advice from Charlie Hollis who said, "If you want to be a champion, you'll have to top spin your backhand." From there, it was done by feel.' The advice gave him confidence to persevere with the top spin regardless of the consequences.

Steve Davis said that his manager, Barry Hearn, was like a brother. 'He helped me mature as a person and grow up a lot quicker. Because of the fact that you only play snooker, there's no childhood, no teens, you're lacking in other ways and you have to grow up quickly and he helped me to do that.' Steve also mentioned that Barry was the one who introduced him to the need for total physical fitness.

Clive Lloyd was significantly influenced by Fred Mills whom he referred to as his mentor. 'He was a very brilliant man, a barrister, and I always wanted to be a barrister; in fact, he was a QC. He gave me the inner strength and confidence. He looked after me. When I first played first-team cricket in Guyana, aged sixteen, I remember the rest of the team going off to the pub at the local hotel. Fred would give me some money and tell me to take my girlfriend out or something, letting me know that he thought I had exceptional ability and not to waste it.'

Some performers reach a point in their careers where they generally know what is the best for them. However, they value having a knowledge-able sounding-board or someone whose opinions they respect. Joan Benoit Samuelson cited Bob Sevene, the Athletics West coach. Peter Scudamore cited the help David Nicholson had been in showing him videos and talking through what to do.

Experience counts and Steve Cram is grateful for the reflections of Brendan Foster. 'That extra 10 per cent was very worthwhile. Jimmy Hedley couldn't have told me what it would be like in the Olympic final. Brendan could, so I was lucky.' Clive Lloyd's cousin is the West Indies bowler Lance Gibbs. Clive said that his cousin advised him when he was fourteen not to aspire to play for Guyana, but to set his sights higher, to play for the West Indies.

Another important part that advisors can play is giving advice on personal financial matters, or helping to find financial assistance from another source. Financial backing can be a very valuable asset for the performer. Harold Guiver was just such an influential person in Billie Jean King's life. 'Harold believed in me from the beginning and said that he would pull together the money to get me to Wimbledon. I said, "No, I haven't earned it yet."' It was not too long before she did. For Rod Laver it was Wally Best at Dunlop in Brisbane who gave financial backing. 'He wanted to know how I'd done and would ask if I needed anything – he was like a second father.' Ginny Leng mentioned the financial support from her uncle and her sponsors. Sponsorship can be a great benefit to today's sporting achievers. In most cases that support is invaluable but in a few the tail wags the dog and commercial interests can run across the best interests of the performers.

TEAM-MATES   Team-mates and training partners have assisted in a variety of ways. Rod Laver talked about the encouragement from team-mates Roy Emerson and Mel Anderson. 'I worked well to encour-agement and I responded well to the positive example.'

Cricketers have no coach at national level, so they rely on advice from fellow team members.

Mixed training with both men and women seems to have helped the women significantly. This may take the form of combined or competitive exercises. Mary Rand referred to the fun of blatantly taking a flier (leaving before the gun) in starting practice against the boys; Heather McKay,

Billie Jean King and Chris Evert all mentioned the significance of playing against males.

Stefan Edberg mentioned the benefit he felt he had derived from being stretched while growing up in a very small town. 'I was lucky because I got to play with the older players. I was the youngest among the juniors in the club.'

PARTNERS   Almost everyone in the study referred to the support which they had from their partners. Ian Botham and Viv Richards both cited the understanding and support they receive from their wives. This support is very important considering that cricket and rugby tours take the players away from their families for weeks and even months at a time. Without the backing of partners, it would be difficult for the individuals to embark on such trips.

Squash champion Geoff Hunt valued his wife in a role which went beyond normal support. 'My wife helped to keep my performance in perspective and I think that's important. She doesn't tolerate bad behaviour on the court and the odd times where I'd show any form of disagreement, which usually wasn't bad compared with others, she would pick me up on it. She would never come out and abuse me or really praise me. She had confidence in me that no matter what predicament I was in, I was going to get out of it. It was also what she expected me to do . . . because she knew it was what I expected of myself.'

The women were no less grateful of their partners' support, encouragement, backing and baby-sitting. Heather McKay said her husband often travelled with her and not only supported her activities, but was involved with the necessary encouragement in training efforts.

Lucinda Green pointed out the quality of relationship developed with her horses. 'In the case of coaching support, there are so many people who have been vital parts in the jigsaw on the way up, five or six or seven coaches with valuable input, that it's unfair to name one or two in particular. It's the horses that are most important to me.'

TEACHERS   Several of the athletes spoke about their school teachers who had played an important role in their initial introduction to sport. In Gareth Edwards' case, school teacher Bill Samuel was mentioned as the significant coach, but in most cases the teachers were simply the ones who introduced the sport and kindled an interest in it,

Sean Kerly celebrating a goal against Pakistan in the 1986 World Cup; success in sport has increased his self-confidence.

Duncan Goodhew accommodates the Press during the 1980 Moscow Olympics. The astuteness of his parents and coaches must take some credit for his dedication to swimming and his success in it.

1984 gold medallists Jayne Torvill and Christopher Dean epitomize the expressive side of sport; they think of their bodies as shapes and designs.

Clive Lloyd, inspirational West Indian captain for sixteen years: 'My personal belief in Christ helped me quite a lot . . .'

Nick Faldo's ability to muster complete concentration when required is crucial in this most cerebral of sports.

Ken Read (left) and Jonah Barrington; top class practitioners in two sports requiring very different types of concentration. The downhill skier has to focus on several things at once, while the squash player only takes his eye off the ball to study his opponent's movements for clues about the return shot.

Gareth Edwards feeds the ball out for Wales against England in 1974. His impassioned performances on the field were in contrast to his detachment immediately before a game.

1990: Sir John Whitmore in his new CanAm McLaren at Silverstone more than twenty years after his retirement – a remarkable and victorious comeback.

David Bryant, no less successful today than he was back in 1972 when he was caught in action in the National Championships. An easy-going, phlegmatic exterior conceals a master at applying pressure.

Kip Keino (left) used to aim for a personal best, regardless of the competition. Here we see him fighting for the lead against his great Finnish rival, Vasala, in the Munich Olympics.

Rod Laver, one of the finest touch players to grace the game of tennis, seen here at Wimbledon in 1972. He used to practise against two opponents at once to perfect his singles game.

A more recent arrival on the tennis scene; as a teenager, Stefan Edberg worked hard to develop a positive attitude – there is nobody but yourself to help you on court.

You may have talent, dedication and the right temperament but, as Ginny Leng (seen here with Priceless in 1985) is the first to admit, in some sports you need to find financial sponsorship.

Bill Beaumont leads out the British Lions in 1980. He needed no extra incentive to compete: 'Money would probably have made me a dirtier player!'

Increasingly, snooker seems to be a young man's game. In a sport where a major flaw in technique can easily develop into a major problem, both Steve Davis (left) and Stephen Hendry are fortunate in being able to detect their own faults and work on the remedy alone.

Friends, rivals and instinctive competitors, Ian Botham (left) and Viv Richards have the vital ingredient in their make-up which makes them relish a challenge. Botham happily admits that he never knows when he's beaten; Richards always aims to demoralize the opposition's bowlers.

either through the way they presented it or, more importantly, through their personality and enthusiasm. There are thousands of such teachers who see young talent and encourage the children in their sporting pursuits. Mary Rand spoke of Miss Saunders at her secondary school, Mr Bromfield at Millfield and club coaches Alf and Mabel Cotton. The chain of people has been there for almost everyone, but their importance often goes unrecognized. It will be noted in a later section that a large proportion of these high achievers saw their progression as a series of steps. The teachers and club coaches have been a vital part in putting youngsters on the first rung of the ladder.

OTHER INFLUENCES   Daley Thompson has Doreen. 'When I started out, my aunt was really helpful in everything I did; she just supported it whether it was right, wrong, indifferent or anything. She's just been really helpful and supportive – everything you'd expect from your parents and more. So that's been great. If I'd tried to do everything I've done without her, it would have been twice as difficult or perhaps I might not have been able to do it all, because with her, I've always had home stability and all that kind of stuff and I spend so much time away from home. I need someone back there to be solid and dependable. I like being at home, I like my friends and I get homesick.'

Medical back-up is another important facet in the sports person's life. Joan Benoit Samuelson said, 'I must thank the doctors who put me back together. People were saying after my knee surgery that I had this miracle cure, electrical therapy, but if Stan James hadn't performed successful surgery, neither therapy nor a strong mind would have helped, and the same with Dr Leech who carried out my Achilles tendon surgery.'

Valeriy Borzov believed that the support of the Press, as well as friends, was a positive influential factor. He said that the Press had always been good to him. Significantly, it was not uncommon to hear the Western athletes in this study say that they had stopped reading the papers because too often they were misquoted or run down by the Press. As in other areas, constructive criticism along with praise for what has been done well is far more likely to promote higher achievement than negative criticism and cynicism.

Nick Faldo talked about the support of Gerald Nicklan. 'He always put things to you well. He caught me throwing a club in a temper once and rather than give me a rollocking, he said, "I used to do that. It never got me very far." Rather than ticking me off, which others would have done, he had turned it round and it was just the right approach to this.'

How important to you was a sense of humour and what purpose did it have? The overwhelming response of 90 per cent of all the performers interviewed was that it was vital and basically relieved tension. Performers enjoy being around humour even if they are not humorists themselves. Kip Keino said that it encouraged everyone to be a part of the team, helping to keep it together. David Bryant saw it in a similar light; as skipper, especially, he thought it provided team unity. Sean Kerly pointed out its importance, particularly with a group you haven't been with before.

Lester Piggott said that with all the travel required in his work, a jockey must see the funny side. Peter Scudamore said that the weighing room was usually a very funny place. Because of the imminent danger humour relieved the tension.

Another dangerous sport is motor racing and John Whitmore saw humour as 'Crucial! I don't think a racing driver would survive without a sense of humour and racing drivers are renowned for a good sense of humour. I think it's a release of energy from the dangers involved. Also I would say that because racing drivers have to contend together against the common dangers that we all share, the level of camaraderie is quite high. One might not imagine that in the light of the Senna–Prost revelations but I would say that that's the exception rather than the rule.'

To Daley Thompson, humour is everything. His humour, however, often gets him into trouble outside the track environment. For example, a sponsor's wife told him, 'Daley, I can't tell you how much pleasure you've given me.' Daley drily replied, 'Thank you, but you'd better not let your old man hear you say that!' Carl Lewis sees humour as a form of creativity, while Ken Read felt that it gave perspective.

Lucinda Green said, 'I don't see how you can exist without it and still enjoy yourself.' Billie Jean King responded by saying, 'It's essential. You must have resilience, and humour helps that a lot.'

Steve Ovett and Steve Cram said that they saw the funny side of things even during training sessions. Ovett said, 'There are occasions when Matt [Paterson] and I have actually had to stop training because we've been laughing so much. I think if you don't have a sense of humour and you can't laugh at yourself, you are not really enjoying it as much as you possibly could. Some of the hardest sessions are when the funny occasions arise. I don't know whether it's because mentally you're alert, you're concentrating and therefore anything seems funny. I think part of you accepts the lunacy of it all, saying, "What the hell are you doing this for?" When training is really hard and people are doubled up on the floor or throwing up, you'll hear, "It's only pain but you'll get used to it." It's not the sort of thing anyone wants to hear, but it's funny at the time . . . Middle-distance runners are very similar and there's an empathy and a closeness that brings understanding of the training or the environment or whatever the circumstances. It only needs something to get you going and it triggers everything off and everybody else can immediately identify with it, it doesn't have to be explained.'

Steve Cram reflected on his need not to make his training too competitive. 'I hate people getting too serious in training. I see lads destroying themselves being too competitive in training and they sometimes get miffed if we're having a few jokes. It helps me enjoy it a lot more.'

In contrast, Herb Elliott took his training time very seriously, saying that he could not remember laughing during the sessions or even finding humour in their intensity. Nick Faldo said that he's acquired more of a sense of humour but 'when things are going wrong and people are trying to make fun of it – then I haven't got a sense of humour.'

For all the glamour of national and international sport, it can be a very tense scene. The Olympic Games, for example, come once every four years, and many people aim for them with such passion and intensity for so long that they become highly charged within their environment. Yet in the midst of the Olympians, one man, Al Oerter, reflected on the scene from a different perspective. Instead of the shared humour with others which he also valued, Al talked from the perspective of one who has been at the top and is then able to relax and enjoy the scene. 'It's always necessary to have a sense of humour. You can't stay in an intense climate, including the Olympic Village, and be unaware of what's going on. There's something about the Games themselves. They're the most intense environment in sport and they're comical at times because these architects build these wonderful venues with award-winning housing and they're wonderful things to behold . . . the first thing the competitors do is hang their underwear outside! In fifteen minutes, it looks like a tenement building. They'll wash out their jocks or their shorts and go out and hang them on a statue to dry!' Al also reflected on what tension does to the performers. 'It's funny to watch people who were absolutely normal just fifteen minutes before, conversational, talking about their kids back home or about where they're from, and minutes later they're on the floor of the stadium, before the competition – pacing, sweating heavily and looking so concerned. This is to be enjoyed; this is why we're here and why we've worked for four years. If you don't enjoy it, why did you work the four years?' Al was able to reflect on this because he sees the Games as a journey and not as an end in themselves. Each day's training was a step forward, regardless of the final result. Was it possible that he acquired this more relaxed view following his first success? 'Maybe you're right; maybe it was that way my first time in 1956. Certainly, since then, it's something to be enjoyed.'

Oerter is certainly expressing a view which most can see intellectually but few are able to follow mentally. There are few actors or actresses, musicians or dancers, who do not feel nerves at a time when an important performance is about to be judged. Singer Vera Lynn once said that 'You're only as good as your last performance . . . I didn't really enjoy the feeling beforehand . . . I only felt relaxed after it was over.' It is part of the human response and Al Oerter is certainly a fortunate man to be able to enjoy his competitive times before and during the performance. Few, if any, are forced to compete. They do so because they have to and want to. It is a self-expression, and afterwards the athletes are happy to have fulfilled their task with distinction.

Al is not entirely alone in being able to keep matters in a light-hearted vein, even during competition. Barry John talked about an incident near the end of a rugby union match. He said that his team were ahead by a substantial margin and he knew that making another score was not going to be fully appreciated by the fans. He said that he would rather give them something to talk about and go home with a smile on their faces. So when a high ball was coming his way, he saw that it was going to be very close between him catching it and getting hit head on by a 6ft 5in, fast-moving defender. He kept his gaze up toward the ball but drifted to his right. The defender naturally followed him. The ball landed with a thud several feet to one side while he jumped clear of the attacking forward. The crowd loved it.

In their own way, each type of assisting person is significant. It may be through sharing humour at different times, or having a role model to set a standard of temperament or behaviour; it can be a person with insight into talent, taking the trouble to give assistance – or to offer a guiding word or helping with finances; it may be a partner or a friend who understands the struggle or is simply there to go through difficult times with them. The roles are many and varied but the end result is the same: the performer is supported in mind, body and spirit.

Summary of learning points:

- Role models are inspirational for up and coming youngsters. That puts a great deal of responsibility on the top performers to behave in a manner which they would like to see followed.
- Humour should be valued and used for the many positive roles it can play – to relieve tension; built team unity; relieve boredom; break the ice with new groups; give perspective; allow for creativity; provide fun and enjoyment.
- The types of ways that people assist others are very varied. Everyone has something they can provide to support another person's aim to get the best from themselves.
- No teacher, parent, friend or supporter should ever assume that their help will be too little to count. In the eighteenth century Edmund Burke made a fine statement: 'Nobody made a greater mistake than he who did nothing, when he could only do a little.'

12
INSTITUTIONAL SUPPORT

Those in the West often think of state support in sport in terms of the Eastern bloc countries where total control was administered by state subsidy of their performers and facilities. With the breakdown of communist rule in Eastern Europe things will change greatly. The brilliant results which came out of East Germany have come to a close with German reunification. Several hundred coaches and scientists from the GDR's Institute of Sport were laid off and investigation initiated into their use of performance-enhancing drugs. A new order will evolve but one wonders whether the same search and control of talent will take place. Many Westerners recoiled at the thought of the Eastern European performer's lack of choice, but most did not have a completely accurate picture.

SPORT IN THE USSR Young performers in the USSR are screened for their physical and psychological aptitude for sport. Those who fit the highly successful sports profile are then given the choice to attend a school. These are normal educational schools which also have a specialist training in specific sports. It is considered an honour to be chosen and offered such an opportunity, similar to being offered a tuition scholarship to university in the United States. Most youngsters willingly accept but it is their choice. Once secondary school is completed, almost all Soviet sportsmen and women will go on to study their sport and related disciplines at university. This has proved to be a very successful system, up to a point. But Jayne Torvill and Christopher Dean pointed out a drawback of such early screening. 'They always get very good performers because they've chosen somebody with the right physique and they always have pretty girls skating, but they almost never get that fantastic, spontaneous performance because maybe it's not coming directly from within them. Some have strong personalities, like Olga Korbut in gymnastics, but we find that they have a lot of very bland people and they work like robots.' They went on to say that some of their top performers have rebelled in some way. 'The Protopopovs defected and Olga herself was very outspoken . . . Rodnina [who was best known in her partnership with Zaitsev] was different in that she's a party member and she chose who would be her partners and she could also decide when to finish skating.'

Due to the large numbers involved, there are bound to be some entering the sport who find that it is their form of self-expression, but Jayne and Chris's point was that only if the choice of sport is made by the performers themselves can one expect to have individuality and personality fully expressed in a performance. Perhaps the choice of sport is being made too early for the generally gifted, who could turn their talent to another sport later on. Certainly the screening helps to identify talent and to match them up with well-qualified coaches. But what happens when the sports person is no longer in the peak of condition and is unable to continue his or her sporting career?

Valeriy Borzov made a personal comment. He felt that the system in the West was very unfair to their high achievers, as they could participate for their country and even win a gold medal but at the end of their sporting career, there was no guarantee from the government, or private sector, of any job. He felt that there must be some amount of insecurity in the minds of Western performers not knowing if they are perhaps sacrificing their early career days. He posed the question of injustice; while devoting a great deal of time and effort on their own behalf, performers also devote their energy and talent on behalf of their country, and at the end of the day can be left with nothing. He reflected specifically on Tommy Smith, the US sprinter, who had won the 200m in world record time at the 1968 Mexico Olympics, and returned home to unemployment. Tommy is now a junior college coach, but Valeriy believes that there should have been no time lag.

It is certainly a point worthy of reflection. One reason there was not this problem in the Soviet Union is that they have had full employment by the State and almost all sports people attend state universities. Many of them will become well-qualified coaches by the time their active career is over. Of course, this may not be wanted by all the Western performers. However, it would be reasonable to consider that the performers who are currently receiving a subsidy for training virtually full-time should have a responsibility to give something back to their sport. It would be a valuable inspiration to future generations if each subsidized high-achieving performer took a coaching qualification during some of their free time, so that on retirement, or before, they would be able to visit schools or clubs and teach as well as inspire. It would take financial backing to underwrite their travel and payment, but as qualified coaches they would be in an excellent position to engender enthusiasm and to pass on sound basic advice.

SPORT IN THE WEST   How do individuals choose the right sport? For most youngsters in the West, choosing the right sport is more by luck than good judgement. If a school teacher happens to recognize talent and has the expertise to assist or direct a youngster towards good coaching, then the young person is fortunate. Usually, the young performers must rely on the right facilities and decent coaching being close to where they live. The high schools in the United States are very well set up to afford a variety of competitive opportunities with excellent facilities; however, most of their coaches are teachers who, although they have played in their time, have no coaching accreditation. In most cases, this is not the coaches' fault: few coaching certification programmes exist. The teacher training colleges teach the physical educationalists the rules and general state of play in a wide variety of sports, but even there, no individual sports have instituted a test or specified priorities in coaching and training techniques. Most coaches come up through the ranks of experience: they are usually self-taught and have had no formal instruction. They apply their own thoughts to old methods.

In Great Britain, greater emphasis is placed on coaches having sport teaching qualifications but there is far less provision for sport indoors than in US schools. Another difference is that Britain has most of its sport based on clubs centred in each town. Most of the US provision is centred in community schools. In recent years a support service for an introductory course to international coaching has been established in the UK. The National Coaching Foundation provides all levels of coach with a comprehensive coach education programme. No sport-specific skills are taught but there is everything else a coach needs to know, from how to develop speed, strength and flexibility, through nutrition, injury prevention, fair play, the use of video, mental training and a lot of other areas, including our effective questioning course. In a very few years the NCF has done much to raise awareness of what coaches need to know and has provided the opportunity for them to learn. Many sports have taken advantage of this common programme and have integrated it into their own sport-specific courses on skills, tactics and rules. Many countries are now looking to the NCF as a role model.

A disturbing trend for those of us who believe that children need physical development and can learn much through physical reaction is budget cuts for school sport. In several local authorities, sport in school is played on only one afternoon a week and three different sports are rotated. Ian Botham recounted that his son is very keen on soccer. Thursday was assigned for sport but if it rained, that activity week was cancelled. This happened twice in succession on soccer weeks, which meant that there were nine weeks between the one day for soccer! This is no way to allow young talent to develop. Sport is so important to youngsters as they grow and learn to master their bodies and themselves, it must be hoped that the trend is reversed and that learning through the physical is rediscovered for the gem it can be in developing our youngsters and helping them grow. A reduction of this opportunity is regrettable and short-sighted.

CLUB COACHES IN SCHOOLS   The trend towards less teacher involvement in coaching may promote the club coaches to spend more time linked with schools. This would have two obvious advantages, the first being that each coach would have specialist knowledge, the second that interested and gifted children would feel inclined to link with clubs to continue sport after their school days. Perhaps combined funding from governing bodies of sport and education authorities could support more coaches coming into schools on a regular basis. I would also love to see top PE specialists for the very youngest in schools, learning the fun and joy of movement.

SPORTS SCHOLARSHIPS   The British Football Association at Lilleshall National Sports Centre and the Lawn Tennis Association at Bisham Abbey National Sport Centre have a few youngsters attending local schools and practising their sport under senior coaches, in the hope of developing top quality international players.

A few independent schools offer scholarships. Millfield School, which Duncan Goodhew, Mary Rand, Gareth Edwards and J.P.R. Williams attended, in the west of England, along with other schools in more recent years, has given scholarships for the development of excellence in sport as well as for academic subjects, music and art. Many schools offer financial assistance to top academic scholars; a few awards exist for music, and even fewer for art or sport.

Some independent schools in America give aid to a few talented sportsmen and women, but in whichever Western country one names, the backing usually comes from a keen headmaster rather than from any coherent government policy for the backing and development of sport. Sixty per cent of high school graduates go on to further education in the US. The academic spectrum is a very wide, Harvard and Yale, Stamford and others at the top end swapping professors and students with Oxford and Cambridge. The lower end in the US spectrum could be like GCSE level work. Of the more than three thousand colleges and universities, hundreds partially or wholly subsidize the cost of education for their better sportsmen and women. University teams are provided with world-class facilities, equipment and professional coaching. Travel is underwritten to participate in local, regional and national competitions. Few talented high school athletes are not offered the chance to study the academic area of their choice in exchange for representing their university to the best of their sporting ability. It would be difficult to conceive a better opportunity for eighteen- to twenty-two-year-olds to participate on a regular basis, at all levels of competition. Most of the US Olympic representatives come from this pool. The problem is, however, that there is practically no club system to progress to once university is complete and only a few, very elite competitors are chosen to play for professional teams. The vast majority finish participating when they leave college or university. In a sport such as athletics, where the trend is to reach a peak around the mid-twenties to mid-thirties, many of the better athletes have finished competing years before fulfilling their potential.

The best of both worlds is available to non-American performers going to the US on a scholarship. They have the training and competition during the university days, possibly competing during the holidays in international competition. Then after university days they return to a full club and international programme. In exchange for competing for the university, the sportsman or woman may study the academic area of their choice, assuming that they qualify for that university's entrance standard. Individuals such as David Wilkie, Duncan Goodhew and I attended universities in America. We were fortunate to find coaches who helped in our development rather than merely exploited our talent on behalf of the team in inter-university competitions. This element needs exploring before signing a commitment to any institute.

It is worth asking the question: would it not be possible to create a British universities structure which took the best from the US system, involving more students and providing greater opportunities for competition? The gathering of all-round talent is not the same here as in the US; they take an average of three times as many from every school and that presents one problem. That also brings into question the whole system. Is it realistic for our schools to have the role of helping our youngsters to grow and develop in order to fulfil their greatest potential *and* at the same time be involved in an academic screening process to find the top 20 per cent? Does this not leave the remaining 80 per cent with some feelings of inadequacy? Given the fact that the sporting elite have so many late developers I am pleased that one evolution in education has been to maintain a more broad curriculum. Previously, too much emphasis for every student had been placed on the narrowing channel to the end goal of the exams which are taken after three years at university – an approach which was only tailored to the top 20 per cent.

Public and personal sponsorship in the form of donations is another form of sport subsidy. Indeed, in many Western countries from club to Olympic level, donations from the general public are essential in order to finance the country's top performers and ensure their participation in major events. In the UK, the Sports Aid Foundation assists those with major games medal potential with personal grants. The founders recognized that an athlete needs assistance in the years running up to the Games as well as during that crucial year. Several Winston Churchill Fellowships have also assisted sports representatives and coaches. And in recent years the NCF has also begun to give study scholarships to coaches.

In UK soccer, Bobby Charlton pointed out that the better clubs, of which Manchester United is one, require that their young apprentices continue their studies or attend technical or trade school while they are learning their soccer trade. This is a practice I strongly endorse. Too often the boys who leave school at the earliest possible age of sixteen sign away their education in the hopes of glory on the field. Unfortunately a large proportion never attain their dreams and are left with no qualifications and an incomplete education. Even a successful professional could be developing other skills which could be used once his or her playing days are complete.

COMMERCIAL SPONSORSHIP Commercial sponsorship is another area which can underwrite sporting participation. An ever increasing number of companies are willing to assist performers, often for the publicity acquired by being associated with them, and at times simply for goodwill. Sponsorship in sport has become exceptionally big business for the few outstanding achievers at the very top of most sports. Commercial companies have seen the advantage of associating the well-known and admired performers with their product, for example Linford Christie with milk, John Barnes with Lucozade. Most of the top achievers have their own agents who link them with the commercial opportunity, usually for a commission in the region of 20 per cent. The best known of these is the International Management Group run by Mark McCormack. However the number of companies in that area continues to grow. Sponsorship is now a key ingredient in the presentation of sporting events. Several events now bear the name of the company or product in their titles. This is particularly true in Britain when the event is to be televised. The caution which agents and governing bodies must have is to find the balance of mutual benefit. Sport can certainly use the money, but the question of what is in the best interests of the performer and the sport must be kept in mind. There is also the problem that, as agents force up appearance fees for the super elite, the distribution of available money to the up-and-coming, more needy performers is lessened. Television plays a vital role for sport. Sports which receive a good deal of exposure attract major sponsorship money. A positive feedback situation exists. Lesser exposed sports cannot find as good funding and do not develop as rapidly or to the level they might with more sponsorship.

GOVERNMENT SUPPORT In the UK at present the main funding for most governing bodies comes from the annual government grant made through the Sports Council. I sincerely hope that, at some time in the future, the broader potential of sport will be recognized. School is an ideal place for learning for life. What is positive health and how can we pursue that? What can we learn through the physical? How do we increase competence in leading ourselves and others? This could be linked with art, music, dance, etc.; it might also be cross curriculum but the intention would be to support the development of learning, growth and excellence through sport and PE.

Summary of learning points:

- Guidelines as to sport aptitude would be helpful for children, but the choice of sport should always be that of the performer.
- Those who have had their sport choice imposed on them tend to be more mechanistic, less creative.
- Is it possible to ensure work for those who have competed successfully for their country?
- Those competing should also be preparing themselves for life after full-time sport.
- The US has the best facilities but few coach education programmes.
- Britain has excellent coach education opportunities and gradually improving facilities.
- Can we evolve a better use of qualified club coaches to work with schools?
- Could Britain evolve a university structure which took the best elements of the US opportunities to study and participate in sport?
- Scholarships and sponsorships can provide valuable support for a limited number of performers.
- Schools should be the places for learning for life, including health and learning through the physical.

13
SOCIAL LIFE

Do you feel that you sacrificed anything in order to pursue your sport? Two-thirds thought that they had not. It was a matter of choice and many underlined how much they had gained rather than what they had lost. Pat O'Callaghan answered, 'I would regret it if I hadn't done it. I would always have wondered what I might have done.' John Whitmore said, 'It wasn't a sacrifice it was a privilege.' For some, although there is no regret, sacrifices were great. Kip Keino put it simply, 'Money for food'. Many sports are still completely amateur. One wonders what Kip Keino could be earning were he running today. When I interviewed Sean Kerly the time away from work through hockey was pressing him financially. He was searching for a job. But he still pointed to all the benefits. 'I feel more of a person. It's given me a lot of self-confidence. It's enabled me to travel the world; see the character of nations and how they're organized. I have friends where I could stay around the world. And my ambition was to be an Olympian and to have fulfilled that is amazing' (to say nothing about his being instrumental in getting a gold medal at the Games!).

What might seem to be a sacrifice to an outsider may be nothing of the sort to a dedicated performer. Individuals who did not want to devote themselves to becoming the best could often be seen accepting an extra pint at the pub; to refuse would have been a sacrifice to them. To the aspiring achiever, saying 'no' was not always considered a sacrifice, because it was what he or she felt was right and would help the quest towards the goal they had set. Everyone has to make choices as to what they will do with their time. These individuals made their sporting goal the top priority and other things, in varying proportions, were fitted around that aim.

Stephen Hendry said, 'Parties, but I loved playing snooker, so I didn't see it as a sacrifice.' Rod Laver said, 'I wouldn't call it sacrifice. I could have got a better formal education or spent more time with my family, but my friends are spread around the world.' Billy Beaumont spoke for most sportsmen and women when he said that the rewards outweighed the sacrifices. But he said in his case, both business and social life suffered.

The social sacrifice in many cases included the family, and several performers said that their families sacrificed as much as they did. As was mentioned previously when referring to partner support, several sports involve individuals or teams travelling for extended periods. Rugby, cricket and hockey tours were mentioned as lasting weeks and even months, but the tennis circuit is now virtually a twelve-month proposition. The US professional sports have extensive 'road trips' scattered throughout their seasons. Today, sport at the top is not too considerate of home time. For Ken Read, pursuing the best meant travelling from Canada to Europe and when the Europeans went home for two to three weeks between races, he could not. Obviously, family life went by the board. On the subject of skiing, Carl Lewis's coach pointed out that Carl had sacrificed his winter hobby in order to avoid being reckless. Speaking during the winter before the 1984 Olympics, Carl said, 'There's no way in the world you'll catch me on skis because if you've got a goal you don't want to have anything divert it.'

Chris Evert referred to the loss of her teen years, but also said that she felt amply rewarded. It was her choice and she could have stopped if she had chosen to. Ginny Leng referred to her sport being unsociable, since it takes place on weekends. You wouldn't have a boyfriend unless from the same sport. And for the first ten years (16–26) she didn't go out. She also referred to the sacrifice of education as a whole and would like to have done business studies. This is a point worth noting. To be a world-class performer, while at the same time studying for a degree and having any social life, places a heavy demand on the individual. The same applies when trying to combine progression in a work career with elite training. If the performer is going to try for the top, the physical preparation has to be the number one priority. It requires considerable additional effort to pursue absolute achievement goals and retain a balanced life. Is it an impossible target? Some sports are far more time consuming than others. Athletics is probably the kindest to the individual life style as many athletes only need to pull on their kit and run out the door. A distance runner will complete 20 miles in two hours and much more than that in a day and the body won't recover adequately for the next day's session.

One prime question to be answered is whether it is necessary to have an imbalanced life in order to achieve any significant level in sport. These sportsmen and women were asked whether they considered that their pursuit of excellence in sport caused their lives to be imbalanced in any way. Eighty per cent said that they had managed to retain a balance, and most expressed their belief that their sport had added to their lives rather than the opposite. The 20 per cent who felt that their life had been imbalanced pointed out that it was chosen rather than forced on them.

However, it is concerning to read about ex-world boxing champions becoming alcoholics and penniless down and outs; and individual waste is in no way confined to that sport. One might well question whether sport does provide the essential elements for learning about life. The answer is that the lessons are there for the taking, but the key as with many aspects depends upon those who are guiding them – family, coach, manager or friend – and whether they themselves have the perspective that sport is there as a learning experience. This group of achievers was fortunate to have had a good degree of support and constructive advice on retaining a balanced view of themselves and their sport.

Ideally one would like to think that the top performers are able to set an example similar to Renaissance Man, integrating mind, body and spirit. Seb Coe, the only man to have retained the Olympic 1500m title, expressed the view that it is not only possible but essential that the performer is encouraged to be as mentally and physically balanced as possible. Indeed, Seb is one who has demonstrated that it can be done. While running he completed his degree, developed an interest in politics, maintained interest in music, art and other sports, and was involved with several promotional activities. About his sport participation, he said, 'I'm inclined to feel that far from taking me into imbalance, sport adds a sort of balance to the equation.'

Ron Pickering expressed his opinion that it was important to let the young performer know that it is possible to reach the top and qualify to do other things. 'There is no track and field athlete who cannot get to the top with a balanced programme of work of two hours of intensive effort a day. Now I don't mind them taking four hours to do two hours of intensive work. I don't mind them telling me they spend all day training – I have yet to see it! But I still want the aspiring athlete to know that it is possible to be a first rate carpenter or a damn good brain surgeon and be a damn good athlete at the same time.'

When this balanced view of achievement was lost, Barry John decided to hang up his rugby boots. He said that it got to the point where he did not know what people wanted of him. He was expected to be an after dinner comic; he wanted still to be one of the boys but he was expected to stay physically fit and, as it is an amateur sport, he had to work as well. Barry said that there are four parts to life; family and social time, work time, personal time and sport time. When sport became too large, he dropped it. He was being called King Barry and while at one public appearance, feeling tired and haggard, a little girl curtseyed to him. For him, that was it: he knew it had gone far enough.

The vast majority viewed their life as enhanced by their sport. Some were inspired to care more about their body, living a cleaner life and as the Bible says, using it as a temple for a spiritual existence. Whatever imbalances there may have been, the responses came back that at least for this group, the experiences of sport were worthwhile. In Daley Thompson's word, 'priceless', and Chris Evert said that she would never trade it. Bryan Robson said that rather than cause an imbalance it had given him sides to his life that he probably would not have had without soccer. 'It's a fantastic job to be paid for what you enjoy doing.' Bobby Charlton would not wholly agree with Bryan that one does not have imbalance. His view was that the professional players have so much done for them that they are sheltered and cosseted. 'Everything was done for you. When you've finished and you have to start doing it all yourself, I think some of the lads have found it very difficult to adapt.' He realized that organization was necessary for the team, but he thought it would help many players if they were given more personal responsibility.

Rod Laver put forward the view that most people would stamp his life as imbalanced. He readily agreed with the term, saying, 'It was tennis morning, noon and night. You slept it, you ate it but that was never forced on me. I would get up at 6 o'clock in the morning to ride my bike, eight or nine miles sometimes to get to the club matches. We'd play all day and people would say, "Weren't you tired after cycling all that way?" Well, that wasn't even thought of. It was just the opportunity to play.'

Travel, and having to live out of a suitcase, was viewed by Lester Piggott as producing an imbalanced life. Another drawback is the delay in developing any other career. Peter Snell was one of several performers who felt that their career progression was slowed by participating in their sport, but it was the chosen course and it was not regretted. He showed how times have changed in terms of pre-sponsored amateur athletes. He said that during his competitive days, he did not leave work until 6 o'clock in the evening. Had he been given time off before the Rome Olympics? 'Yes, I was given an extra half-hour at lunchtime. An hour and a half was enough to get in a speed workout.' Since his three Olympic track golds from Rome and Tokyo, Peter has gone on to receive his doctorate, and has been doing research and teaching at Texas University.

Although questions in this survey did not investigate academic intelligence, over 40 per cent of these sportsmen and women obtained undergraduate degrees and some have further degrees. For example, J.P.R. Williams is a medical doctor and Pat O'Callaghan is a veterinary surgeon.

Lucinda Green made the following observation which is very true. 'Sport is a university of life really. You may go to university and learn an awful lot about the Greeks or the Romans, but this following of sport can teach you so much about life because it's never going to go as you expect it to. Among other things you are going to have to learn to take very many disappointments and learn to take success, which is just as difficult sometimes.'

There is widespread belief that top performers are often selfish individuals. In many ways, that implies that they are not very nice to know. The definition of selfish is being deficient in one's consideration of others, thinking chiefly of one's own personal profit or pleasure. Placing sport above personal relationships seems excessive behaviour but it prevented Rodney Pattisson from marrying. He stated simply that he chose sailing over marriage.

There are many performers, and several have already been cited in this chapter, who would not see themselves as selfish and they would say that it is certainly not necessary to be inconsiderate towards others. The term which is perhaps more appropriate in describing many achievers is egocentric. The very nature of their endeavour and the ends to which they have to go almost forces that state upon them. Intentionally, they place themselves in the centre of a pursuit and much of their mental and physical effort goes into self-improvement. Not only are their thoughts often on themselves, but so is the attention of their coach and supportive cast. In such a situation, it takes a very balanced person to keep themselves and their needs in perspective. No doubt that is why Barry John related the value of going to hospital and seeing children whose bones were crumbling, looking so ill. This insight allowed him to see his own difficulties in their true light. Yes, the quest is important. It is one of the few remaining frontiers open to everyone. We cannot all explore space or the structure of sub-atomic particles, but we can see how much our personal frontier can be moved, and, for a few, that means being at the frontier of human endeavour. When the individual is a performer and is at the forefront, striving, public attention is massively focused. Whether it is the world land speed record attempt by Richard Noble, Steve Cram in the mile or John Harvey Jones turning around ICI, humans focus their attention on what can be achieved. As fellow humans, there is an identification with achievement. These individuals represent all of our needs for self-mastery and mastery of our environment. In so many ways, people are confined and restricted by choice and otherwise, so when achievers break new ground, they lift the horizons for all of us.

As a result of this interest and public attention, the individual is under added pressure to produce. The focus of the performer is in many ways forced to be egocentric. The sportsman or woman is often in the position of being the 'body' under discussion, whether that discussion is about their effort or execution. They are being channelled and manipulated or indeed they are doing it to themselves, all in an attempt to better their performance.

In fine-tuning the body, the slightest twinge means that the 'machine' may not be ready for absolute service. When this sensing or concern is put into words, the performer is seen as a hypochondriac. However, to the achiever, anxiety about health is easily justified. The performer's life, emotionally, physically, psychologically, and often financially, is largely bound up with trying to improve. If anything or anyone comes in between the performer and his or her goal, then it has to be avoided or removed. The whole self-image of the achiever is tied up with being in top condition. Is it any wonder then, that with this thought uppermost in the performer's mind, he or she will often appear imbalanced? For Ron Clarke, the Australian distance runner, it took a shock situation to give him a balanced perspective. He had been attempting to break the world 10,000m record and had come very close, but failed on successive occasions. He was on a training run on the beach and in frustration at his inability to achieve his target, he came to a standstill at the top of a sand-dune. As he looked out over the sea he noticed some creatures flopping and squealing at the edge of the water; then he saw a ball and so he went closer to investigate. He saw that they were not animals at all, but a group of paraplegic children, laughing and squealing with delight as they attempted to play volleyball, with the water supporting their paralysed lower limbs. Ron said that he looked again at himself; here he was in the best condition of any runner on earth, yet carrying a burden of frustration. This simple experience changed his whole perspective. He came away determined to enjoy his health and strength and be thankful for it. Ron recalled this story at the end of his most successful season, having broken not only the world 10,000m record, but also half a dozen other records besides.

How do you get on with others generally, and with teachers, opponents and peers specifically? Eighty per cent said that they had no problems getting on with anyone. The words used to describe how they got on generally varied, but the intent came across as being the same. It was apparent that, in most cases, these athletes got on well socially. They were relaxed within themselves. Steve Cram is a typical illustration. His response to the question was, 'Very well, I'm a social animal.' Those interviewed were not pushy people. Their communication was straightforward, honest and often tinged with humour. They were enjoyable people to sit down with and reflect with, on general issues as well as those which involved their quest for achievement. It should be noted that no one said that they did not get on at all well with other people. Within the 20 per cent who did not simply say 'very well' or 'fine', some explained their communication problem areas. Daley Thompson referred to not getting on well with authority. 'I hate being told what to do. I don't mind being asked but some people are a little more pushy than others.' Duncan Goodhew said that in his younger days, he had conflict with life in general. Some responses were mixed. Seb Coe said 'reasonably well', and Ed Moses, 'pretty well'.

Several performers made the point that they still had many of the same friends with whom they had grown up. This was true even for a jet-setter like Jackie Stewart who has moved countries. Both Billie Jean King and Chris Evert said how difficult it was playing against friends. Billie Jean rationalized the situation by pointing out that it would not be a battle with a friend but a focus on, and battle with, the ball.

Some sportsmen have had quite open confrontations with their administrators: Ian Botham is just such an example. He is aware of taking some raps for others and that in turn, some peers have taken raps for him. His view is that the reason for the conflict is that too often the administrators of British sport have lost touch with the realities of today. In cricket, the view is still held that you do not complain about an umpire's verdict. Ian complained that the administrators do not stand up for the cricketers. To them, it is more important being a good loser.

It is worth following up Ian's point here, as there is a generation in Britain who have grown up believing their own words – that they are good losers! I believe the original intent was that if we lost it was taken with good grace, but it has rebounded with some expecting to lose! At the turn of this century, Britain introduced a number of new sports to the world. As the British were winning consistently, they preached the importance of being a good loser and proudly became humble winners. And when they did lose, it was not hard to act as a generous loser because they knew that they were in fact more frequent winners. Time has changed the luxury of this position. Over the last fifty years, relative affluence has opened up opportunities in sport for many individuals throughout the world. State and private money has increased sporting facilities and coaching, often to a greater extent in other countries than it has in Britain. If Britain or any other country is wanting to compete at the sharp end of international sport, then they are forced to travel the same road. There is a requirement for provision of quality indoor and outdoor facilities, competition at home and abroad, highly competent, qualified coaches, sport science back-up, and full-time qualified, supportive and understanding administrators, for every level of development from introductory fun, grass roots level through to the world-class achievers, striving for excellence.

Is it important what others think of you? Has this ever changed?
One of the issues which females have often had to face has been the stereotyping of physical success with masculinity. Some sports have been inherently more acceptable than others: for example, gymnastics, diving, dance and figure skating all allow the female to project her body gracefully. At the other end of the sporting spectrum is ice hockey and rugby in which female participation has been suspect. Attitudes are rapidly changing as a good cross section of the female population takes part, but in the recent past, if men and women have competed against each other in sport, the unwritten rule for the female was, 'never beat a man'. The female was expected to be passive and gentle and was allowed

to cry. If she was relatively strong, assertive, confident, tough and did not cry, there had to be something wrong with her! It takes many years to alter social bias, but the successful female performers of the last thirty years have forced some enlightened change. Physiological research has also helped. For example, it is now known that the greater quantity of active burning fat in the female body makes them more suited than men for ultra endurance performances. For centuries, men assumed that weakness was a female characteristic. The first time women were allowed to run 800m in the Olympics was in 1960, the 1500m in 1972 and finally the marathon in the 1984 Games.

The responses from interviewing the female performers show their awareness that they represent the image of their sport as well as themselves. Heather McKay said, 'The image of sport is important. I always tried to look as good as I possibly could and as feminine as I could. I'd play the game fairly, and with good sportsmanship. I would put myself out if I was asked to do something for the sport because I felt that a lot of people had put themselves out for me.'

Nearly 90 per cent of these performers did think it was important what others thought of them. Clive Lloyd referred to the responsibility he felt for his image in sport. Clive said, 'As an example for youngsters, you've got to conduct yourself in a good manner because you never know who the people are who idolize you. People look up to sportsmen whether you like it or not . . . I'm not really different, but some of the younger sportsmen don't want the responsibility of acting correctly. Kids need to have heroes, someone to look up to, admire . . . more so now. You can help people! As a person, well liked because of what you're doing, you sign autographs, open things or whatever. They expect that their heroes should maintain certain standards. Ninety per cent of those idolizing expect you to live to high standards . . . and if you have to be smoking, drinking or whatever, do it in private.'

Stefan Edberg traced how he changed himself. 'I like people to like me. I think that's very important. Nobody's perfect but I try to improve myself, not just as a player, as a person too, because when I was sixteen or seventeen I was sort of grumbling a lot on court. I was miserable on the court and I've changed that attitude a lot. It affected my game in a way that I got down on myself. It was a negative thing which I have tried to change into a positive attitude. And that's kind of lifted me both as a sportsman and as a person.'

Kip Keino, understanding how transitory fame can be, seemed to have no attachment to others' opinions. 'I'm so and so today, tomorrow there's somebody else'.

Some commented that they enjoyed being liked. Peter Snell thought that he probably placed too much emphasis on what others thought of him. Peter Scudamore said that it shouldn't matter what others thought but it did, and that he judges by what he reads in the paper. Both Wayne Gretzky and Bryan Robson were bothered by unjustified criticism. Wayne said, 'I take offence over some things written. My parents say don't worry over what other people are saying. I'm saying, "How can they say that? They don't even know me!"' Nick Faldo said he also was sensitive to what is said: 'I've been seen as a hard, single-minded person, as if I had a channel and nobody must get in the way. I blame that on the concentration factor. If I'm concentrating – wanting to do something and have got a direction to go, I can have someone standing right by my left ear saying, "Nick, Nick, Nick, over here", and I honestly won't hear it.'

For others their feelings have evolved. It was more important being liked earlier on in their careers. Jackie Stewart said, 'It gradually became less important.' His racing colleague John Whitmore said, 'As I thought more of myself I was less dependent on what others thought.' Des Drummond felt that a person must face him or herself: 'it was more important what I thought of myself'. That sentiment was echoed by Sean Kerly: 'We all like to be liked. It is important. I'm a bit hard now. As far as I'm concerned I know when I've done all I can do and that's more important to me than what others think . . . because they don't necessarily know. What they think they see isn't necessarily what's happening.'

Three performers qualified whose opinion it was that they cared about. Both Daley Thompson and Ian Botham said, 'Only family and friends.' Herb Elliott said, 'The ones who I did care about, did matter – the rest of them, I didn't give a damn.'

Five of these achievers, Duncan Goodhew, Viv Richards, Lester Piggott, Steve Ovett and Al Oerter, said that it was not important to them what others thought of them. Duncan explained his perspective. 'It was as a kid I learnt, because of having no hair, that if people were so narrow-minded to think a certain way and not give you a chance, then there was no point in worrying about it, but I suppose I've always wanted to be a nice guy basically.' Al Oerter said that he found secondary school years and going through puberty very difficult, but that from the mid-teens on, 'I just have not given a damn what others thought; if I did I'd have been a football player, driven a large car, this kind of nonsense . . .'

Two others gave qualified answers. Ed Moses said, 'Not so much, I'm a loner.' Shane Innes said, 'It was not that important, but I did try to be good.'

Whether or not top performers like it, they are going to be role models for others. Some of today's televised heroes seem unaware of their influence. On the other hand quite a few do see the impact they can have. The fact that sport's household names are largely accepted regardless of the viewer's or their own gender, race, religion, politics and class means that they can have a significant role to play in social integration.

Wanting to please others is part of Maslow's human needs hierarchy – the need for the esteem of others. I asked whom they were trying to please. The other need at this level is the need for self-esteem. Inevitably one prime motivation to do anything is for oneself. It can be reasonably argued from a religious-philosophical stance that one is acting for the glory of a creator, God. This can equally well be extended to say that if God is in all things and man is made in his image, then man's quest for the positive development of his talent is both for the glory of the Almighty and for self-expression. A view from Eric Liddell in the film *Chariots of Fire* was that he could feel God's power running through him. In personal, egocentric terms, there is a school of thought which says, 'If it feels good, do it.' Either way, it comes down to wanting to satisfy one's own desires and needs.

In the religious form, the quest is elevated to a spiritual plane and this will be discussed later on in the book. If a person is from the Soviet Union, it is done for the benefit of the State, the party and for the good of the whole nation. In Hitler's call to the Germans, it was all for the Fatherland, and in the West, the spirit of freedom enables the personal choice to be one for personal satisfaction.

Maslow made the point that in terms of human striving and need fulfilment, unless the individual is travelling on a self-fulfilling path, he or she will be frustrated and discontented. In religious terms, that fulfilment would include the application of the parable of the talents.

Of course, pleasing oneself does not preclude pleasing others, and more than 90 per cent of these achievers said that they wanted to please others through their sport participation. Ginny Leng's response was most typical; the opinions that counted were those of 'parents and friends'. In some cases, the response sounded like a revelation – 'Deep down, I really always wanted to please my Dad, or my mother.' Often it was simply 'my parents'. This underlines the closeness of the family ties for most of these performers and also shows that they appreciated the support shown them by their parents.

The next most frequently mentioned person was the coach. This is also not too surprising as in the close coach–performer relationships, it became a joint venture. There was a partnership where the intent and aim of both individuals was fused into a goal to break new ground together.

There were several who mentioned more than one person, or a group of people. Apart from parents and coaches, there was mention of spouse, team-mates, training partners, friends, managers, sponsors, owners, fans, everyone and anyone! Shane Innes and Peter Scudamore said 'everyone'. Peter Snell and Rodney Pattisson used a similar expression, wanting to please 'anyone'. Snell also said that he had great difficulty saying no to any requests. I closely identify with that. Duncan Goodhew said that he never wanted to let anyone down, and Steve Cram thought that he may have gone a little overboard in trying to please 'everyone'. He had allowed himself to be exploited, slightly; an easy thing for any new arrival in the limelight. Rarely are sports people prepared for the blitz of media attention which follows any exceptional performance. Paul Gascoigne suffered instant deluge following his brilliant performance in the 1990 World Cup. If the image is suitable, then the performer can be hounded by requests to do everything from more competitions to speech-making; from opening supermarkets to judging beauty contests; and from advertising dog food to endorsing religion. The image of a winner may be short-lived but it is very powerful. The vision of human greatness elevates the spirit and our emotions are touched. No doubt that is why advertisers in the West use the known achievers and also why the Eastern countries spent so much to improve their image through the success of their sports people. Valeriy Borzov was another who wanted to please 'everyone'.

Apart from family, Bryan Robson specifically mentioned the fans. 'Not just my own club but all soccer fans.'

Jayne Torvill and Christopher Dean are the only ones in this group who are judged and marked by others in order to determine their measure of success. Not surprisingly, their focus for pleasing was on the judges.

Quite a few of these responses show the extent of responsibility felt by the athletes: not only for themselves but for a wider circle or cause.

Only four commented that they were not aiming to please anyone but themselves. Coe: 'I wanted to please myself.' Ovett: 'No, not even family. I just did it because I wanted to ... getting the best out of myself for all the effort I'd put in.' Kip Keino: 'No, myself.' And Daley Thompson: 'It's just too much hard work to be doing it for someone else. You can only want to do things so much and you know how badly you're going sometimes. You wouldn't do that for anyone, other than yourself.'

There is little doubt of the work effort which success entails, which in turn requires motivation to come from within the athlete. It also follows that unless they enjoyed what they were doing, they would not make such extreme commitments. No one claims selflessness, but the majority seem to approach the effort in a social context. Generally they are not pursuing their ends in a totally isolated mental framework, but it is done for more than just personal satisfaction. It is also apparent that most feel personal enhancement from the fact that they are sharing the intensity and motivation with others.

Summary of learning points:

- Life is largely concerned with making choices. These performers believed they had chosen well, and if they had sacrificed anything it had been worthwhile.
- We cannot all explore space or the structure of sub-atomic particles but we can see how much our personal frontier can be moved. For a few that means being at the frontier of human endeavour.
- In order to pursue excellence in sport it will be necessary to make that your top priority. That should not exclude other interests or cause lack of balance in your life. It will mean prioritizing time and action.
- Sacrificing an extra beer can enhance your chances of reaching your best and will help your health. Self-responsibility is required for what you put into your system.

- Egocentricity is understandable in top performers but that should exclude neither consideration nor concern for others.
- We should not believe the old words that we British are (good) losers. We can take losses and wins with good manners but please don't believe that we are losers!
- In order to compete with others at the top, internationals today require: full-time, qualified, understanding and supportive administrators who will assist with excellent indoor and outdoor facilities; equipment; competition at home and abroad; coaching and sport science back-up – from grass roots to world class.
- Only in very recent years have the power and stamina of the female been acknowledged. Today there is more recognition that the qualities of grace and fluidity are not mutually exclusive of those of strength and endurance.
- Those in the public eye have a responsibility to live by the best qualities they are able, because, like it or not, youngsters will model themselves on their behaviour.
- Sport provides a tool for recognition and self-confidence, for self-esteem and the esteem of others.
- Unless the human is travelling on a self-fulfilling path, he or she will feel frustrated and discontent.
- Performers are working for themselves and their own advancement but in most cases they acknowledge their quest is a shared one.

14
THE MIND IS
KEY

If I had to choose one area of this study of achievers and say, this is the main area, I would have no hesitation in turning to this chapter and the seven which follow it: the part of the book which examines the mental approach of these top performers.

There are several types of intelligence. In the West, the IQ test has become almost synonymous with the level of academic intelligence of a youngster, but according to some educationalists, these tests simply measure how well a person does on IQ tests! It is intended to test the aptitude for logical reasoning and other formal educational skills. However, it is necessary to look at the term 'intelligence' in a wider context. Certainly if youngsters living in a highly industrialized urban country were thrown into the outback or a jungle as a test of their intelligence in survival, very few would pass. Intelligence is not limited to qualifications in the academic sense alone. There is recognized genius in music, art and drama and no less in the more physical performing arts of dance and sport. Moments of creative genius are apparent to all who have watched Paul Gascoigne play football; Larry Bird play basketball; Lester Piggott ride a horse; Jackie Stewart drive a car; or Torvill and Dean perform on ice. Some ball players 'read the game' so well that they always seem to have more time than others or they have the repeated ability to find a space in order to give or receive a clear pass.

Paul Gascoigne was likened to a chess player who saw several moves ahead. He sees, in the flowing pattern of play, the upcoming advance of a team-mate. His timing, control and placement can create a spectacular opportunity unseen by others. Basketball player John Havlicek once made a comparison between his team-mate Larry Bird and Albert Einstein. 'Larry has been called the "hick from French Lick" [which is his home town in Indiana] because he doesn't use the right words in speech from time to time. Put a basketball in Einstein's hands and he wouldn't know what to do with it, but if you put a mathematical equation in front of him, he'd devour it. Put a maths equation in front of Larry and he'd say, "What's this?" but give him a basketball and he's an Einstein. Lots of people judge performers unfairly because of their actions off the field of play.' Larry's exceptional skill is apparent in every game but a particular illustration of the genius to which John refers was witnessed by millions who were watching one of the Celtics' games on television. Larry put the ball into play under his own basket and took off at full speed towards the other end of the court. A full court return pass was overthrown and was going out of bounds under the opponents' basket. Larry, still running, left the floor heading out of bounds. In mid-air and in one quick motion, he caught the ball with his right hand, passed it to his left hand which had not yet passed under the backboard, and successfully shot the ball off the backboard with sufficient spin to score. Bob Cousy's commentary at the time was, 'You can't teach that! It was impossible! Absolutely fantastic!'

The sections which follow identify some of the important mental aspects which have made a difference to the high achievers' performance levels. They have held together well in competition. What were they thinking? The average performer may have been born with slightly less natural ability, but much can be learned from the experience of those who demonstrate sporting genius.

To what extent was the mind involved in playing your sport? The unanimous verdict was couched in words like 'immensely', 'totally', 'that's the whole game', 'you play with your mind', 'that's where the body movement comes from'. And as a minimum, 'It's equal to the body.' There was an added element raised by Lucinda Green and Ginny Leng as they pointed out that it was not only important to be in tune with themselves but also with their horses. Just as a coach must be aware and sensitive to the moods of the performer, Lucinda explained the similar requirements. The addition is that they're both performing. 'You've got to read your horse like a book. You've got to know exactly what he's thinking and exactly how he's feeling and not think, "Oh, today we're going to do such and such because that's what my rough programme says, so we'll do it." He might not feel like doing it. I think you've got to be totally in tune to be successful with a horse. To me the root of success is how in tune you can be and how you interpret being in tune. You are always looking at the horse as you walk to the yard and asking yourself, "Does he look happy, is his coat right?" And when you're riding, you're thinking, "Is he feeling right, is he happy?" You're always asking yourself questions, you never just sit there. I suppose it's through experience that you know when it's not quite right and little danger signals warn, so you change the food or do something different with the exercise or give him a week off.' Ginny added, 'You must ask all the "What ifs. . ." to make sure you've thought of all the possible negatives and positives; to be aware of the unusual and be ready and know what you're going to do.'

Shane Innes referred to the need for body awareness, being in tune with her muscles and the need for concentration on what she was doing on each stroke and recovery, in every inch of the pool. Arnold Palmer gave a response which was alluded to by many of these achievers. Given the physique to play, he said, 'You play from the shoulders up – it isn't all important, just 90 per cent . . . and it may be over 90 per cent.' Nick Faldo went further: 'Once you've got the physical bit, then it's all in the mind. Targeting the shot, executing it and believing you're going to execute it.'

Billy Beaumont pointed out what he saw as required in rugby: 'The intelligence that's needed is to know how to train well; to react within the team; to read situations; you've got to be quite sharp . . . the ball is constantly moving and you have to switch and change all the time.' Sean Kerly added, 'I think the mental side of a team sport is more important than the physical. If your team is physically fit yet not in tune with what's going on, not switched on, not aware of what can be going wrong or what you need to do to be right, then you will lose. But if you have a mediocre team but you all understand what each other is trying to do and can apply yourselves to overcome the other team . . . it's almost a battle of wills against somebody. You can force yourself over another team, physically and mentally. You out-think them. They're in trouble if you're not wilting in a big-time situation.'

Some competitors used other sports to describe similarities. Jackie Stewart said, 'I saw the sport like a giant snooker match where I always put the other drivers in a position where they could not retaliate; I would always have them behind the ball. If they did retaliate and therefore involve me, they would be the ones who would be the most embarrassed. They would be the ones going off the track or hitting the barrier.' Steve Davis and John Newcombe compared their sports, snooker and tennis, to a game of chess. John described it as follows: 'For two, three or four hours there is a great battle of minds going on, which is like a chess game and also an enormous physical contact of minds. It's gladiatorial really – one on one, thousands watching in the arena and millions more on television, and here are two people standing on Centre Court, firing tennis balls at one another but it's really firing rockets from the mind and using your ability to hit the ball to take that message from your mind. So there's a huge clash of mental prowess out there on the sportsfield. Your game is the weaponry you have to play with.' Steve Ovett likened the contest to an animal stalking its prey. He used the terms 'cunning' and 'having the understanding of other animals'.

Stefan Edberg's response to this question drew out several important elements of the process of handling difficult situations. The performers must know what they want. In Stefan's case it was to change his performance to put himself in with a chance of winning. He has to be aware of what's going on, then look at what his options are for change, then finally take responsibility for executing his plan. He said, 'The most important thing is to have belief that you still can win even if you're down. Winning from coming back once, believe you can do it twice, believe you can do it again, and again, and again, which is very important. Everybody can play when they're playing well, because it's running for you, it's easy. But when things are going against you, then the mental aspects come in. Can I still win? Do I believe I can come back? Yes I do. I never give up, because I know there is a chance that I can come back. And when you're out there and everything is going wrong, you've really got to start thinking. What can I do? What have I done? What's gone wrong up to now? What can I do to change the situation? During the game you've got to be thinking. In tennis you have ten, fifteen, twenty seconds between points and one minute in the change-over and you've got time to think, and that's what I think is the wonderful thing about tennis, there's no coaching allowed. You've got to do it all yourself. Nobody can help you. You're just out there by yourself and you're going to have to think and change things yourself. It's a lot easier if someone else tells you, who is watching, but from my experience, most of the time I know what to do. Sometimes you can't do it because it's not your day. You can't change your game too much but obviously I try to do different things.'

Alan Beggs, a sports psychologist at Nottingham University, has been working with Britain's top sailers to enhance their mental skills. During

1990 he proved statistically the enormous part the mind plays. He had the ranking list of the laser fleet for the year. With these he correlated the results of the psychological questionnaire developed by Lew Hardy at Bangor University. This test looks at how performers maintain confidence and concentration; how they handle competitive stress, etc. The result was staggering. Mental skills accounted for two-thirds of the variance of the performance measure.

Many performers demonstrated their desire to know all they could about their sport or event. They tried to learn from their coaches and had read all they could from books – history books and biographies as well as instructional books, and they also spent time talking to those who had experience.

It is perhaps most surprising that coaches with eager young athletes do not direct themselves or their fledglings to the people who have most recently been at the top. I was quite surprised that almost no local coaches had asked Billy Smith what sort of programme he had evolved en route to producing an Olympic champion. Steve Cram expressed the same surprise, saying that he was hungry for information. Steve said that he talked a lot to experienced athletes and coaches. Most of the information divulged could be left, but the odd helpful thing picked up made the search worthwhile. 'Everyone needs to learn and yet no one is asking, "What do you think about this?" They don't take the opportunity to learn.' Certainly it is not possible to have one programme exactly suit another individual; the physique, physiology, mind and temperament of each individual is different, and the aptitude at birth may not have been as great, but there is a wealth of experience from which to learn. Young athletes should not be shy to ask for advice while it is available to them. And if any-aged performer or coach becomes unwilling to advance their learning, their performance will stagnate. The performers who have made it to the top are all eager to learn. John Newcombe said, 'I talk to some of the top juniors and you can tell if the kid's got the potential to be a champion because when you're talking, you can almost feel them absorbing everything you say.'

Seeking knowledge extends beyond how to perform. Many American teams spend hours reviewing films of their coming opponents, looking for weaknesses or clues to give any advance notice of what the opposition are about to do before they do it.

Jonah Barrington's method was to make extensive notes on his squash opponents, even the ones he was not playing, and keep them on file. 'I could refer back, say five years, and would always find there were common denominators with a player throughout their whole career. So I could make myself aware of them and prepare before a game; I'd never leave it to the last moment.'

Only two achievers said that they were slow in adapting to new skills. Duncan Goodhew said that he found it difficult to change swimming techniques, while Lucinda Green said that she felt unable to change her plans quickly during a cross-country event. She added, 'And as far as teaching me goes, anyone who has tried will tell you, it's a nightmare, because I find it very difficult to re-adapt.' On learning new skills, Ed Moses said that he was prepared to work at it. Apart from these few, all the rest, well over 90 per cent, were what is often referred to as 'naturals', i.e. they learned the required movements fast and naturally.

From my own experience as a coach, I know that academic intelligence does not correlate exactly with sporting intelligence. One study said that, in general, top performers have a little above average academic intelligence but the spectrum is varied and therefore analogy pointless. During my seven years of coaching hundreds of students at Boston University, I discovered that it made no difference whether or not the athletes were good at their studies: some who were receiving top honour grades had great difficulty translating verbal descriptions or physical demonstrations into personal changed actions. Others may or may not have been average in their academic performance, but they picked things up as if they had a mental picture even before the instruction was complete. These were generally the better athletes.

Tom Tellez said that he thought Carl Lewis was an athletic genius. He only had to see another athlete attempt something or hear a few words from Tom, and he was able to execute the new action. This does not mean that it instantly becomes second nature, but the action was almost a perfect imitation. Herb Elliott had such a clear communication with his coach that he picked things up before Cerutty finished what he was saying.

Christopher Dean said that there was such clear communication between himself and Jayne Torvill that it would only need a word from him. 'Some people say something to us that I see straight away. If Jayne doesn't quite understand, I can just say one word and Jayne will understand straight away, because we think along the same lines.'

Arnold Palmer referred to being able to copy easily. 'I could watch a good player like Sam Snead, who had a great golf swing, and could go and concentrate on what he was doing, and then in my own mind, maybe not in yours, but in my mind I could go and swing the club just like that. And that was all I needed. It didn't matter whether I was doing it but I could imagine that I was doing it and I'd get the results I wanted.'

As with all motor racing drivers, Jackie Stewart had to sense what he needed. He pointed out that motor racing requires perfect coordination between hands, feet and eyes, but unlike other sports where you can observe how it is done, the cockpit of a racing car is such a confined space that you cannot even see how the others do it. 'I liked the way Jim Clark performed. I thought he was smooth rather than busy. He never seemed to be in a hurry to do anything. It was always a nice, smooth, gliding motion and he never seemed to be going quickly, whereas the others looked spectacular but never seemed to be going anywhere. If there was nobody else on the track they looked wonderful, but I realized that controlled motion and the elimination of heroics was a very important ingredient. Therefore, I applied myself to becoming smoother and smoother and as a result, the physical movement was cut down. But it took a lot out of me to make that happen, so I was draining one side to play up the other.' In order for Jackie to learn his skill, he had to observe himself and sense what was needed to execute his image of a 'Jimmy Clark' performance.

What are the attributes necessary to have things come naturally? Inevitably there are physical factors such as physical coordination and the right bodily structure for the sport. There are emotional factors too – the nerve to try, as well as emotional stability – but the greatest key to success at the top is having the mind for it. They had heightened sensory awareness, the link of mind and body, being able to feel, see and hear what was needed and when. These top performers employed mental control and could use their imagination to sense themselves performing an action before they did it. This ability will be discussed more fully in the following chapter on creativity, visualization and imagery.

Summary of learning points:
- The mind and body are linked. What the conscious or subconscious mind thinks the body responds to.

The Mind is Key

- Intellectually gifted and non-gifted can have sporting genius. The performers in this study were highly aware and articulate.
- Before an event performers should cover all the positive and negative 'What ifs . . . ?' so they will know what to do if one of them occurs.
- A team which is mentally prepared, understanding and supporting each other in what they are trying to do will perform better than a fitter but mentally unprepared team.
- Turning a difficult situation into a better one requires knowing what you want, discovering what's happening, reviewing what could be done differently and taking responsibility to make a change.
- Most top performers were eager to soak up as much knowledge of their sport or event that they could glean from books, film, video or other performers.
- If any-aged performer or coach becomes unwilling to advance their learning, their performance will stagnate.
- Most top performers can learn new movement and adapt quickly. When learning, many could sense and mirror the movements of top performers.
- Partnership communication and coach–performer communication were clear and rapidly comprehended amongst members of the sample group.

15
CREATIVITY, VISUALIZATION AND IMAGERY

Did you always think that you were going to achieve at a high level? This question was asked to see if the dreams of youth were present in all those who reached for the top. More than half answered positively, saying they had always thought that they would reach a high level. A few said it as if they saw it as their destiny. Herb Elliott and Wayne Gretzky said that there was 'no doubt' and 'no question'. John Newcombe said, 'I knew it was my destiny.' Sebastian Coe responded, 'No age, five or six, I knew', while Daley Thompson said, 'Yes, at something.' Several others sensed that a high level of achievement was for them, but only when they were a little older. Peter Sterling said that by the age of seven he wanted to do well, but he had no doubt at all by the time he was thirteen. For Duncan Goodhew, the realization came when he was fourteen years old. He stepped out of the pool one day and told his school mates that he was going to the Olympics. Billie Jean King was eleven when she first held a racket. She said that she knew from the first day that this was it, she was going to win Wimbledon!

The remainder, just under half, of the group gradually realized their capabilities to achieve. They described their experience in terms such as 'it evolved' and 'it was like steps', or 'there was just a gradual progression'.

Steve Cram confided that he had only set short-term goals, but he also mentioned an important turning point in 1981 when he was racing Steve Ovett at the Talbot Games in London. 'I didn't want to go past him in the home straight. I felt I shouldn't try to go past him. After the race, I made a conscious decision, saying to myself, "You're now good enough to beat them if you really want to."' He had to consciously change his attitude about his own capability. A very similar deferment had taken place in the mind of Ben Jipcho, the 1972 Olympic steeple-chase champion, who had not felt that it was right to try to pass the great African runner Kip Keino in a 1500m race. Both Steve Cram and Ben Jipcho had not yet taken the final step. At the times they were referring to, they were still thinking of 'them', on the top step, rather than 'us'. As Steve Cram pointed out, it takes a conscious recognition that one is just as capable of competing with the people on the next level up. The way in which people perceive themselves affects their whole approach to doing anything. Joan Benoit Samuelson is another who never thought that she would achieve the heights she has in spite of the hard work she was prepared to put in, but she did not see herself as different. 'I really enjoyed long-distance running and was willing to work hard at it. I don't think it was innate talent by any means . . . I still consider myself an ordinary everyday person.'

Lynn Davies drew attention to the fact that motivation can determine success and that if your aim is enjoyable for you to pursue, then you will be more motivated. 'I was tremendously motivated towards sport – I wasn't motivated academically. I believe if you spend two or three hours a day over a long period of time at something which you enjoy doing, you become very good at it regardless of what it is, but you have to tap what it is that motivates you, that you enjoy doing.'

It is apparent that either from when they were young or by way of a gradual progression, these performers have accepted a very positive and balanced view of their capabilities. In most cases, they see the top as just another plateau which they have found attainable. Sometimes, it was a frightening thought of taking those first steps but in each case they were willing to make the effort and had the confidence to face the next challenge. Whether a person is in sport, business, or any other challenge, gaining the confidence to achieve anything is critical to success. Confidence is often only gradually acquired.

What these performers did consciously or subconsciously was to set themselves a goal or target, and it would probably be helpful here to say something about this. It has already been stated how important it is that the coach and performer have similar levels of aspiration. It is also invaluable that the goal is set individually or in concert with a coach or team, but it must be pitched at the right level. Set it too low and the motivational value is lost. There is no challenge if something is too easy to attain. Equally unproductive is the goal which is set too high. The individual or team can be tempted to give up because the target is unattainable. At best a good effort is made but the result inevitably is failure. A realistic yet challenging target is therefore the aim.

Very high achievers usually have a dream, a hope, even an aim to get to the top. This long-term target is a large motivating factor but along the route there are many smaller targets. Each target can be seen as an end-goal in itself; for example winning a title, a trophy or promotion. These are not largely in your control, whereas your performance improvement is. Improvement is usually the best route to end-goal success. And there is a process of work of some kind to achieve performance improvement. The attraction of the next-step goal can be a significant motivating factor in the difficult training and preparation times ahead.

Sixty per cent of the athletes were able to give specific dates or ages when they truly felt that they had the capability of setting a goal to make the top. Most of them were two or three years away from their greatest achievement but the time varied up to twelve years in advance of realizing their goal. The remaining 40 per cent stated that their progress was step by step or that their success just evolved. The aim for the top had not been a long-term aim, it just became a natural progression.

Lynn Davies certainly had the latest revelation of a goal to win. He was more than half-way through his Olympic long jump final! The realization added more than six inches to his jumping and he won by less than two inches. The build-up to that was as follows. 'I had worked very hard in the winter before the Tokyo Games, and in May I won the Inter-Counties tor the first time with over 26ft 4in (8.03m) and the 100yds in 9.5 sec and I achieved a new level of self-esteem as an athlete. I walked into the Tokyo stadium feeling I had a right to be there, whereas at the European Championships two years before, I was letting things happen, I wasn't controlling the situation at all. In the Olympics I was aiming to make the final and possibly the bronze. I went in thinking there was no beating the American Ralph Boston or the Soviet Igor Ter-Ovanesyan. The weather conditions were really bad and the performances were all down. I thought I could jump further than was being jumped in those conditions, and suddenly I had a perception of their vulnerability. I was sitting there watching them, perceiving that it was possible to beat them. It was then my fifth out of six jumps and I jumped into a six-inch lead. It showed that the bad conditions had been having more of a psychological than physical effect, and the others came back to within two or four inches, but it was too late; I'd seen the opportunity and snatched it.'

Do you feel that sport is a form of self-expression for you?
Performers are expressing their thoughts, enthusiasm and will in a physical action. In the introduction to this book, John Whitmore gave his deep reflection on what sport self-expression had meant to him. Virtually all these high achievers did see their sport as a form of self-expression. Some saw that sport contained an element of creativity. Others acknowledged that it had brought them out of their shell. Stephen Hendry simply said, 'I enjoy what I do.' Sean Kerly: 'Yes, I liked being good. It was something I could achieve in.' Peter Scudamore said, 'It's become one.' Ginny Leng spoke for many in recognizing the growth potential through sport: 'It's taught me a lot about people. It's made me grow up a lot . . . do things I thought I couldn't do – like giving a speech. It's a terrific education.' Jackie Stewart acknowledged that his sport had been done better than anything else he'd done or was likely to do in his life. 'If you like, it's the signature of life.' He went on to say to me, 'I doubt if you can honestly believe that any of the other things you've done since, you've done better.' I replied that that was true and that for me my running felt like the best integration of my body, mind and spirit. My body and mind were in such condition and attunement that it just felt as though energy was flowing through me. As my mind thought, my body executed. Jackie went on to say that even if someone's good at sport, he didn't think they thought, 'Right I'm going to make my mark by expressing myself through sport.' He said, 'It's something you do. I don't think Arnold Palmer ever thought he was going to be the greatest name that golf ever had; he performed to the best of his talent in every avenue and he became a golf legend, as Keilly has done on skis, as Pelé has done in football, as Borg has done in tennis, and their expression, their interpretation, their endeavours have left their signature all over the place . . . I've worked for safety because I thought it was so darned important for the sport – I had seen the good and the bad. You see little crevices to improve . . . then what you do is a self-expression of course.'

A couple who have taken self-expression to an art form are Torvill and Dean. Christoper Dean recognized the unusual opportunity his sport provided, and took it. 'We can do things we would never normally do in other walks of life. I mean we're just ordinary people off the ice, but we can go into another world, we can dress up, which automatically changes you into someone else. I think everybody needs to express themselves.' Jayne saw it differently: 'I love skating. I enjoy it. I don't feel that I need to express myself. There's nothing crying out in me that's got to come out, it's just that I adore skating and it does come out.'

Are you creative in experimenting with your training or technique? It has been said that the need for creativity is one of man's basic needs. Some years ago I listened to a professor attempting to criticize the pursuit of sporting excellence on the grounds that it often involved little creativity and was repetitious. If this is the case then both coach and performer are to blame. There are, of course, certain constraints within any event or sport, and practice must involve a certain amount of repetition. However, the greater the degree of control the performer achieves over their movements the greater their freedom of expression can become. Once the fundamentals are sound, then they can be used as building blocks to allow for individual creative expression.

Nick Faldo said he was experimenting 'all the time'. Stephen Hendry gave a similar response: 'I would always try new shots and experiment.' John Whitmore referred to 'working on myself and the car. I would try new things, going outside the boundaries set. I hoped I was getting enough information to report back accurately during preparation time, but I was certainly adding in a lot of my own work.'

Barry John said that he was constantly attempting to be creative and experimenting with his play, kicking drop goals with either foot, and catching the ball backwards if they had a substantial lead in the game. He said he tried to make the game fun. His rugby union team-mate Gareth Edwards, having a soccer background, could kick the ball into touch wherever he liked with either foot. 'I didn't think anything was impossible. I worked on the reverse pass, going one way and the ball going back the other, and a few different things like bringing the ball around behind my back.' Gareth referred to this last move as schoolboy stuff, but it was enough to confuse the opposition at international level!

As Peter Scudamore recounted, he was having a tremendous run when he got hurt. When he came back he said, 'I had to sit back and improve again. At twenty-one I averaged 120 winners. Things drifted off and in time I altered my technique and by the time John Francome gave up I had become a much better rider, a more complete rider, although you never become a complete rider. You're always struggling to achieve . . . and the more you experiment and struggle the more you find what there is to find out. I really believed I was riding a horse not only more aggressively but I found more ways of getting the best out of the horse. I watched Jonjo O'Neill a lot.'

Wayne Gretzky credits his father with part of his creativity. He said that his father had been clever in giving him a lot of different things to work on in both training and technique.

As just stated above, perhaps the most obvious exhibition of creative art in sport is ice skating. The performances by Torvill and Dean gave the world a new vision of how drama, art, humour, music and sport may be integrated. Jayne said, 'Christopher is very creative. He's the one who comes up with all these weird and wonderful ideas which I have to learn how to do. We both think along the same lines, that we want to do something new every time.' Chris said, 'At the end of the day it comes down to the discipline of training technique. However, I think of our bodies not just from a physical point of view but also in terms of shapes and designs, the lines our bodies are creating. I see pictures in my head.' Chris added that he can be watching a film and suddenly he would see something which could be integrated into their programme. He would mentally note it, then go back into the film. Torvill and Dean included ballet as part of their creative learning work. They are not alone. Other top sport performers are turning to this discipline for added strength, balance and flexibility.

Creativity comes through the mind, and positive visualization is a powerful and valuable use of our creative thought. A Californian-based company called Syber Vision published a series of tapes based on interviews with high achievers from all walks of life. Visualization was considered by them to be the most important aspect which these achievers had in common.

To be most effective the performers must use their imagination to sense the successful performance of their ambition. The greater the clarity and the more senses you are able to involve, the more effective the visualization will be. Most top performers imagine the sounds, sight, feelings and sometimes even the environmental smells of the coming challenge and its successful outcome.

The sports achievers in my study were also asked if they had used visualization or mental imagery. Eighty per cent said that they had used this mental exercise. Several had never talked about it; it had just been an intuitive, natural part of their thought processes. Others had learned the skill but a few still had to execute the task physically. Jayne Torvill said,

'Chris can picture moves of where we are and where the legs will be, whereas I can't picture them without actually doing them.' The mind becomes accustomed to an action by physical practice. The concept of visualization is that in addition to a performer's physical practice, he or she can perform valuable practice by rehearsing their action in the mind. It is important that the action is as close to perfection as your mind can conceive of your body performing. This action has three advantages. Firstly, the process allows the performer to have 'been there' before the event and therefore some of the fear of the unknown can be resolved. The performer will be more familiar and at ease. Secondly, the required competitive action has additional practice time in perfect execution, i.e. a successful personal outcome. Thirdly, and perhaps most importantly, the individual can sense and understand that a new action is possible and may be successfully executed. By doing this well the performer is not only improving their physical action potential, through their thoughts, but also enhancing their self-image and thereby their self-confidence. And confidence is all important in performing well under stressful conditions. The mind is rehearsing personal control of successful actions.

Of course, this process can be applied to all areas of life, personal or professional. In sporting terms visualization and imagery allow the mind to take the body into differing competitive conditions or even different form. Differing conditions might include varying weather conditions (if the competition is held outdoors), different opponents, differing surroundings, varying ground conditions, and so on. It might also mean performers imagining themselves in calm unhassled surroundings when the actual pre-competition surroundings are anything but calm. Imagery can even be used during training to imagine qualities such as springing like a tiger, which can free the inhibitions and release more of the performer's potential. When we were youngsters, how many of us imagined we were fast cars, or our favourite international player? This enabled us to play up to those ideal images. What is suggested here is a 'conscious' use of just such positive images. Many people are still unaware that the images they hold in their thoughts can substantially control their heart rate and other automatic systems. Apart from visualization and imagery a variety of relaxation techniques such as deep breathing and progressive relaxation can affect the body and have it respond as the performer needs it to for top performance. The main point here is that individuals can have more control of themselves than they realize and can give themselves a better chance of determining their future success. The performers who have not imagined what they will do in varying competition conditions are more likely to have their results dictated to them, which may well not produce the results they wanted.

Do you use mental rehearsal and imagery? There is not a sport or an activity to which mental rehearsal cannot be applied. Dr Christiaan Barnard, the world's first heart transplant surgeon, said that he believed man could achieve anything within the scope of his imagination. I heard him say that in a speech during a dinner in 1966. It struck me that the first four-minute mile by Sir Roger Bannister had first to be mentally conceived as possible; similarly, for man to walk on the moon, it had to be thought of as a serious possibility. All that then remained were the hours of dedication and intelligent application of time, effort and resources to achieve the goal! This thought helped me in my own quest of bettering what had been done before in my event of 400m hurdles. In the months prior to the Olympic Games, apart from the hours of physical practice, many more hours were spent mentally rehearsing the effort distribution, pace judgement, stride pattern and hurdling technique to break the world record by half a second, which I hoped would be good enough to win the Olympics. Even while lying down, the visualization was so clear that my pulse rate and breathing would come close to what I would actually experience in a race.

Peter Sterling related how he visualized successful moves the day before the game. 'Lying in bed at night, for a while I'll be looking at myself doing something at full speed, doing it correctly and simulating the situation in my mind as close to a game as possible. I'm sure it's helped my game, but if I only think that it's helped it's worth it. The only time I see myself defensively is if a man gets loose and I come up with a good tackle but it's mainly when I've got the ball in my hands, I think of doing something that's directly involved in what I'm going to do ... Sometimes your sub-conscious comes in and you do something bad, so you repeat it without the error.'

In motor racing the driver has the problem of controlling a potentially lethal situation. Jackie Stewart said that the greatest requirement was to eliminate the sensation of speed. 'What I did was to de-synchronize to the element of speed, where it was all slow motion.' In an interview for

Playboy in 1972, Jackie had said that he was always impressed when he saw Rod Laver return a serve. Even when returning a 'cannon ball', there appeared to be no rush. He returned it almost as if it was an insult that one should send such a 'dribbler' into his court. 'That's what I mean by synchronization, and that's more than just fast reactions. I can't see one of those serves. In my case the synchronization is to a race track.' Most people have travelled in a car for extended periods at some speed and find that the sensation of any great speed is lost. The cues seem to be coming in slow motion so that when one leaves a motorway exit and slows down to 25 m.p.h., it feels as though one could open the door and get out. In cold anticipation, Jackie Stewart eliminated the sensation of speeds approaching 180 m.p.h. before the start, and thereby dominated the early laps and took control of the race.

In John Whitmore's last race, the biggest sports car race of the season, at Silverstone 1990, he was driving an 8.5 litre Lotus, capable of 300 m.p.h. on a long straight run. John said, 'I mentally practised taking Charlie Ag [his team-mate and top challenger] on the outside of the first bend, because I knew I was better than him on that corner. I practised it time and time again . . . but he got a much better start than me and I wasn't close enough to operate the manoeuvre. But on the second lap I did take him on the outside at a place on the circuit which the commentator and spectators thought was extremely exciting. It was on the fastest corner on the circuit, and passing on the outside is not a common thing. We approached that corner at 195 m.p.h. But my level of anxiety about making the manoeuvre was zero. For one thing I didn't fear the manoeuvre and, besides, I knew it was going to be successful, and I don't think either of these would have been true had I not mentally rehearsed it in other circumstances.'

Billie Jean King said that her own rehearsal was of what she would do once the ball came onto her side of the net. Her focus did not include the opponent, just how she needed to react and what she would have to do.

Kip Keino said he just daydreamed it, 'imaging myself winning in different circumstances'. Steve Cram liked to put himself in the shoes of the other top competitors, such as Seb Coe, Steve Ovett and Said Aouita. He liked to have game plan options. He would imagine how he thought they might like to run the race, and how he would like to run it. By the time he had run through the possibilities he had a few options. 'I think that's good because then when I get out on the track, I've been through it and I don't suddenly have to think, "What am I going to do now?" If you react too slowly your chance has gone. Things happen very quickly in the 1500m and these days you can't give anybody two to three yards.' It is perhaps unfair to make comparisons at this elite level, but it may be significant how often the vastly talented pair of Coe and Ovett have run themselves into tactical trouble. They are two of the 20 per cent who did not use mental rehearsal or imagery. They both expressed, and exhibit, a heightened awareness while running but react to their surroundings rather than having rehearsed options.

At every major sporting event, there is the tension relating to the occasion. Prior to coming onto court at Wimbledon, John Newcombe would mentally rehearse the first five to ten minutes so that it was familiar. 'I'd imagine walking onto the court, tossing for serve, photographers are out there, go down, I'm going to serve, he's going to return like this. He's going to serve, I'm going to return like that. The night before I'd just run through in my mind and make a check-list on everything I knew about the guy, any titbit of information and then I'd go to sleep.'

Nick Faldo said, 'You have to picture the shot. Are you going to move it left to right or right to left? I'll picture shots in competition mode even when I'm not.' Advance planning is a common thread. Arnold Palmer said, 'My most successful events were those that I had carefully planned and imagined throughout the entire day imagining what you're going to do, how you're going to do it, what the course is like, which is similar to saying what the opponent's like and how you would attack him or the golf course.'

In the same way, Lucinda Green said that she walks the cross-country course before an event. 'You start getting the science right behind you when you walk it and soon before I start to ride, I will find a completely quiet place, shut my eyes and think. Starting from the beginning, I'll go right through and see every single bit of land I'm going to cover and every single approach at each fence, like a film.'

Al Oerter used to visualize the Olympic competition during his training sessions in the weeks leading up to the Games. 'I've always been able to simulate competition. I may be by myself out in the field but very easily I drift into a simulation of an Olympic discus event. I can mentally picture myself competing with the other people in a training session.' He added a positive philosophical note. 'Some people compete because they have a compulsive need to beat someone and like getting someone else down – that's negative and will ultimately force someone out of sport. But those people who use competition as a natural extension of the training environment, just to test their capabilities, they become positive and bring you back into the sport. If you don't think you've done as well as you possibly could, all you do is go back and change the training programme and if you improve, the programme is working and you push it into a higher gear.'

Even from these few descriptions, it can be seen that there was variety in method and intensity. Some athletes watch themselves as if they were watching a film, others are able to take it much further and live the event in great detail. The more senses used the greater the impact on the system. Mental sensory experience can be a powerful tool for anyone wanting to fulfil their potential.

How can imagery help one to control nerves before a big event? How can it assist a performer's preparation? One aspect of imagery is to help the performer come through difficult training sessions. Herb Elliott said that on training runs where he wanted to slow down, he would call up a mental picture of Merv Lincoln, another fine Australian runner, who would be on his shoulder. Herb would not allow himself to slow down or to be passed in this imaginary race.

The emotional stress before competition can be extreme. Jackie Stewart described how he felt and how imagery was used to defuse the tension. He said that prior to a Grand Prix race, the image he had of his emotional state was that of an over-inflated beach ball; he felt as though it could bounce out of control. During his emotional countdown towards the race time, he would gradually deflate the ball. If bounced, it would come back to his hand. This process continued until the ball was completely deflated and Jackie was virtually emotionless. 'By the time the race came, my rubber ball had deflated; I wasn't going to get choked and I wasn't going to get angry either.' Jackie had eliminated all emotions and was clean and cold on the starting line. He had become almost numb, a protection of his nerves against the atmosphere of tension and anticipation before the race.

Duncan Goodhew used imagery to centre on his target and to keep himself focused. 'I broke my race into quarters. I visualized my target times on a big wall of paper and I'd smash through it into the next one.'

Soviet athletes are prepared psychologically before competing.

Valeriy Borzov spoke of his autogenic training. To control his nerves before his Olympic 100m semi-final, he used the rehearsed image of a forest and a river, relaxation being the key point. The different moods required for each occasion were linked to his own experiences in life. High points with great emotion and successful outcomes, and very quietening times of complete emotional relaxation. Before the final, his thoughts were uplifting ones. Visualization was of success, winning in perfect form of course! Valeriy said, 'For success, first performers must have talent, second they must work and third they must have control of the mind.'

One requirement for all sports is that the performer feels able to cope with their surroundings during the competition. John Newcombe related how he had been introduced to a few things that helped. 'Let's say I had to play on the Centre Court; before I left Wimbledon the night before, I would walk up to the back of the stands and look down on the court and I'd imagine my arms enveloping the net posts and the court, and I'd close my eyes and have a mental picture of the court and myself being one – familiarity, so that when I came out to play there I felt right at home.'

Stephen Hendry said, 'During practice, I'll make a break and in my mind I'd be saying, this is for the World Championships.' Many athletes are familiar with mentally simulating major competitions during training. How many have used someone walking on the street and imagined that the finish line of a major race is the telephone pole you're both advancing on? The other person doesn't even know they're in a race but the performer is busting a gut to reach the line before them!

In many sports such as golf – when putting, basketball – when shooting, and baseball – when hitting, there are chances for success or failure in every attempt. Any run of negatives can create psychological pressure which in turn can tighten the performer physically and adversely affect his or her performance. Daley Thompson said that he spent most of the last two or three days before competition lying down. 'I spend an hour or two going through every decathlon event and in each event putting myself in a pressure situation. For example, I imagine myself standing on the high jump area having had two failures and the bar is at 2m 10cm, so I've been there before.' He said he knows how he is going to approach it and will not be afraid of it because he has actually been there. This practice may well have saved him in the Los Angeles

Olympics. He had two failures at his opening height in the pole vault, then successfully cleared the bar on his third and final attempt. He expressed his relief to the world with a back flip on the landing area.

Pat O'Callaghan used imagery during his Olympic hammer competition. In training he had used physical targets. He would walk out and place flags at the distances he knew his competitors had thrown in the summer prior to the Games. 'I'd walk about saying to myself: "Three throws to qualify for the final". I never left the field without beating those fellows flags . . . You can reverse that, when they're shouting at you at the Games, you can stop and think, remember the flags outside.' The image of the contestants' flags was used to get him 'psyched up' in training, and the same image was used to calm him down in the pressure of competition. He knew he could surpass the flags because he had been there before.

Prior to major competition, nerves can cause performers to go 'over the top' and lose their self-control. On the warm-up track in Mexico prior to my Olympic final, I was sitting down to change from my jogging shoes into spikes. As I looked up I saw the pre-race favourite, Geoff Vanderstock of the United States, take a practice start around the first bend. He flew! I felt my throat tighten and recognized the first stage of inner panic. I knew that it was vital to maintain my sense of personal control. The grass on the infield was damp so I left my shoes off and while taking an easy stride, took myself back to where I was running in a few inches of water, on the firm sands of Powder Point Beach in Massachusetts. The sun was on my back and I felt the sensation of my body flowing with health and strength. The image was so strong that my mind was totally blank as to what I had just seen and I was back on to my personal performance. Imagery can be used to heighten or lower emotion. It can be applied to real or imaginary situations. As long as the performer is in control of the imagery, it can be a valuable and powerful tool. It should be noted, however, that it can be equally powerful in a negative frame of mind. Certainly in everyday life the imagination can be used just as effectively to think of reasons and create images as to why something cannot be accomplished. I had a personal experience of creating a negative reaction without intending to do so. Prior to the Munich Olympics in 1972, I thought that it was important to face the possibility of losing. It was a thought that I had never before entertained but as I was older and possibly past my prime, or so I thought, I considered that it would be a prudent and a mature thing to do . . . so I ran race after race mentally imagining that I was beaten and although I anguished over being a loser, for the couple of months I was imagining these races, I finally became numbed to losing such a race, virtually programming in the statement, 'It's okay, you're just going to try your hardest and do your best.' The result of my negative thinking was it killed my adrenalin (so needed for a fight or flight response). I woke up on the morning of the final, completely flat. As I walked into the stadium I tried pressing my nails into my hands saying, 'Wake up, this is the Olympic final', and the programmed voice came calmly back, 'Yes, and you're just going to try your hardest to do your best.' It caused an uncontrolled response from me during the race. I put in a sustained all-out effort, where normally I would try to conserve my energy while still running high on adrenalin. I realized my error too late and found myself treading water in the home straight. I hung on for a medal but the gold was gone. I have no idea whether I could have won that race. Injury had also been a factor shortly before that Games, but I am very well aware that the negative mental rehearsal had an overwhelming bearing on my subconscious on the crucial day – so much so that I could not consciously will a change in my emotional level. It is often said, 'As you train, so will you race.' I believe one must add to that, 'As you pre-think, so will you react!' If one wants to gain positive results, positive thinking is one key element.

Summary of learning points:

- The belief that you can achieve at a high level may be there from when you are very young or it may just evolve over a series of stages.
- It helps to have a dream of making it to the top.
- At some point you must recognize and accept that you are capable of more, and that may mean becoming the best.
- An obvious point: you will become very good at whatever you enjoy and practise for 2–3 hours per day, over a long period.
- Performers should clarify their goals, making them challenging and realistic, positive, measurable, time-phased and agreed upon.
- Motivating 'end' goals need to be pursued through measurable 'performance improvement' and 'process' goals.
- Ultimate performances come from personal alignments: absolute clarity of thought concerning aims, 100 per cent enthusiasm and total commitment, all put into action – training and performance.

- The greater the control the performers achieve, the more freely they can express themselves. Creativity is an important ingredient in self-development.
- Positive visualization is a powerful and valuable use of our creative thought.
- The greater the clarity of sensory imagination the more effect the visualization will have.
- The advantages of visualization and imagery are:
    1. They allow the performer to experience the unknown, thereby decreasing fear and increasing familiarity.
    2. They complement and enhance physical practice.
    3. A performer can sense and understand that a new or advanced action may be successful.

    Their use will enhance the performer's self-image and confidence.
- Visualization and imagery may be used to mentally experience various competitive circumstances; to take the performer away from a stressful environment; to provide an image stimulus which extends his or her potential, etc.
- Positive mental rehearsal creates positive results; negative mental rehearsal creates negative results.
- Imagery may be used to control adrenalin.

16
CONCENTRATION AND CONTROL

In competition, how would you rate your ability to concentrate on a scale of 1–10? Never one lacking in self-confidence, the response from Daley Thompson was predictable: 'Twelve!' Daley was certainly not the only one to exhibit confidence in this area of concentration, Lester Piggott, Kip Keino and Ed Moses used the word 'total'; Ken Read said 'absolute'; and Herb Elliott referred to it as 'dramatic'. Just over one-third said things such as 'very high', 'in the eight or nine range'. Joan Benoit Samuelson rated herself nine and added that it was her strongest asset. Nick Faldo said, 'I'm labelled for that now, 9.5. When I really need it most, it's very good.' A few added that they'd never score themselves ten as there'd be nowhere higher to go.

For most people there is a limited period of time in which concentration can be razor sharp. Sean Kerly said, 'It's ten but not all the time; eight to nine for seventy minutes.' Des Drummond passed on his experience related to tiredness in the game when he said, 'I used to get tired in a game when I wasn't mentally prepared. My concentration used to last for forty minutes and the game's eighty minutes. If you have a positive view of the game before you go into it, you can last longer.'

Bryan Robson tackled the same problem of total concentration from another standpoint. He said that the more tired you become the harder it is to concentrate, underlining the need for a high degree of physical fitness. I have also found this applies to studying and work.

In some sports such as cricket and tennis some performers find it possible to switch on and off, e.g. to re-focus as the bowler gets back to his line or as the player is about to serve. The conscious breaking of concentration is clearly seen in the play of Arnold Palmer and Lee Trevino. Both men are able to laugh and speak with the crowd between shots and then go back and completely lock into the task of the next shot. Ian Botham attributed the longevity of Lee Trevino's career to that ability to relax in between shots. Ian likened it to his ability to turn on and off on the cricket field. He also showed how his ability to concentrate but carry on a conversation won him a battle. 'In one game against Northamptonshire, a good mate of mine Geoff Cook was trying to intimidate me by fielding really close. So I thought, right, I'll play him at his own game. I'd just come in to bat and they had a spinner on and just as he came in to bowl, I started talking. "Have a good night last night, Tosh? It's nice down here, isn't it?" I wasn't looking at him, so I wasn't going to get out. He went! He was wasting his time! I had won!'

Stefan Edberg identified his ability as nine to ten, adding, 'If you lose concentration a lot of things can happen. Tony, my coach, might say, "You've got to go out and concentrate on every point here today." You've really got to stay focused when you're out there. You should keep your concentration even if someone screams out just as you're tossing the ball up.'

Billie Jean King was one for whom the concentration varied, increasing as the title came nearer. That meant she was more vulnerable to being beaten in the early rounds. The further on the tournament progressed, and the further into each game she went, the nearer her concentration moved towards ten.

Another reason for less than ten concentration came from Peter Scudamore. 'It varies because we're competing every day, many times a day. If I turn into the straight and I'm twenty lengths clear, concentration can start drifting. It's better now. I've got to be on top of my job all the time.'

John Whitmore said it was 'Absolutely as required – 100 per cent when needed. When I was well in the lead I might look at the girls at the side of the track, or whatever it may be, which I did sometimes, and waved to photographers, things like that.'

Billy Beaumont said that he concentrated well because as a forward, he was always in the thick of things. He added with a bit of humorous needle, 'Whereas if I was a winger, I might have been daydreaming and thinking about how I could keep my kit clean for next week!'

Duncan Goodhew was harsh on himself because of a break in his concentration while competing, and with good reason for concern. He said that as he turned, half-way through his swim at the World Championships, he said to himself, 'Come on Duncan, you've got to do well, your mother and step-father are here all the way from Britain, you've got to do well. I wonder what we're having for dinner tonight?' At which point he realized that he wasn't quite concentrating fully on what he was doing. In his Olympic win he said that only in the last 25m was his concentration absolute and everything was right.

Many performers become so intense in their concentration and effort during the competition, they find it difficult to unwind. Late into the night they will be re-living and reviewing the day. High intensity is quite common among the highest achievers and will be discussed later in this chapter.

What was your focus of attention while you were competing?
Inevitably the range of answers was diverse because the sports varied so greatly; however, there are many similarities within groups of sports. At various times individuals will require a different focus. It may be appropriate to be internal at some points, sensing and assessing what is happening within your body. At other times the main focus must be on the external environment, assessing what's happening. The other spectrum is whether your focus is broad or narrow. The performer can consciously control the change in focus. Billie Jean King said that her focus would constantly switch from a broad perspective, assessing where the opponent was on court, then to narrow on the ball as it crossed the net; as the ball left her racket she would immediately broaden her focus again.

This change of focus is true for all team ball sports. A player who has the ball must at times have a narrow focus on that, and as they pass there may be an instant or two when the focus is internal; however they must maintain an awareness of what's happening in the constant changing movement of their team-mates and opponents. Then a broad external focus is required. Sean Kerly said, 'I'm thinking what I can do to help the inside right or the left wing . . . always being aware of where the ball is and asking myself, "Where am I supposed to be in relation to the ball?"; "How can I support my player with the ball?"; "Where can I position myself?" And not switching off when the ball is up the other end of the pitch and the full-back's got the ball, or all of a sudden the ball comes whizzing up and you think, 'Oh shoot, I should have been positioned correctly. It's just concentration for 70 minutes.' Primarily an internal focus is held by the top marathon runners who are monitoring their energy output and effort distribution. A mainly external focus would be held by the yachtsman who must constantly be conscious of outside elements.

For illustration I will use the 400m hurdles to show that performers often use all four types of focus during competition. The hurdler's primary focus of attention is narrow–external, paying attention to the lane and the upcoming hurdle. A broad–internal focus is held to allow the subconscious to assess the stride lengths required to reach the next hurdle in the proper position for a rapid, balanced clearance. In addition to stride length the subconscious is taking account of the effect the wind, track conditions and pace are having on the stride pattern for clearing the next hurdle. The performer must also see whether their chosen pace is sufficient to maintain good position against the other competitors. That is using a broad–external focus to consciously assess where one is in relation to all the other competitors in the race. The narrow–internal focus is the personal monitoring of effort and pace judgement. At any one moment in time, any of these factors could be critical. The point being made is that even in a relatively uncomplicated activity the performer is required to have varied focuses. In sports where opponents are aiming to interfere with you and your team's progress the ability to focus appropriately and maintain concentration is highly challenging. However it is possible for the performer to remain calm, alert and aware, if they can remain in the present, and assess the most appropriate single focus for every instant. If we could live our lives with that level of consciousness we would be awesome performers.

One problem for individuals who need a broad focus, such as the American football quarterback, is that generally a performer's focus narrows when pressure increases. With mammoths descending on them at high speed is it surprising to see even highly paid quarterbacks forcing a pass between two defenders, when another man in the open is waving his arms to show he's unmarked in the end zone?

'Selective attention' was identified by the Salford University researchers as accounting for the predictive mental state of competitive cyclists. In their study the cyclists were being taken into stressful fatigue. There are different ways of dealing with these feelings of discomfort. Some choose to distract themselves by thinking about other things. This may be helpful but if the discomfort is reducing the performer's ability to concentrate then it is more useful to focus fully on the discomfort. Most top marathon runners are fully focused on their internal sensations. The following is a personal illustration of how this process can be useful. I intended to have a hard distance run over ten miles while training for the Olympics. I set out faster than usual and at about the seven mile point I got the message, slow down. Before doing so I checked where the thought had come from. I found that the primary area of discomfort was in my abdomen. My lungs had been heaving and I felt a bit sick. Then without slowing down I rated the feeling of discomfort on a 1–10 scale. I gave it a 7.0. I then asked myself, if 10 would put you in hospital what could you endure. The answer for me was 9. So I continued to run at the same pace and monitored how the feeling gradually rose to 7.1, 7.2, etc. As I reached the ten mile finish point I was only up to 7.8. I felt both exhausted and very high; astonished to recognize that I could have gone another mile at that pace if I'd had to. And I could so easily have eased off and given in to a level of discomfort which I would have had to face in races. Occasionally it's invaluable to practise holding on when hurting.

Using this 'discomfort zone' scoring tool helps performers to realize that they really can cope; things are not as bad as they originally thought. Sports like athletics, where this is part of the necessary training, involve the body and mind gradually learning to build up a tolerance. Herb Elliott believed that his training was, for the most part, producing an adaptation to pain tolerance.

Billy Beaumont said that his focus was primarily on the ball and the opponent . . . and sometimes on the referee! Middle-distance runners have to monitor their internal response during the race, but in traffic they must maintain a broad–external focus. In the light of the fact that neither Coe nor Ovett uses mental rehearsal, it is not surprising to see the exceptional degree of awareness with which they run their races. Coe said, 'You're concentrating on what you're doing and have an awareness of whatever else is happening around you, sensing how other people are breathing, whether they're breathing hard and whether their feet are coming down heavily – that way you respond to a break. The one thing about 1500m and upwards is continually being aware of how somebody is responding to what you are doing. If I look back to the 1500m in Los Angeles, there was an occasion when 250m from the tape, I felt Steve Cram wasn't responding as well as he should have done and that made me realize that if I could perhaps hit him with two or three more surges before we got round to the bottom bend, each time the response would be slightly less. I throw those surges into races just to see how people respond. It's that and also it's just concentrating on not allowing other things to start clouding what you're trying to do.'

John Whitmore admitted, 'I think in my early days of racing I focused on the wrong things. For example I might have focused on the person behind me in the mirror – which I don't think helps. I wouldn't do that now. I'd know where the person was, but I'd be focused in front. My focus would vary from the instruments, to the tyres as well as the job out there, aiming the car as far ahead as I could see.

When I asked Peter Scudamore how much of his attention was on himself and how much on his horse he said, 'Primarily on the horse. I look at the fence take off line every time. It's all to do with momentum. You're always pushing him forward even if it's long or short. Say I'm on the third favourite, I'm always aware of the better horses.'

Any contest where the competitors are moving towards the same finish line with no lane restrictions, whether it is a foot race or with bikes, automobiles, yachts or horses, there is a need for a broad focus of attention. Lester Piggott left school at fourteen, with sporadic attendance for another year. He said that he and academics never really got along, but in terms of his trade, his intelligence is unquestionable. Lester said that he sees things that are going to happen before they happen. His focus is on the other horses and jockeys around him. He said that he would be taking in how much space there was between the inside horses and the rail and between the other horses; he would be focused on what the other horses and jockeys were going to do before they did it. He would be assessing how much each horse had left, and aware of a jockey getting ready to make a move, and he would attempt to cover the action before it happened. He would know the form of each horse from reading the form book before going to the start and he knew from past experience how the other jockeys raced. He said that he had a minor focus on his riding position and how much energy his own horse had left, but the main focus was anticipation and knowing his options. His racing record sets him apart. Where most would be holding on and trying to steer at 40 m.p.h., Lester gives us an insight into racing genius.

Ken Read said that he identified strongly with Lester. He said, 'Your focus of attention is on yourself, your space and your positioning, how you're riding the ski itself, how it's reacting, but you're planning ahead, five or six seconds, which at 80 m.p.h. is quite a distance. You're planning your trajectory, how you plan to come into a gate, coping with the terrain, working with the centrifugal force, trying to get a good curve and gliding the skis as well. So your focus of attention is ahead of you as well as around you and within.'

Awareness is another important factor in where to place one's focus. Seb Coe's awareness often had to be on those behind him, and while leading down the home straight in the 1500m final at the Moscow Olympics, he kept control of his position by watching the shadows of his competitors on the track!

In games like squash and tennis, the way in which an opponent approaches the ball can tell much about the coming shot. This means reading the game before it happens. Jonah Barrington said, 'If you are taking in what an opponent's doing with his racket swing and with his body, it's much easier to assess what stroke he's going to play. When the ball is on the other side of the player, so it's not visible, you have to anticipate what's about to happen through what's taking place with the body and those who read that better and earlier than others will immediately be far better players.'

Kip Keino also referred to reading bodies, 'When you're racing you have to read others – you read their movement and you read their mind, while they are running; especially in distance racing. You see how they are and how they move. From their movement you read the event, as the race develops. You're watching them. I would run behind and see how they move. Sometimes you try them. You set them up, by increasing the pass; you push for two or three laps and you see who is next to you and then you know with whom you're competing. And the focus is still mostly on myself. I'd test them and then check myself. Then you decide what to do – do we go for a sprint or can I steal again, go ahead and set them up? Racing is mental. An athlete's mind has to work like a computer – every step is calculated. He should know what speed he is going, how fast he is moving and correct the mistake as he goes on. You're there doing it, there to correct and react quickly. I would only move ahead with three laps to go.' Kip agreed that he kept very focused in the *now*. It is the only time we have. Life and the race is always now, and it's being present and controlling what we do in the now that determines our progress, the quality of our performance and our lives. Sport provides a highly motivating time for quality 'now' monitoring and action.

During the first British Superstars, former England soccer captain

Bobby Moore showed how slow he was over 100m, and by exposing that, he told us that his situation-reading intelligence was extremely high. During his career, he read the game so well that he was always in the right position when the ball came into his field of play. Bobby Moore always looked as though he had extra time. For those who have to manoeuvre and change direction rapidly, returning a tennis service, slalom ski turns, etc., simply 'imagining you have more time' can take away the overtense motion which results from 'trying too hard'. The affirmation 'imagine you had more time' may just provide the space to keep a cool head.

At one end of the spectrum is Rodney Pattisson who said that he was thinking all the time, reading the wind, studying the tide, watching other boats, keeping on a permanent look-out and constantly changing the feel of the boat with the strength of the wind. At the other end of the sailing spectrum another top performer stays relaxed, responding automatically with an open mind. Those in the middle do neither very well, and they are not the top finishers.

Performers who are in their own lanes such as sprinters and swimmers must have a focus which will draw them out. They may be able to react to the challenge from others but it is also necessary to have a personal target or focus. For Ed Moses in training it is the hurdles in his lane and how he feels, but he added that in competition everything was automatic. Duncan Goodhew spoke of his focus at the start. 'There is a cross at the end of the pool and I used to stare at it and physically try to draw it towards me. I was concentrating absolutely so when I actually entered the water, I got a real feeling of speed with this cross coming towards me and I focused to nothing.' Duncan explained that because of this, elements of the race were practised in training and they became 'one'. Then he practised clearing any extraneous thoughts from his mind while competing, which combined to produce a 'focus to nothing'.

Duncan Goodhew's description of 'focusing to nothing' and allowing his subconscious to simply execute the known action is very similar to the actions taught by Timothy Gallwey in his book *The Inner Game of Tennis*. He wrote of two basic principles: 'trusting the body' and 'quietening the mind'. Trusting the body is allowing the subconscious mind to perform the appropriate actions. As our conscious mind controls only 3 per cent of our internal and external body functions, does it not make sense to allow the other 97 per cent, which manages to integrate and harmonize the 'whole' body, to get on with the job? The best function the conscious mind can perform is to hold clarity of intention. For example, by being clear and focused on our intention to get up and take a certain route to a door, the body will follow that thought. We give the command consciously but we don't usually interfere with our way of walking by thinking about which arm we'll swing to balance the opposite leg, etc.

Too often coaches over-instruct; telling performers what they should do and how they should do it. Some of that is fine, particularly using the coach's experience to help the performer clarify the rules or their most relevant focus. The coach retaining total control has drawbacks. For example, performers don't advance beyond what the coach tells them. If the coach is taking all the responsibility, is that preparing the performer for taking full responsibility when they compete? Is the performer being given the best chance to grow?

Many generations ago Socrates taught through questioning. In sport that means asking what the performer is wanting to get from the training session and what their long-term aims are. When that is clear, the aim of further questions is to have the performer discover their most relevant and appropriate focus. That may be different for each performer, but the task is not complex. In the present moment what is the performer discovering to become more aware and self-responsible? Questions which increase appropriate self-awareness and environmental awareness will improve performance.

Tim Gallwey pointed out that the body taught itself to walk and talk and yet our egos want to take over, when in fact we do not know what alterations are necessary to achieve our target. The player is asked to keep his or her competitive mind in the present and not to dwell on self-critical aspects or past mistakes. Gardeners do not force seeds to grow into beautiful flowers. Similarly, inside each human is immense potential. The role of the coach is to support, encourage, and feed as required. Sunlight draws the plant up and out. The questioning process can do the same for humans.

Some will question whether it's possible to allow the subconscious to compete, while the performer simply holds intention of the aim in mind. Ayrton Senna's experience provides illustration of what can happen. A preview of the book *Grand Prix People* by Gerald Donaldson came out in *Formula Magazine*, July 1990. In his interview Ayrton Senna said, 'I do try very hard to understand everything and anything that happens around me. Not only in the car but in my behaviour as a professional on the circuit, outside, in the garage and so on, and it takes a lot of energy . . . There are some moments that seem to involve only the natural instinct that is in me . . . When I am competing against the watch and against other competitors, the feeling of expectation, of getting it done and doing the best, gives me a kind of power which at certain moments when I am driving actually detaches me completely from anything else as I am doing it . . . corner after corner, lap after lap. I can give a true example. I experienced it and can relate it.

Monte Carlo, '88, the qualifying session. I was already on pole and I was going faster and faster. One lap after the other, quicker and quicker. I was at one stage, just on pole, then half a second and then a second and I kept going. Suddenly, I was nearly two seconds faster than anybody else, including my team-mate with the same car. And I suddenly realized that I was not driving the car consciously. I was kind of driving it by instinct, only I was in another dimension. It was like I was in a tunnel, not the tunnel under the hotel, but the whole circuit for me was a tunnel. I was just going, going, more and more and more and more. I was way over the limit but still able to find even more. Then, suddenly, something kicked me. I kind of woke up and realized that I was in a different atmosphere than you normally are. Immediately my reaction was to back off, slow down. I drove back slowly to the pits and didn't want to go out any more that day. It frightened me because I realized I was beyond my conscious understanding.'

Senna's experience provides a great illustration of the 'tunnel vision' produced when a performer is focused in the present with absolute concentration. Mike Murphy and Rhea White's book *The Psychic Side of Sport* has documented several cases of sport producing exceptional perception and performances. It is interesting to note that Senna was leading that Grand Prix by nearly 50 seconds when he crashed – inexplicably. He later acknowledged that he lost concentration when his pits ordered him to slow down. A good question is 'Why tinker with something which is working?' Coaches need to be aware and sensitive as to when to intervene and when it is best to let the performer simply get on with their practice or performance.

Do you experience emotional pressure in sport and, if so, how do you deal with it? If an occasion is very meaningful, whether it is a social encounter, a business deal or a sports contest, there is almost always some apprehension. In the case of the high achieving sports performer, for a period of time their top priority has been focused and centred on achieving a goal. There is a heightened sense of anticipation, responsibility, and in many cases, anxiety. The ones who walk tall in these situations are those who have managed to withstand the pressure and maintained emotional and mental control.

From discussions with this sample of top performers, they believed that it helped immensely to be capable of high emotion. A competitor without emotional intensity is not going to live long in any competitive arena. It may sound like a dichotomy but the intense emotions must be more than matched by the ability for self-control. If there is intensity without self-control, either players erupt and are doomed to disqualifications, bookings, penalties or fines or they 'choke', cracking up under the pressure of the occasion.

During competition Steve Davis often appears as cool as ice, but when I interviewed him, Steve said that he was a very emotional person, and that he might be shaking like a leaf inside as he walks to the table but he would never show it. He said that he thought there was a need for that emotional intensity within every great performer but that true greatness came from their ability to control that emotion. This summary was repeated to all subsequent interviewees and was unanimously supported.

David Bryant's sport of bowls would be seen by many as a quiet and relaxing game; however, David said that his sport was all about pressure: who can take the most pressure, being able to apply pressure, and choosing the right time to apply it. 'One good shot or one lucky one can completely wipe out five minutes of good careful build-up by you, and there's no outlet. You can't get stuck in as you could on a soccer field. The pressure is all in the mind. You have to have great self-discipline and take it squarely on your shoulders and rise above it.' David referred to the qualities of Bjorn Borg and Chris Evert, citing them as ideal professionals. They never let their opponent see when they were getting to them. David said that he will always appear confident although he accepted that one can lose. He quoted Borg as saying, 'If you're afraid of losing then you daren't win', but David and almost all the other top performers are at their best when the pressure is greatest. Frequently they produce an unbelievable comeback when they are in trouble.

The pressure referred to is a strange phenomenon because it mostly exists in the mind of the athlete. Nevertheless, the performer is only too aware that the outcome could determine his or her future. Since the days of the ancient Olympics in 776BC, sport has carried a high degree of prestige. Today, many lucrative financial contracts can depend on the outcome of events, as may any appearance fees or prize money that might accrue. However, money is not in the mind of the competitors when they are about to do battle. The emotional pressure is caused because the performers have invested themselves entirely in the outcome; their self-image, self-esteem and credibility are laid on the line. Those who *intend* to win usually do. Many would like to but the intent is missing. The mental or emotional pressure comes from the uncertainty of the outcome and the fact that the outcome has such personal importance. There is a strong desire not to let themselves or anyone else down. The emotional pressure is so great that it is rather like having a baby; they want the end result but they would often rather not embark on delivery!

The need or desire to prove oneself is a strong motivating force. The response to a challenge may be fear or anger or enjoyment. Whatever the root cause of the heightened emotion, the key to success is learning to maintain mental and physical control. Some performers have become angry with themselves, others direct it towards the equipment, hating the shot or the hurdles and trying to overcome them. Those who direct anger towards their opponents, the officials or the crowd are, in my view, lessening themselves. They may have every justification but their actions will cost them in the long run. The Nazarene's words, 'Love them that hate you', have a psychologically and socially sound base. How else do you break the cycle of 'I'll get you back!'?

Almost inevitably the name of John McEnroe came up in conversations on personal control. Everyone had their own views as to whether his outbursts were gamesmanship or involuntary. Billie Jean King said that she identified with John as a perfectionist because she had suffered from similar outbursts. 'One side of me was telling me to shut up for making such an ass of myself and the other half was still going, telling the guy where to get off. Afterwards I'm totally upset with myself for being such a jerk. I can feel part of me trying to bring myself back but it's like a volcano going through an explosion. Afterwards, I get over it quickly and I'm sorry I did it. I think John's that way. I saw him yelling at Cliff

Drysdale for putting Fred Stolle on a rival television network at the same time as the Davis Cup. He was going crazy. One minute later he was back, apologizing and saying he shouldn't have said those things.'

John Newcombe saw it differently and said that McEnroe never behaved like that against Borg. 'I think it's his way of creating a presence on court . . . [to] dominate the occasion. My way of doing that was in the way you played the game. If someone hits a winner against me, I'd say, "great shot" and smile and then come back and play the next point like it was match point. It was just a subtle way of letting the opponent know this guy's not afraid of him. I was leading the applause and then attacking.' John said he wished he was still at the level to play McEnroe. He said, 'The first thing I'd do when he starts bitching about calls is wait until he'd finished, and then I'd walk up to the umpire and ask for the referee and I'd say, "My opponent's trying to intimidate the linesman and trying to put me off by stalling and I ask you to stop him straight away." I'd say it loud enough so it went into the microphone for the people to hear. I wouldn't talk directly to him until I'd finished, then I'd say to him, "Look, John, every time you do something, I'm going to do something. You want to see who's the best tennis player, get on with the game or do you want to carry on with this . . . ?" I don't know whether he understands this himself but what happens out there is that when he blows up, the whole centre of attention is on him and the umpire and referee. His opponent's down there unimportant. Everything is centred on John and it's a tremendous psychological presence. Almost every time he does it he breaks serve straight away. That's why I'd wait until he'd finished his show, then I would become the presence so when we resumed play, we'd be even, but I'd finish up with the presence being on me.'

Time has been devoted to McEnroe as his name was brought up by a number of performers as an example of how not to behave because he lacked personal control. Each sport has its problem players, but the percentage of these achievers who did not care about self-discipline and behaviour was negligible. Quite the opposite. Heather McKay reflected on the worlds of squash and racketball. She was concerned about the deterioration of court manners in a few of the younger players. There was a definite bias towards old-fashioned standards. In the final chapters, there will be further reflections on standards related to cheating, gamesmanship, drug-taking and other disturbing issues which face the players of tomorrow.

It has been outlined previously how relaxation, concentration, focus of attention, mental rehearsal and imagery can all help the athletes to maintain control of themselves. Without that control there is a possibility that they will go over the top. It can best be depicted as a wave with the curl overhanging. If the performer can stay on the crest of the wave then they are carried forward with the flow of adrenalin. However once they fall off the top they cannot be lifted back up. There has to be a time of re-establishing and rebuilding.

Most performers have an automatic nervous system response as competition approaches. Anticipation of the upcoming event can produce a great deal of stress and anxiety as well as pleasure. Some of the physical responses to stress are increases in muscle tension, breathing rate, pulse rate, urination, sweating as well as feelings of nausea and so on. Prolonged concentration becomes more difficult with increased stress. The mind tends to jump from one thing to the next. If the tension and anxiety go unchecked, performance can be negatively influenced.

The purpose of discussing the topic of performance under stress is to draw attention to the fact that there are techniques, used by top performers, which allow them to control their arousal levels. Illustration of the use of imagery was given by Jackie Stewart, deflating his imaginary beachball. He took away his heightened emotions. Borzov used images of being in a relaxed environment and also used the repeated self-suggestion of a winning self-image. Physical relaxation is used. Progressive relaxation is one technique of tensing muscles to bring awareness to them, and then consciously relaxing them. Following one's breathing can be extremely helpful, used as a way of staying mentally present rather than scattered, and by deep slower breathing, slowing the system down. Mental rehearsal is used to give the performers a sense of personal control and mentally letting them experience the idea of a successful performance beforehand. The focus of attention is on personal control and not on what others may be doing. Concentration was helped by good physical conditioning and having a clear view of the intended goal. The goal is set at a realistic but challenging level. Self-confidence certainly helps to control stress levels, and it is no secret that confidence comes from having done the preparation work. All of these factors can assist the performer to remain at the crest of the wave.

A host of other factors may have been responsible for an individual not being ready for his or her test. In the case of the sport performer, apart from laziness, other reasons can include injury, bad coaching advice, or unrealistic goal-setting.

There are two separate conditions of anxiety. Trait-anxiety refers to the perceived level of danger or fear which we all carry around with us on a daily basis. Some people are more highly strung and will jump if a door slams unexpectedly. Others are quite laid back and take life very much as it comes. The other anxiety level is referred to as state-anxiety, which is the response or reaction to a particular occasion or state in which one is centred. Obviously a World Cup penalty shoot out, an Olympic final, or the last round of the Master's golf championships produces a heightened state-anxiety level. If individuals have high trait-anxiety levels, it will not take much state-anxiety to nudge them over the top of the crest of the wave with the resulting drop in performance. For the highly strung individual there is even greater need for control techniques, but in all cases there is a need for control of anxiety levels. Before a big event, performers need to understand what they must do and how they should think in order to maintain their control. In addition coaches can help by remaining calm, and reinforcing a positive belief in each performer's capabilities. Most coaches who are seen screaming on the sidelines are primarily releasing their own tension.

As the start time approaches the sensations which anxiety produce can be most uncomfortable. A performer can either try to avoid these or welcome them. That only means a change in perspective, recognizing that the sensations are signalling that the body is readying itself for fight or flight. Personal bests are created out of that state.

Pressure often starts to build up some time before an important event. Many people have difficulty in getting to sleep, the night before, because their minds are racing. One technique for getting to sleep is to mentally watch your brain, encircling it and every time a thought escapes, pull it back. In no time at all the brain gives up and sleep results.

Learning to control one's body responses is something which takes practice. Equipment is now used to measure the degree to which a performer is achieving success. Machines have been developed which measure physical responses to symptoms of stress. Biofeedback is the term used for the measurement of such things as pulse rate, finger-tip sweat response, etc. The feedback come through digital monitors or audible notes which change pitch as the performer's stress is more or less controlled. This feedback give the performer and coach some objective information as to the beneficial results of relaxation and mental rehearsal techniques. The British National Coaching Foundation has produced several tapes for use in this learning. Of course, subjective assessment can be equally valid, as the performer can learn to give accurate feedback on their responses. Valeriy Borzov referred to his 'autogenic' training. This has a growing following among those who are concerned with stress management. As the mind is the key to improving performance, biofeedback can provides a useful measure of personal control and help to ascertain which form of visualization, imagery and physical relaxation technique is the most helpful. The equipment simply gives indications of the degree of control which one is achieving. In the past, no such information has been available to the coach or performer.

Summary of learning points:

- All top performers recognize the importance of concentration.
- At different times a performer's focus may need to be internal or external, narrow or broad – monitoring oneself, the opposition and the event environment; assessing, analysing, deciding and acting.
- If discomfort is distracting from performance, 'enter' the discomfort, rate it (1–10 scale) and monitor its changes.
- An ideal state for performance excellence is to hold clear intention in the conscious mind and allow the subconscious to integrate the necessary physical actions.
- A high degree of emotional intensity will enhance performance but it must be coupled with mental and emotional control.
- Intending to achieve an aim is more committed and powerful than wishing, wanting and hoping to do so.
- You get what you give.
- As emotional arousal rises performers need to employ their best methods of emotional control, through mental and physical relaxation techniques.
- Biofeedback can be useful in assessing stress levels and demonstrating which forms of relaxation technique work best.
- Sleep can be induced by mentally watching the mind and pulling back thoughts.
- Uncomfortable pre-competition feelings can be welcomed rather than avoided, because they signal readiness for heightened performance.

17
PRE-COMPETITION

Did physical or emotional relationships affect your performance?
For many years, the world's Press have congregated at sporting events where some of the world's youth are on display in excellent physical health and attractive condition. Most people find a well-toned body appealing. It does not take long before one or two openly friendly women cause rumours to fly around the world, about sex at the Olympics or whatever the particular gathering may be. These tales were certainly enhanced in the sixties when a certain US diver and an even more successful Australian swimmer found that pre-competition sex relaxed them and they performed better in the pool.

However it would be accurate to relate that there is less sexual activity at an Olympic Games than there is on any university campus. It is also fair to say that in every large group, sports performers or not, there will be a cross-section of personal habits. The responses of the performers who had to peak for one special occasion, such as a world championships or an Olympic Games, differed from those who compete in frequent league or other competitions. The response of those whose sport is a regular fixture was that life proceeded as usual. The coming competitions made little difference to how they normally led their lives. Most of the individuals who were peaking for a long-term event said that they usually abstained from intimate relationships prior to those events; this ranged from a day or two up to several weeks. The reason behind this abstention was that their emotional focus was needed to produce a peak performance on the day of competition.

It is understood that with any meaningful human bonding, emotions are tied in with the physical aspects of the relationship. The question of emotional upheaval was asked as a separate question in order to get the performers' reactions to a situation of emotional distress such as a quarrel or news of misfortune. The question was asked to find out whether their subsequent performance was adversely affected. More than three-quarters of the achievers were able to shut themselves off from their problems or concerns once they entered their sports arena.

Stephen Hendry firmly said, 'In tournaments, nothing gets in the way.' Wayne Gretzky used the expression that he was able to 'block out' everything else. Seb Coe said that he had the ability just to switch off.

As one who was affected, Joan Benoit Samuelson said that although she felt that she was an emotionally stable person, upsets certainly did alter her performance so she attempted to avoid a situation which might hamper her emotional or physical state before a major race.

Clive Lloyd mentioned an aspect which was relevant to several sporting individuals who came from small villages or small countries – that they felt somewhat overawed by a move into the big time. He mentioned that he felt that the West Indians in general did not see themselves as good enough. That inferiority complex was something which Clive helped to turn around. He started with himself, working on attaining a professional attitude which was needed when he lost his place on a team. Having conquered his complex, Clive dedicated himself to helping other players gain belief in themselves and their capabilities.

Being mentally prepared for an important event is essential. The performers interviewed were asked whether or not they were able to distance themselves before a competition. As an important event nears, was there a need to put a cocoon around themselves in order to focus and concentrate on their performance? It is the most difficult time for the performer: similar to entering an exam, with the results being publicly put on display. Inevitably there is apprehension as to whether the preparation has been sufficient. Fears are magnified at such a time. Questions circulate in one's head: Am I in a good enough condition? Will any recent injuries inhibit performance? Will my body perform as I want it to? Will my performance live up to my own expectations? What about the fans, the judges or the clock?

One way in which many individuals behave before major tests is to avoid involvement with other people. Of this group almost three-quarters said that they took themselves away from distraction either mentally, physically or both. Often the reactions are involuntary, as Lucinda Green pointed out. 'I don't mean to distance myself but I think I do. It's not done purposely but I notice people saying, "Mind what you say because it's only a week to Badminton." So I then realize that I must have been difficult.'

Gareth Edwards was one of those for whom it was business as usual, but he explained that he was almost in a dream world, detached from the current situation. He would be greeting friends in the hotel lobby before going across the street to Cardiff Arms Park to play; 'I'd talk to them and see them but I didn't see them.'

Quite a few needed to be quiet and by themselves for only the last half an hour or so before their match. John Newcombe said that at Wimbledon, he would retreat into the toilet because it was the only quiet place. There was too much noise in the dressing room. J.P.R. Williams said that the team would change about thirty minutes before the game. By then he liked to have all the preparation done. He said, 'I liked to have half an hour or an hour before I went to change, just concentrating on the game.' Peter Scudamore would finish the day's racing and could switch off that evening, but liked to be left alone the following morning before the next day's racing. Nick Faldo likes to have the hour and a half before going out to get his mind in sync. Nick laughed at himself: 'As a youngster I heard that you should lie perfectly motionless – deep breathing – for eighteen minutes or twenty-eight minutes or something like that. I did this first thing in the morning and I didn't play till 2 o'clock in the afternoon . . . I still do that sometimes, going to sleep, letting my body go like lead, absolutely still to relax, and sure enough, it usually knocks me off to sleep.'

For Wayne Gretzky, the lead-in time started the previous evening. He said that the night before a game he would have some food at about 7 p.m. and by 8.30 p.m., he would shut his door and unplug his phone. 'I can't carry on a conversation on the afternoon of a game. I'm awful.'

Individuals' comments varied as to the amount of time that they needed prior to competition. It was often more prolonged for those who were tackling a long-term occasion such as the Olympic Games. Lynn Davies said, 'I used to cut myself off. For a week or so I was anti-social. I just wanted to be by myself leading up to an event. I think it's part of the process. You train very hard and you withdraw into yourself. I think you seek inner strength and you can't share yourself with people. If you want to be the best in what you are doing, then it's probably got to be the most important thing in your life at the time. If you're going to be number one – you can do other things but the focus of your attention has to be on competing.

Jayne Torvill and Christopher Dean both avoided socializing the week before competition. Jayne said that Chris would only say 'hello' or 'good morning'. Chris replied that he avoided long conversations. They both declined invitations to join a group for lunch, preferring to eat alone together or with their advisor Betty Callaway. If they were caught at a table, Chris's desire to escape was high. Jayne said, 'In a way I don't show it. It's obvious that he doesn't want to talk to someone and he leaves, but I'll stay and be a little more polite and say, "How are you and how's it going?" and all that and I'll make a bit more of an excuse why I'm not going to join in. As long as we're in competition we like to be quiet.'

At the other end of the spectrum are those who need to socialize and want to talk in order to relieve tension. As can be imagined, this can cause problems on a team when other members need solitude. Two of those interviewed, Billie Jean King and Viv Richards, liked to mix and needed to talk. In the middle are those who simply lived life as usual. This group, just over 25 per cent of those interviewed, did not separate themselves from encounters with others although in some cases they were aware of becoming a bit edgy. Steve Ovett mentioned this last point, but in general he felt that his balanced and more relaxed approach to his competitive encounters had helped him to perform consistently over a ten-year period.

How did you spend the day of competition? In a sport such as cricket, competition progresses throughout the day, but with most sports, there are hours of waiting and apprehension. The question was asked to see what the athletes did to occupy this time.

David Bryant spoke for many saying nothing was overdone; it was a time to settle oneself. Gretzky, Snell, Moses and Coe all talked about taking a doze during the day. John Whitmore might lie down and could sleep before an event but his preferred way of getting away and being alone was to go for a walk in woods in the morning before the race. Gareth Edwards said there would be a team talk at 11 a.m. Following that he would talk with his parents whom he met in the hotel lobby. There would be tickets to distribute and autographs to sign while all the time he would be preparing himself mentally, not wanting to fail. On the way to the field he would move down the corridor alone thinking how he would feel on the way back. He said it was a case of wanting success.

Bobby Charlton referred to his routine as business as usual, and J.P.R. Williams said that he would try not to do anything different from the previous week. Both he and Bobby mentioned getting enough sleep. For a weekend match, Bobby never went out for a drink after

Wednesday of that week, and J.P.R. said, 'No alcohol for the week before competition. I don't say it made any difference but mentally it was important to me, it got me in the right frame of mind.'

Many of the performers referred to their day being made up of small segments of activity. Billy Beaumont indicated a number of activities such as watching television, having a short walk, talking and checking the kit for the match. Some listen to music. Jackie Stewart liked to read, while Rodney Pattisson said that he would go for a run in the morning to clear his system from the night before; then there was a great deal of equipment checking to be done. Billie Jean King said that she was very conscious of enjoying the process of getting ready for the day's play.

Each in their own way occupied their minds and bodies in what might be termed planned trivia, being active with time-consuming activities until it was time to move into the serious business of competition.

In physical terms, there is a general belief in reducing the volume and intensity of training in the lead-up to competition. Most top performers work towards a peak in preparation for any major event. Performers who drive themselves right up to the day of competition are only draining the emotional resources available to them. Soviet research has shown that following a long period of training, a week to ten days of light sessions will allow the performer to produce their best performance in explosive events.

Do you see yourself being able to adapt to sudden change during or just prior to competition? For example, what would the outcome be of a changed start time, a delay because of the weather, altered conditions, equipment failure or other similar interruptions?

Ken Read said that he was bothered to a limited degree and saw that as one of his faults. Wayne Gretzky said that he was upset by changes because he liked routine. Lynn Davies said that it was never comfortable to have things changed on you.

Bobby Charlton made the distinction between playing conditions and other aspects. He said that he was never thrown by frost or other pitch conditions, but that because he had been in a very stable club where changes were not expected, it threw him if the managers changed or coaching techniques changed. He would adapt to it but not overnight. Well over 90 per cent of these top achievers felt that they were very adaptable to change. I came to interview Stephen Hendry on the day that his cue had been stolen. He had had it since he was thirteen and had issued a £10,000 reward. It was in the early rounds of a major championships. In spite of this problem he was remarkably calm. 'It's tough, but you've got to try to put it out of your mind and concentrate on the game in hand.' This is an extremely important point – *focus on what can be controlled*. By contrast, how many individuals have wasted emotional energy and time worrying about aspects over which they have no control? Fortunately Stephen's cue was found, and he went on to win the tournament.

An amazing reflection came from Ginny Leng on being adaptable. She said, 'You have to be. Anything can happen – a dog can run in front of you . . . in fact at one competition a women with a pram was behind one of the fences. It was too late, we were a stride off it so I said "DUCK!" She did and we went right over the top!' Geoff Hunt reflected that he was adaptable because he changed his style for different players. Steve Davis also said he was adaptable to sudden change but he did not like it.

Throughout history, man has always had to adapt in order to survive. It is not unreasonable therefore to assume that sports people would be adaptable and be able to cope with pre-competition changes. However, it is quite common to see the physical manifestation of a performer's panicked thoughts: the actions become hurried and jerky, and the deliberate calm and control have been lost. It is a matter of mental control under stress. In general the high achieving performers have been adaptable and have coped well under stress. What actions they took to achieve that state of control will be discussed later in Chapter 20 under 'getting an edge'.

What do you do to cope with pre-competition stress? A few top performers said that they did not feel under any stress. Ginny Leng said 'I don't find it stressful – I find it exciting.' Daley Thompson felt similarly: 'I love it. I just look forward to it.' While Al Oerter said, 'That's what all the training's about.' Kip Keino also did not feel precompetition stress. 'I never felt under pressure. You take everything as it comes. If you pressurize yourself it doesn't help anything. You have to play it cool. If you put on a lot of pressure you become tense. You have to relax. If you are not physically fit then you have pressure that you're not going to perform well. So you prepare yourself on physical fitness; then you're ready.' I couldn't help feeling that this was an ideal attitude to life. 'When you reach the time of competition, you need to have a very cool mind, a relaxed mind, ready and prepared only for the event. If you are pressurizing then you may not perform very well.' Stefan Edberg said, 'I'm lucky because I'm competing almost every week. It's not like I'm waiting for the Olympic Games. Even Wimbledon feels nice. I'm looking forward to it more because I can live at home, which is one big factor. I know I have to work hard, and if I work I know what the achievement can be. So that sort of makes me look forward to an upcoming event. The day that I fear going on the court it's time to quit, because you've got to go out there and enjoy it, that's important.' All the performers interviewed who did feel stress coped with it very well. They held together and performed best in the most demanding and high pressure situations. Some of the shared illustrations of these experiences are in the following chapter.

Some techniques of controlling stress have already been discussed in previous chapters dealing with mental rehearsal and imagery. It was also mentioned that these performers felt that their exceptional physical preparation gave them a great deal of self-confidence. Prior to competition many of the performers liked to be on their own, collecting themselves and their thoughts, whereas a few liked to talk a lot to calm themselves down. Reference has been made to the benefit of self-control gained through relaxation and autogenic training. A few performers have included a prayer for help. Many of the performers referred to maintaining a routine on the day of competition. Sean Kerly mentioned the 'rituals' of warming up: 'jogging, stretching and drills'. In a lot of cases performers referred to the excitement of 'being there'. Billie Jean King said, 'I like the pressure, the challenge – it's exciting, I chose to be here!' Al Oerter's comments were similar, loving to be on the hot spot in the Olympic discus circle. Jonah Barrington declared, 'I love the competing. I get fired up, no panic.'

Lucinda Green spoke for many who have questioned why they compete as the feeling of nerves is so uncomfortable. 'It's just a question of keeping control of yourself; you come into the start box and you still say to yourself, "Why do I do this?" It's stupid in many ways and you wonder why you're doing it . . . but the nerves are important. Some genuinely don't have them but I don't know how they get anything out of themselves.'

Herb Elliott said that stress was one of the unpleasant pressures of competition and training. 'Nevertheless, I was aware of the strength that you develop out of nervous tension. I used to try to get away into a forest to feel the serenity and the greatness and the distraction, if you like, of things that have been there for hundreds of years, to take my mind off tiny little insignificant events like winning a running race. There was quite a lot of careful handling of yourself mentally, to be able not to ignore the importance of the event but at the same time not to get it out of perspective.' Others spoke of their ways of coping with stress and what they had found worked for them in bringing out their best performances. Ian Botham referred to music taking him over before he goes in to bat. 'My metabolism is slowed completely – a pre-death state. I can be totally unaware of my surroundings, someone could drop a cup and I wouldn't know. Someone has to kick me to let me know a wicket's gone and it's time to go. The music matches the mood of the day.' Jackie Stewart mentioned that he would avoid eating heavily. Certainly the anticipation before a major test will often inhibit the desire for food. 'I just have a very light breakfast. I never eat before a race. As soon as I had food in my stomach, I'd feel satisfied and the edge would come off me, I'd get lazy ... less aggressive and less desirous, less hungry ... I wanted to hold that strength. Some skiers told me that they didn't want to shave or shower because they felt that the hot water seeped away some of their vitality. If they did shave and shower it was with cold water; the hot water takes away the edge. Although I might not have a cold shower, I certainly wouldn't lie in a hot bath.'

David Bryant expressed his thoughts on holding together under pressure. 'It's a discipline of doing things right and the way you do that is firstly to have confidence in the mechanics. To that you apply your concentration. You must be able to read the conditions in which you're playing and you must be able to pick things up quickly, which comes through concentration.' For Pete Sterling the requirement for holding together under stress was as follows: 'Confidence in your ability, confidence that you've done the preparation, confidence that you're better than the other side, confidence that if you do the simple things right then you'll win the game, and not panic . . . We just thought if there was time on the clock we could still win the game.'

Lynn Davies said that in his experience, many athletes try to do too much training prior to a major championships. Lynn has acted as team manager for the British Olympic team. 'It was an effort to restrain some of them in the last week before the Olympic competition. I now realize that if one took a week off and did nothing, it would probably be better but it's hard to recognize that at the time.' The point made by Lynn is that many athletes who have been training intensely throughout the year do not have the confidence to do very little, but if they did, they could produce a higher level of performance.

J.P.R. Williams said, 'I think you've got to be self-critical, especially when you've stayed at the top for a long time. You have to work on little things. It's easy just to go through the motions and people probably wouldn't notice that you're not trying the odd thing and it's very easy to be lulled into being very safe and not doing anything spectacular. On the other hand, you can get criticized unfairly; you're trying everything and you have extra people marking you and the critics say you're not doing anything. I think once you stop learning something, then you should start worrying!'

Ken Read spoke of the time directly before competition. He would read a good book and follow a routine for the day but when he arrived at the course, there was a pre-race routine. There would be a warm-up and relaxation time with a bit of horse-play to avoid thinking about the race, but at some point he would go into his cocoon, thinking intensely about what was to come. 'During the last few minutes before the race, I concentrated on rehearsing the run – two minutes at race speed – then I relaxed and tried to drain my mind so that it became blank and ready to race.'

Lester Piggott pointed out that the frequency of racing precluded him from getting too nervous. 'When you're doing it every day I don't think it comes into it – if you start worrying too much you can't get the best out.'

Summary of learning points:

- Most performers who have their competitions infrequently modify their intimate social/personal lives to put their emotional focus on the upcoming contest. This is for anything from a day or two, up to a few weeks.
- In the last twenty-four hours before the event, most top performers tend to cocoon themselves, taking themselves away, physically and/or mentally for a minimum of half an hour.
- A small percentage of performers need to be more verbally or physically sociable.

- Most top performers plan the waiting time before competition. Some distract themselves with trivia, others go inside themselves, some sleep, still others use the great outdoors, such as the woods, to gain self- and life-perspective and calm. All abstain from excesses.
- Being adaptable to change obviously helps a performer to cope. It has been said that change is the only constant in life! Mankind has had to adapt in order to survive.
- Avoid energy and time loss caused by worrying about what you can't control. Place your attention and energy on what you can control.
- Take everything as it comes. If you pressurize yourself it doesn't help anything. Too much tension will inhibit performance.
- Being well prepared physically builds confidence.
- Nerves can be valuable; the adrenalin heightens response. However mental and physical coping strategies are essential, e.g. positive thoughts, routines, being well prepared, no excesses, mental rehearsal, solitude, relaxation, etc.

18
HOLDING TOGETHER UNDER PRESSURE

If two performers or two teams are quite evenly matched, the difference between who wins and who doesn't is largely due to who holds together best under pressure. We've seen two of the world's best snooker players chasing the last ball around the table. We've agonized watching internationals putting their soccer penalty wide of the goal. We often see performers lose events in which they are favourite. In discussing this with members of this sample group some performers simply referred to the event which they class as their most memorable win under pressure. Others included what they saw as being needed in their situation.

The most obvious example of performing well under pressure is the 'comeback' – the gaining of a victory despite having been in a losing position. Seb lost the expected Olympic 800m title to team-mate Steve Ovett in Moscow. He had a second chance in the 1500m and managed to lift himself above the disappointment and refocus on the new goal. His 1500m win was memorable. Several other individuals referred to being in potentially losing situations and making a comeback which meant a great deal to them. Both snooker players referred to times when they came from behind to win. Steve Davis recalled his first come-from-behind win. Playing Cliff Thorburn in the 1981 World Championships he had been leading 6–4 but fell behind 8–6, then pulled it back to win 16–10. Stephen Hendry mentioned a semi-final comeback from 5–0 down against John Parrott.

David Bryant spoke of twice being behind 20–17 (with 21 being the finishing point) in the World Championships. Both times he won. He said, 'When you're playing badly and you're behind, you have to have a plan to get out. You have to play conditions which suit you the most. Keep it as simple as possible. Don't be dictated to by opponents and be taken off your best hand. You must also learn from your previous bowls.'

Gareth Edwards made the all-important point of not giving up when you're behind. He said, 'For example, against the All Blacks you might be behind at half-time 13–0 or you've used the wind and you're up 13–0 and hanging on in the second half, tackling everybody and absorbing pressure. It's pushing yourself when it hurts and not wanting to lose.' Ian Botham made a similar point: 'I'll never admit defeat until the last ball has been bowled. I'm a survivor . . . I believe no situation is beyond repair . . . half the battle with stress is you think you're under stress.'

Within many sports there is sufficient time to determine a more positive course of action or attitude. John Newcombe recalled the 1969 Wimbledon final with Ken Rosewall. 'I was playing someone who at ten years of age I'd looked up to and the crowd were 90 per cent on his side. The whole aura of the occasion – he won the first set. Then I was blowing him off the court, 6–3, 6–2, 3–1 and the crowd got to me. They started clapping double faults and everything and I hadn't done anything wrong and you know Centre Court, out there is electric. I just got caught up emotionally in why they were against me and five games just went like that. Suddenly it was 6–3 to him and the crowd went crazy and I had just sixty seconds changing ends to get my act in gear and I just said to myself, "How badly do you want to win this match?" The answer came back, "Well, I really want to win it, so you'd better put yourself in some sort of zone where you just see Rosewall and the tennis ball and that's it." Within sixty seconds I put myself in a cocoon. I just thought – I had to do it. I beat him 6–1 in the fifth set. Everything he did, I knew he was going to do it before he did it.'

From squash both Heather McKay and Geoff Hunt talked about being down and staying under control. Geoff said, 'You've got time. It's not as if things are running away from you quickly and therefore you can think about what you're doing, where you're falling down and you can try and change it, so you change your pattern of play. That might not work, so you try something else. You've got to go through the process. There's not much point in going on playing in the same old way unless you know what you're doing will eventually allow you to win, but it's very rare that it happens like that, in my experience, anyway.'

Heather referred to the US Racketball Championships where she had won the first two sets, lost the third in a nip and tuck battle, was blown away in the fourth set and came back to win comfortably in the fifth. 'You have to stay calm and also know what you can do and do that. Just stay calm and be patient.'

John Whitmore's is a comeback with a difference. 'It was a tremendous challenge to return 21 years later, with nothing in between!

And because I ended up in '66 as a success, in any kind of comeback I had a lot to lose. People had an expectation of me and that I began to buy into, so that became quite a pressure – and also wouldn't it be wonderful to win my first race after a 21 year gap. I did and it felt terrific. Then I won my second race and that expectation grew again. One of the reasons I retired had been that, particularly in saloon cars, I won almost every race I did. And if I came second people would say, "What was wrong with you?" So I was now stuck again with that expectation to win, which was not fun. However in 1990 there was a new challenge. I was asked to drive a car that was more technological, more advanced than anything I'd driven in my career, and therefore was more difficult for me to drive and required me to learn some new techniques, and learning new techniques is not something that one imagines will be terribly easy at over fifty. So the whole season was a build-up, inexorably step by step, and the adrenalin was there all the time. I didn't get off the adrenalin between events because the moment one event was over or one practice session was over I was immediately starting some anxiety towards the next one. And that was largely because it was a very big challenge for me to take on this car [8.4 litre CanAm McLaren, capable of 300 m.p.h.]. I was on such a high after I won the last race I did and then retired, because I'd had a very long period of a lot of adrenalin, that had really run from two weeks before Christmas 1989 with a build-up to July 1990. It seemed like one event and included a lot of work to get myself physically fit. I recognized the difference of what was needed now. It was quite a strenuous regime and I'm fitter now than I've probably ever been.' Daily John swam 1000m, ran for up to an hour and a half, did thirty minutes of sit-ups and springs for the upper body, and was playing competitive squash.

Lester Piggott's comeback is similarly astonishing. To retire at nearly fifty and have five years off, in such a demanding physical sport, and return to win again is an inspiration and a challenge to the average forty-year-old who believes they're past it.

One's own expectations and those of the public create another type of pressure. It is said that pressure is self-inflicted. We are only responding to what we perceive as a pressure situation. We know what it's like to win and we know what it's like to lose. Top performers accept the challenge and apply their will to winning.

Nick Faldo recalled rekindling his own personal expectations, 'It was the week after the British Open in '83 and I was exhausted after it. The Open really drains you and I thought, it's a good time to chuck it in, go home and have a rest, that's what I need. I was just about to throw in the towel and my caddy said to me, "Come on, I've never seen you throw the towel in", and I pulled it round and woosh! I ended up winning the tournament. I came from nearly missing the cut – one over par, to 64, 62 on the last two days and won the tournament.' Nick's illustration is a valuable reminder of how often we call our limits before we have to, and also the remarkable powers of resilience within each human. But the choice must come from within. That's the challenge to the performer's mind, enthusiasm and will.

Ed Moses mirrored a comment made by Herb Elliot saying that he put pressure on himself by never expecting an easy race. Before the 1984 Los Angeles Olympics, Ed felt the additional pressure of public expectation to maintain his immense winning streak, which he did. The pressure was also on Carl Lewis before those same Games. Carl was heralded as the modern-day Jesse Owens. Reporters left him with no option but to repeat that astonishing feat of four gold medals or be labelled a failure!

Another Press-created pressure was placed on Shane Innes who held every freestyle world record from 200m to 1500m. The press predicted that she would break Dawn Fraser's eight-year-old world record at the New South Wales Championships. The record stood at 58.9 seconds. Shane's father helped set a goal by putting a little sign on her bedroom door saying '58.5 Club'. With the pool area packed, people lined up on the Sydney Harbour Bridge and there was live television. Shane retreated to a pump room to get focused and she didn't hear the official call to the start. An official came to find her, saying that the others were already stripped and on their boxes. 'I raced out, crying by that stage and falling apart inside, the adrenalin was pumping so much when I got on my block.' She swam 58.5.

From 1971 to 1973, Billy Jean King refused the invitation to play the self-confessed 'male chauvinist pig' and 1939 triple Wimbledon champion Bobby Riggs. Margaret Court was financially pursuaded and lost 6–2, 6–1. Then Billy Jean felt she *had* to play him. 'You have no idea how important this match was to me. It's not only about winning and losing when people get that emotional about something. For six weeks before it felt like life and death. I'd never seen him play and I was trying to visualize what it would be like to play him. I finally saw the tape of the Margaret Court–Bobby Riggs match the night before I played him and took it all in.' In front of over thirty thousand people in the Houston Astrodome, with fifty million more watching on television, she beat Riggs 6–4, 6–3, 6–3.

The British *chef de mission* came to Lucinda Green shortly before she was due to ride last in the 1982 World Championships. The team was third in a closely bunched finish behind West Germany and America. His message was straightforward: 'Right, no beating about the bush, if we're going to win this competition you have to go fast and clear.' Only two people had gone inside the time all day. 'I suppose that was about as tall an order as I ever had, and I did end up winning.'

Stefan Edberg said, 'You're under pressure all the time because everyone wants to beat you!' This parallels the phrase used by Ginny Leng: 'The wind blows strongest at the top of the mountain.' It's tough getting to the top and very hard to stay there for any length of time. Stefan went on, 'I feel more pressure playing Davis Cup. I know the team want me to win and I want myself to win. I'm playing for the team; I'm playing for my country. People expect me to win, and I know if I play all right I will win. That's sort of the country behind the pressure.'

Rod Laver reflected on the different situations which can cause stress: for example, an argument with your partner, someone close to you being sick or dying unexpectedly, personal sickness or injury, all increase pressure and stress. 'Sometimes that sort of thing can give you a great desire to do something or it can just make you quit because it's too much to grasp. If things aren't going right, rather than go out there and say, "Look everybody, feel sorry for me", you go out and say, "Well, I've got to try and wipe all this out of my mind and go ahead and play, then I'll continue to worry about it after I've got through . . ."' Rod went on to relate a story of how he won Wimbledon in 1968 with a bruised thumb and sprained wrist. 'I used to put a matchbox on each side and play with it stiff so I couldn't feel it as much. No one knew I had the sprain and my wife couldn't understand why I was doing it. I had to go and bandage up my wrist in a telephone box while no one was watching. I knew that if people knew I was injured, they would make me play shots that I didn't want to hit. As it turned out I got through the first week and after that it was better.'

Just seventeen days before the Olympic trials Joan Benoit underwent knee surgery. On waking from the anaesthetic her first words to Bob Sevene, her advisor, were, 'Can I start tomorrow?' Joan said, 'The trials were on 12 May and a week before them I couldn't even run. The ups and downs, it was just a nightmare. I didn't say, "Why me?" but I said, "Why the timing?" Things had been going so well and all of a sudden, "boom". I was stressed and I was questioning what was going on but I dealt with it and I just tried to find different things to keep me occupied and alternative exercises.' This included pedalling the exercise bike with her arms prior to clearance to do so with her legs. Her determination was awesome. Joan admits that winning the trial so soon after this operation was tougher than winning the Olympics.

In 1983 Daley Thompson carried a serious muscle injury right through the World Championships. 'That was when I was most stressed because even though I was only going from event to event, I still had my goals to make every time. Even though I was injured, if I wasn't making my goals, that made it worse. Although I was achieving some goals, I wasn't achieving others. That was the most stress I've ever been in. But once I'd started, I was fine.'

Al Oerter didn't feel stress except when injured. 'Six or seven days prior to the '64 Tokyo Olympics final, I was spinning on a wet circle from towel to towel, a silly thing to do. I just tripped and went down. I thought I'd hurt myself. I felt it – but I did it again and this time tore a tremendous part of my rib cage. I can remember just before the Olympic final taking phials of Novocaine. They just kept pushing it into me until they had it frozen, then taped it . . . and *it hurt*! Then they gave me these ammonia capsules and said, "Here, take these if you feel nauseous or something." I had to go out and compete in the Olympic final, and I didn't think I could make it out the door! . . . I threw over sixty metres for a new Olympic record. It was amazing. I kept breaking those capsules and smelling that stuff . . . I never want to go through that again but I was able to put up with the stress of an injury.'

Peter Scudamore recalled a fall at the end of the 1989 season. 'I broke my wrist and they didn't pick it up on the X-ray. I came back to ride after about three weeks and I shouldn't have been riding and this horse ran out on me. I knew I shouldn't be riding but I rode the next race.' He wanted to prove to himself that it really was bad enough to require more time away.

Self-control is undoubtedly the most critical factor in successful performance. However that does not necessarily mean trying to control every move. It means that the performer controls the choices and sometimes the choice must be to let go, trusting and allowing the body and subconscious mind to function as an integrated whole.

In the case of Ken Read the choice was to allow himself to step into the unknown and simply try to hang on against every instinct for self-preservation. He referred to the extremely rough ride over a mogul field in Kitzbuhel. The pitch is steep and away and is hit at 70–80 m.p.h. The instinct is to move the arms for balance. The legs are sending crying messages to get out of the crouched tuck, as every hillock jars and potentially throws the skier off. Ken knew that if he did not give in and just held on through that field, he stood a chance of winning. It requires mental as well as physical toughness to hold on while hurting. Ken did and was rewarded by a six-hundredths of a second win.

Dr Pat O'Callaghan showed immense control and calm during the 1932 Olympic hammer final. He discovered that the competition was to be held on a solid circle. He had been used to throwing from grass and his shoes had long screw-in spikes. He was the defending champion but found himself slipping as he attempted to throw. He tried to unscrew the spikes, only to discover that they were rusted in and extremely hard to remove! Between throws he managed to remove more and more spikes. With assistance from team-mate Bob Tisdall, following his 400m hurdle win, he managed to remove the last of the spikes prior to the fifth of his six throws. That was all he needed, winning on that fifth round throw! Everything was taken in his stride.

Viv Richards remained detached before the big games. 'I personally feel that one cannot perform best when nervous or anxious about things. I've tried not to get mixed up in chatting in the dressing room. I don't want to get myself heated or too emotional.'

Bobby Charlton's control provides a lesson. During a semi-final game in the European Cup, 'Real Madrid had annihilated us in the first half. In the second half they slackened a little and it allowed us to get back into the game. We scored but needed another to win. Time was running short and I remember the ball went out of play and there are no barriers in Madrid. A member of the public leaned over and picked up the ball. I thought, if I dash to get the ball from him he might throw it away, which will take more time, so I said to myself, "Just stay calm" and I walked across and put my hand out for the ball and he put the ball in my hand and I took the throw-in. I thought if I had said, "Come on give me the ball!" he might have thrown it down the touchline, which is quite the norm, but he didn't and I thought, "You've done well there", because it was really a stress situation. But you make a lot of decisions like that on the field when you're actually playing, saying to yourself, don't panic, take your time, have a rest, pass that one sideways not forward, it'll just give you that little bit of time to settle down and it'll give our players time to adjust their positions again.'

Ginny Leng recalled her horse Nightcap's last appearance. 'He was a complete nightmare if he heard a noise. He used to go nuts. I had tried to keep him as far away from the grandstand as possible, but a new rule was brought in that the next competitor must be outside the grandstand. I went to great lengths – rent a crowd from the village, a brass band playing in the stable, big, big shows with lots of people and flags. But outside the grandstand he went beserk – almost unridable. I had to go in but this thing was like a charger, trotting around the outside of the arena, going nuts and everybody's going, "Ooh! Aah! Ooh! Aah!" I just said a prayer, "Please help!" and the bell went and he took a huge deep breath and settled and did the best trial of his life. He'd never settled like that in his life. So you just don't know. It was unbelievable; just extraordinary.'

Another example of gaining control of oneself as pressure increased was given by Sean Kerly. In the 1988 Olympic semi-final Great Britain went 2–0 up. But Australia immediately pulled one back and ten minutes later tied the game at 2–2. 'You can think you're going well and all of a sudden you get hit and you've got to be a bit more strong and come through. It's almost more difficult to hold on.' With five minutes to go Sean scored again to put Great Britain on target for the gold.

Torvill and Dean added some amusement to the situational stress. Chris said, 'You've rehearsed everything so thoroughly in practice, you almost know when the other person breathes in the wrong place. It gets down to that fine tuning because you've done it so many times.' Jane followed, 'When we caught hands in the rock and roll routine, my dress bobbed up and Chris took both my hand *and* the dress! I knew that if he tried to release it, I would fall down, but in keeping hold, he might have ripped the dress.' Chris continued, 'So I just held on. But we had a split second when we both looked at each other; she knew I had her dress and I knew I had her dress and our faces were a picture of horror.' Jane said, 'I was thinking, "What's he going to do?" In the end he held on and the dress slipped away, rather than tearing. In retrospect I admit it was quite funny.'

From amusement to the dramatic seriousness of life and death in sport, and an extreme example of professionalism. One of Jackie Stewart's best friends, Jochen Rindt, was killed in practice for the Italian Grand Prix in 1970. 'I wasn't at the track when he had his accident. I was told about it and ran over to see if I could help. I didn't know how serious it was. I recognized that he was dead and they were trying to bring him back to life as he lay in front of me. I had to collect his things, make sure my wife Helen was with his wife Nina. These things are not normal, but all drivers have to go through this kind of thing. Then I had to go back out and practise. I had to go back in the car – to collect myself and start the programme again; to get in and say, "Hang on now. Now you've got to apply yourself." At Monza it's very important to get a good practice time to establish a good grid starting position. I did four laps and put the car into fourth on the grid; it was the fastest lap I'd ever done at Monza and I set a new lap record. When I got in the car, I was emotionally upset. I just had to channel my energies and my resources and control everything, but when I got out of the car again, I make no excuses; I wept. But my drive had no relation to Jochen's accident and when I came to the bit of the track where he had crashed, obviously the tyre marks were still there and some of the engine too; that had to be cleared from your mind, and you have to be able to do that, to discipline yourself to do that. A journalist might say, "Ah, that's a sort of death wish thing." But that's not how it was. It was calculated, calm, clinical and emotionless. I was able to tuck away any feeling in one corner, while applying myself to the job in hand.'

What does it require to come back from the depths or the jaws of defeat? To keep competing when hurting? To stand tall when expectations are highest? And to remain in control while chaos reigns around? The following points are extracted from the attitudes and actions of these top achievers.

Summary of learning points:

- Top achievement at ages considered outside of the normal range should inspire all to avoid limiting their options and potential.
- To win, you have to *want* to win – even when it hurts.
- To succeed you have to believe that no situation is beyond hope.

- Your focus must stay only on the present situation, avoiding focus on disappointment of what has passed, or fear of what might be to come.
- You have to realize that you do have time to be clear and calm.
- You must recognize that the primary sense of pressure comes from your own thoughts.
- You have to have control of your emotions, when that is needed.
- You must be stronger than your fears.
- You cannot be afraid of winning.
- You must attempt to play your own game, the way you can do your best.
- You have to be well prepared, physically, psychologically, emotionally, and even spiritually.
- You need to recognize that you have more reserves, more gears and more options than first appears. Never call your limits before you have to.
- You must take responsibility for your own situation and the choice of what you do must be yours.
- You must strive for your goals even in adversity.
- Being in control of choice can include choosing to let go – trusting and allowing the body and subconscious mind to function as an integrated whole.
- Self-responsible choices will include taking assistance when you need it and being independent when you know it is up to you.
- Control includes staying calm in body, mind and spirit.

19
COMPETITIVENESS

Were you competitive on your own as a child? The answers to this question may show us the key to the greatest difference between those who play for fun and those who *must* achieve. More than 90 per cent of the achievers challenged themselves. It was not only a one-against-one race to the nearest tree, although that undoubtedly was a part of their experiences, but it was an inner drive, a quest for self-improvement and self-challenge.

I reflected on this topic with my brother John, who eloquently pointed out that he saw one basic and significant difference between us: from the age of six or seven, I had set myself goals which had no finite limit. For example, I would beat the number of consecutive jumps on a pogo stick and be pleased each time I broke my own record. My brother on the other hand wanted to complete a task and move on. He was happy with the bike race around the garden with a clearly defined finishing point. He was never interested in any similar open-ended obsession with beating the previous target, regardless of the time and effort involved. From my point of view, the enjoyment was in managing to achieve the new record breaking performance; the number was almost irrelevant, but the process of struggling to extend the limits was infinitely appealing. In one sense this is the essence of the intrigue and challenge of pursuing any world record. There is always a new frontier as proven by explorers who have driven themselves to unforeseen levels through the ages. Sport has a similar appeal of new discovery, both in personal terms and for the human race. The striving touches many areas such as endurance, speed, strength, balance, coordination, control, creativeness and skill. This striving will equally well include the social elements of cooperation, trust, mutual support, and many others. To some degree there must be a parallel in the make-up of explorers and those who enjoy reaching for the outer limits of human capabilities. It would appear that this inner competitiveness is innate. It was with these individuals as early as they and their parents could remember.

Illustrations to prove this point were plentiful. Herb Elliott said, 'If I got a three-wheeler bike I'd try to see if I could ride it on two wheels and then when I had a two-wheeler I'd try to ride on one wheel, and then there were course records . . . yes, I was fiercely competitive, with myself as well as with others.' Steve Cram's response was. 'I'm awful, I time myself driving to training every day.' Ken Read said, 'Ski jumping helped. One would gain confidence to push out a little further each time, pushing your limit out. That helped so much in downhill – you ski within your limits but you're always trying to stretch them.' Arnold Palmer said that he was out playing with a club from the age of three. 'I recall the days when I started out shooting in the sixties for nine holes when par was 35 or 36, and I can recall breaking 50 for the first time and 40 for the first time. I was doing that by myself, constantly.' Rod Laver described how he built a backboard in his yard and put the boards in vertically. 'They warped over the winter, so I had to hit the right ones to get the ball back. I accepted the challenge, I wouldn't tear it down.' Heather McKay remembered volleying the tennis ball against the wall and beating the number she had done before. She would also mark the garage wall at squash court tin height and do a figure of eight routine, where one strikes the ball to hit off the front wall onto the side wall, back to her and then onto the front and side wall on the other side and back to her again to complete a figure of eight. Her record is ninety-nine consecutive hits and she added, 'I still count!'

Geoff Hunt was challenging himself as a child by seeing whether he could walk around the outside of his house on his hands. Peter Scudamore's challenges included 'jumping stupid things on a horse, just to see if I could. And I'd say to myself, if I can walk along here . . . or if I can put this stone in the bucket I'll be champion jockey. If I can nick that stone with this stone, I'll win the Grand National.' Peter said this was at about ten or eleven, so quite specific goal setting was part of his young hopes.

Ed Moses and Steve Davis took it out of the physical realm. Ed would challenge himself to see how many books he could read over the summer holidays. Steve challenged himself playing patience or space invaders. Barry John challenged the use of the word 'competitive'. He said that he did those self-testing and challenging things for inner satisfaction.

If there is some innate quality of competitiveness in these

individuals, what is it that makes one spirit different from another? From the same parents, in the same location, with similar treatment and similar genes, children in the same family are very different. They may hold the same values but the personality traits and the spirit of each is unique. Have the spirits of these individuals had past life experience in which they have learned competitiveness or is it due to a chemical difference in the brain? Whatever the answer, there is little doubt that those who are involved in competitive sport accept the implicit challenge within their activity which brought out the competitive side of their nature.

Did you have trouble passing up a challenge? The question was asked to see whether or not these performers were motivated by challenges from others. The vast majority said that they did have trouble passing up a challenge. Mary Rand recalled how she was always in trouble, not just joining in when the boys said, 'Let's see if we can walk on this branch without holding on' and saying automatically, 'I can', but often being the initiator. 'Let's see if we can knock on this door and get away before they get us.'

Most of the answers were positive. Steve Cram said that even when challenged to arm wrestling by much bigger and stronger fellows, he would still accept the challenge. 'There's no way I'm going to beat them but I'll always give it a try.' Steve Davis referred to playing things which had some element of skill such as darts. 'Not for money but for the thought of doing it. I dived off the top of a boat in Hong Kong for the sake of a dare. I'd never dived in my life but it was great fun and it wasn't that dangerous.' Kip Keino said he accepted challenges such as swimming across a very wide river.

A few performers gave the qualification that they'd accept the challenge if they felt that they were in with a chance. Unlike Steve Cram, they did not see much point in accepting a challenge in which odds were less than 50–50 at the start.

Bryan Robson applied a challenge to recover from injury. Following a shoulder separation, he was unable to lift even a few pounds held at arm's length. His team-mates and physio were ribbing him about his weakness. He took this as a challenge and secretly took home the weight so that he could work at the exercise over the weekend. He returned on Monday successful.

Many referred to the fun of challenges and their unwillingness to give up. Seb Coe referred to a session with his club Haringey. 'I was in no shape to run fast; I was strong and fit but it's club policy to break the middle-distance group into teams for a mixed relay. There were about six or seven groups of four and I ran with a fourteen-year-old girl, a twenty-four-year-old girl and an eighteen-year-old guy. The better runners have to go twice and the course is about 400m on a hilly course around a rugby pitch – just a stupid thing, my team was about 200m behind and I just went out and literally had to launch myself to get over the line to win the bloody thing, and I felt absolutely like death warmed up. I was spreadeagled in the mud and the kids were standing around while I was quietly passing away.'

Seb's story made me recall a sand-dune relay with a similar outcome, involving four athletes, two per side. There was nothing in the race at stake but the fact that a challenge had been set and accepted. It was the 800m men against the 400m hurdlers. The race ended at full speed down a sand hill, legs like rubber from the previous loops. I also dived for the line to ensure the win, bloodied one knee and was absolutely exhausted. The level of our competitiveness bore no relationship to the lack of importance of the occasion. As Seb said, 'You just have to do it.' It is strange but the enjoyment of the occasion, the effort and the win were as important an achievement, in terms of personal fulfilment, as many top track results. It has a lot to do with giving everything to the effort.

Lucinda Green applied the question of a challenge to her work with horses. 'I find it difficult to admit defeat with a horse. It's only just beginning to sink in that not every horse has star quality, as not every person does. I've been lucky because I've got through doors with some horses and nobody else has and I've found that they have got it, which made me feel that I could get through with every horse. I've wasted a great deal of time with some very mediocre horses. In my particular game I find it extremely difficult to give up with a horse because you are always wondering if you're not giving up with a star.' In a way Lucinda has illustrated an important point. If enough time and effort are concentrated then there is a chance to go through doors which were never thought possible. It was once said to me that each person has their own gold medal level. It is a statement worth remembering. The end results may not produce a world record or an Olympic gold, but if life's challenges are accepted and a commitment is made to try, then a gold medal can be gained in personal terms.

Was a desire not to lose the positive stimulant or was the aim to win stronger? It is, after all, the opposite sides of the same coin. It is not asking if the performer was afraid to lose or that they even thought about it. The question assumed that they won reasonably consistently and asked whether they avoided the thought of losing by making sure they did not lose. In a sense this competitiveness was based on fear; it was an unacceptable thought to lose, so it had to be avoided. Fear can be just as great a stimulant to performance as anger or ambition. A little over one-third of these high achievers believed that they were more motivated by their desire not to lose. Just over half were simply aiming to win, and the rest were just aiming to do their best.

Barry John mentioned that a desire not to lose could produce a defensive attitude in some team sports and thereby take away from the game. For example, packing the defence in soccer may produce a draw but it does not make for a very interesting or entertaining game.

Perhaps the best way of describing the avoidance of loss, as it is intended here, is that the performers see that they have their backs to the wall and will fight very hard and long to avoid losing. It is still the will to win but it is taken from the perspective that they are never willing to accept defeat.

All the tennis players interviewed said that they hated to lose. Both Rod Laver and Billie Jean King spoke of the initial intent which was to win but that they both played better when they got behind. Rod said, 'Even if it was 5–1 to my opponent, there's still a chance. If you believe that, sometimes the other player tightens up a bit and that saved me a few times, not giving up. Also when I got behind I'd give them a rough ride. I wouldn't pull up and play safe if I was losing. I'd make the loser or the winner. I'd put it on my racket. I'd also concentrate better and things look a bit easier from behind . . . not that it was intentional!'

Billy Beaumont pointed out another avoidance issue when he said that he wanted to avoid any team loss being attributable to a mistake by him.

Gareth Edwards said, 'In the end the more success I had the harder I'd work at it not to fail, and that was a motivation. I enjoyed success . . . not to pick up the headlines, but just knowing that you've done it and no one can take that away from you.' Herb Elliott's practices taught him to win at all costs and to die rather than lose. He said, 'In training I had a sense of accomplishment afterwards that I had managed to beat my own weaknesses and my own desire to slow down.'

Lynn Davies referred to the fact that sport at the top level is a self-imposed stress which is alien to people's natural inclination. A lot depends on the perspective of each individual. 'One person may perceive the Olympic final as being a life or death situation for them, whilst another person might simply be happy to be there. Certainly at that level of equal physical talent, the one who wants to win most will win. It's the ability to place enormous stress on oneself to do it. I think the great athletes take losing much more to heart than most people. Losing is worse than dying because you have to wake up the next day! Yet the other side of me is the physical education lecturer, believing in the value of sport for bringing out the best in people, character development, personality growth and everything else but that was not the part of me that enabled me to win athletic competitions. I don't condone teaching the philosophy of winning being all-important, but you must recognize that unless an individual possesses that hate of losing and that feeling of discomfort with oneself, then one loses.' Lynn's statement refers to the performers having their self-image so much tied to their sport performance that they need to win in order for the self-image to survive. The fact that the Press and public are so quick to put in the boot makes the performer quite vulnerable. Peter Scudamore pointed out that he races so often on different quality horses he loses often. His record is still astonishing, winning more than 200 out of 600 races. He added, 'Early on I rode to show off. Now I ride to win.'

John Newcombe was aware of criticism of those who failed to win and pointed out that the person to satisfy is oneself. 'The belief in myself instilled in me a pride that carried across to the tennis court, that every time I played I was going to give 100 per cent and because of that I had no fear of losing. If doubt or fear that they might lose enters someone's mind, and if the other person does not have any fear of losing, they are not afraid to lose, then that person will win . . . I'd give at least 100 per cent so there was no fear of losing because if I lost, that meant the other guy was just better than me on the day. The most important thing was when I sat in the locker room after the match, I was happy in my own mind that I'd given it my best shot.' John's point about self-doubt being a crippler is really important for performers to recognize. It is one of the greatest inhibitors of any person's potential.

At times sport has been strongly equated to battle. It certainly has been represented in that light on many occasions. It is hardly surprising, therefore, that the term 'the killer instinct' has been applied to finishing off an opponent. David Bryant used the phrase in a mild way, referring to the stage in a bowls match where he senses that the other team are starting to crack under the pressure. He feels a bit of the killer instinct when he sees a chink in the opponents' armour: 'I'll say, "Listen boys they're keyed up, I think they're cracking; if we can lift our game now, I think we've got them."'

For Nick Faldo the will to win came from the perspective that he couldn't face handing over a title. 'It was very evident at the Masters in 1990. It was the thought that I've have to give him the jacket! . . . and I'm the defending champion. And I thought, that just doesn't seem right. That doesn't seem like me. How am I going to do that with a straight face and smile? And I think that's what really pushed me on on that one.'

No one should ask more of an individual than to give 100 per cent effort to the attempt. If the performer knows that they have given their all, and that results in a personal best under the most intense competition, then the performer has achieved their personal gold medal level, even if that does not result in a win or a medal. This book is about those who were fortunate enough to win consistently. In one respect they are fortunate because they have not had to face too many insults from the Press and public since they were winning. The written word has immense impact and an individual's confidence can be rocked by a few ill-chosen phrases. All those who pass judgement – or even offer 'constructive' criticism – should bear in mind that to reach the top, a performer must put in years of dedicated work and effort, often without reward.

All the achievers interviewed can be classed as winners by any standard; they won consistently and well under the most serious competitive conditions. However, how should a winner be defined?

Tom McNab, ex-national British athletics coach and author, said, 'If we define a winner as someone who tries their hardest to do their best, then we can have a lot more winners.' If one only sees winners as those who finish first and everyone else as a loser, then one is labelling 97 per cent of those who make it to an Olympic Games as losers. They are already the successful few out of hundreds of thousands who have aspired to achieve that level.

An analogy with music may help us to see the absurdity of calling someone who achieves second place a loser. If one had to make a decision as to whether Isaac Stern or Yehudi Menuhin was the world's best violinist, how could you classify the one placed second as a loser?

No plaudits need be omitted for the actual winners. They deserve their full recognition. However, there is no moral justification in denigrating or dismissing all the supporting cast. All the finishers in the New York and London marathons receive medals. Recognition of accomplishment is what is needed. If capable of finishing first, then go for it, but performers and coaches should appreciate personal improvement and ultimate effort.

It was mentioned earlier, but it is worth repeating. There are two ways of looking at competition. One way is to see competition as a kill or be killed situation. You tread on your opponent to reach the next rung on the ladder of success. This is quite a hostile and cut-throat version of sport. At times it is the way things are but in my opinion it is not a perspective which should be fostered. It doesn't enhance the human spirit. Also, someone once wisely pointed out that you'd better be nice to your rivals on the way up because you'll be seeing them again on your way back down!

Another way is to view competition as a challenge which brings the best out of each competitor and as a result enhances the overall performance level of all involved, to a degree which could not have been reached without competition. Individuals or teams are competing for the same prize, with the recognition that only one can finish on top but that there would be no event without other contestants, and that the better the challenge, the more enjoyable the contest is for contestants and fans alike.

On a few very special occasions, Press, public and contestants alike have recognized a contest where there was no loser. The competition itself was more important than the outcome. The excitement has been sufficient to make everyone appreciate the spirit reaching for its highest qualities in human physical action. There was the classic game in 1971 between the New Zealand All Blacks and the Barbarians. It was seen in a mile race in 1981 in which Steve Cram and Steve Ovett were locked in a sprint finish battle over the final 300m. These are only a couple of examples out of many but on these rare occasions no one really loses. Our perspective on winning has been severely clouded by the over-abundance of attention, praise and rewards usually showered only on the winners.

There is nothing wrong with the desire to win. Neither is there harm in acknowledging the achievements of those who show the way and are taking the fresh steps at the frontier of sport. My objection is to the 'all or nothing', 'winner takes all' approach which misvalues and even dehumanizes all involved. This does not mean that one should settle for second best. Striving for excellence is the ideal. If one has the talent to try for the top, then that should be the aim. The request is for a more balanced perspective in recognizing the efforts of all involved. A gesture which symbolized this happened at the 1982 Commonwealth Games; following two days of intense competition, Daley Thompson persuaded all the protagonists to attend the victory ceremony. The first three place winners received their awards, but all the contestants shared in the applause and recognition of the moment.

All the achievers interviewed acknowledged that they were very competitive when it came to sport. There was also a part of themselves tied to the outcome of the contest. Finland's Lasse Viren, 5000m and 10,000m winner in the 1972 and 1976 Olympics, told Ian Stewart, Britain's 5000m Commonwealth and European champion, that at Olympic level he believed it was the person who could least face losing who would win. The competitive situation sets off the alarm system and adrenalin flows. The two natural responses are fight and flight. Perhaps the individuals who see themselves as aiming to win really are seeing themselves as fighting, and those who are 'running scared' are literally taking flight, avoiding the 'chasing bunch' catching them. In both cases the competitors are harnessing the additional power and controlling their efforts successfully.

How did you respond to mistakes, losses or other setbacks?
There are generally three points to be made about responding to a physical mistake. The first point is that the individual must not dwell on it during the game. J.P.R. Williams explained, 'You have to put it behind you as quickly as possible.' The second point is that it must be

a learning experience. Wayne Gretzky said, 'If you learn from mistakes, you become a better person. If you don't learn from what you've done wrong, then you're defeating the purpose.' Mary Rand highlighted another facet. 'You have to have the losses to appreciate the wins. The important thing is to be able to handle them, deal with them and carry on, and not give up.' Sean Kerly had a similar point, believing that, 'You have to have been good enough and lost it, to learn how to win.' He was basing that on the hockey team's progression towards the gold in Seoul. The third point is coming to terms with the fact that the losses are disappointing, and what is the best way to respond to them. Tennis star Chris Evert: 'You have to care about losing. It has to mean something to you. It used to take me three days to get over it, now it's only a day.' Ginny Leng said that she did take losses very badly and that they depressed her. However, 'I don't allow it to affect me. If I had to go to a party that night, I could be the life and soul of the party and not allow anyone to know it was affecting me but inside it would be. The family might know but nobody else would know how I felt about it.'

Some found it easier than others to bounce back. Barry John said, 'I had one golden rule from a young age; if we lost in a big game, I allowed myself one minute to sulk, then that's it. You become a sportsman again and you go and congratulate the opponents and knock it back into perspective. And if you want to examine your performance, you do it later.' Stephen Hendry acknowledged that it hurt him for an hour or two but added, 'It definitely helped my determination.' Stefan Edberg: 'Losing is part of growing up. You can't win and win and win. You have to learn to take losses. Most of the time I take it quite well but there are times when I will be mad with myself because maybe I haven't given it 100 per cent only 97 per cent and if I'd given it 100 per cent probably I would have won.' Learning from losses was done by analysing what happened and attempting to see what could be done to improve next time that opponent or team was faced. Kip Keino said, 'Three-quarters of your running is mental. If your mind slips and somebody goes and you don't react quickly, you've lost it and you have to accept that mistake, and not allow it to happen again. And in the steeplechase hurdling, if you can only hurdle off one leg you may not be able to react quickly enough to a change, so you must train yourself to hurdle off either leg.' Kip explained that he took all the responsi-

Lester Piggott just before his first 'retirement'. Piggott's sheer professionalism, his knowledge of his opponents' form, his ability to read a race and anticipate events – all of these go some way towards explaining his continued success. And as the record books show, these attributes did not desert him during his layoff from the sport.

Peter Scudamore at the Cheltenham Festival in 1989. Added to the riding skills of the flat race jockey, the jump jockey needs to possess the strength of character to resume riding after the falls and injuries which are an integral part of the job.

Steve Cram (right) just holding off Steve Ovett as they approach the tape. The fitness of top track athletes is primed to reach a peak in competition; they were exceptional amongst those in the survey in often deliberately not giving 100 per cent in training.

Valeriy Borzov (left) prepares to receive the baton from Yuri Silov in the 1972 Olympics. Like many Soviet athletes he was coached from an early age; his preparation, both mental and physical, was total.

A golfer with the enviable quality of being able to break concentration and resume it at will. Arnold Palmer playing on his favourite Old Course at St Andrews in 1970.

Rodney Pattisson dressed for whatever the oceans might throw at him. He was among the minority who admitted to being superstitious – but, then again, seafarers traditionally are.

Joan Benoit Samuelson in the Los Angeles Olympics, 1984. Her courage, resilience and determination in the face of severe injury make her stand out, even among the toughest members of this sample group.

Above Ed Moses (third from left) winning a tough final in the 1987 World Championships. Convinced that most people eat too much, he sees a healthy diet as a key part of a winning programme and has been known to fast whilst in training.

Manchester United and England heroes, past and present: Bobby Charlton (right) is snapped whilst playing his last club match in 1973, whilst Bryan Robson (above) shows characteristic commitment for England against Romania in 1985. Both performers pointed out that mental strength in sport is underpinned by physical fitness.

Wimbledon and Chris Evert will always be associated in the minds of the British public; this shot is from 1987. Chris increased the power of her game with weight training long before it became fashionable.

Wayne Gretzky in 1990, still one of the most dangerous forwards in ice hockey. Too much attention from the local media during his teenage years caused his parents to move to Toronto – which may have saved his career.

A victorious Seb Coe in the 1980 Olympics. He has always had a wide range of interests and believes a balanced view of life is of great advantage to sports people.

Daley Thompson getting the feel of the shot in the 1984 Olympics in Los Angeles. Like so many top achievers he is something of an all-rounder and this aptitude is reflected in his chosen event with its wide range of disciplines.

Jackie Stewart and the author, David Hemery; top achievers who share many of the positive attributes highlighted in this study. Both showed awareness that in their chosen field they were often competing against their own limitations as much as against the opposition; significantly, both are associated in the public mind with British Superstars, the televised test of supreme sporting fitness – a true test of character. Jackie Stewart, it should be noted, has reached the top in two entirely unconnected sports, while David Hemery has practised what he preaches by finding professional fulfilment after retirement as an Olympic athlete.

bility for losing. He said that he only lost if *he* made a mistake! For others it might be a case of the opponents playing better on the day, but in most cases the responsibility for not winning was taken by the individual. Gretzky had built-in perspective. 'After losses I always feel disappointed, dejected and feel even worse if I haven't contributed the way I know that I can, but you see we have a mentally retarded youngster who works in the training and locker rooms – he's my girlfriend's brother – and I come into the room and see him and realize how lucky we are. He really perks me up.'

A very different aspect of loss had to be faced by Jackie Stewart. 'Losing a race I was fairly philosophical – there was always another Grand Prix in two weeks and a World Championships every year. I think the most difficult thing to deal with in our business was that of losing friends because most of them went. I lived through a very bad period of motor sport. Most of my best friends were killed – Jim Clark, Jochen Rindt, François Cevert, Piers Courage, Bruce McLaren. They all died ... I became shy of creating deep friendships because suddenly they were all taken away.' Against much pressure, Jackie successfully crusaded for better safety measures for all cars, racing and domestic.

Would you perform any better if there was increased financial incentive? The background to this question came from two sources. The first was that a great deal of media hype goes into big prize money today and it was wondered if performers did in fact try harder if there was more at stake. The second prompt was from watching Jackie Stewart competing head-to-head with heavyweight boxer Joe Bugner during the first British Superstars. The prize money meant nothing to Jackie but the effort being expended could only come down to personal pride and competitiveness. The answers brought out some interesting insights. A view was expressed that money can reduce the fun in sport. It can become a serious business. Two aspects occur to me here. Firstly, having money involved or having it business-like does not rule out having fun. But, secondly, as many complete amateurs will tell you, once a performer commits himself or herself to reaching the very top, it *is* serious business, regardless of finance.

More than 90 per cent believed that money was not the issue in determining performance effort. Professionals will negotiate for more money but the effort in competition was motivated from within, not by external reward. The view from the amateur ranks was no different. In many cases they would like to see a more open attitude to money being available within their sports but they believed that they could not have put in any more effort. Amateur squash champion Geoff Hunt said, 'I couldn't have tried any harder.'

Among the professionals, Chris Evert, Billie Jean King and Clive Lloyd all referred to personal pride in their performance being far more important than money. Daley Thompson related the same view. 'The reason I'm out there is to do good for myself and to win – that's the most important thing for me, so whether I am getting $100,000 or $1, it would make no difference to me. I have a great deal of pride in my performance . . . I enjoy performing well – that's why I do all the training, so the incentive or motivation of money or people watching makes no difference to me at all.'

Des Drummond pointed out that using money as a tool to get more from players can backfire. 'I've seen players trying to perform better because money has been offered as an incentive . . . they end up having a bad game. They should have been prepared to play the game before.' Even if money does work to get performance from a moderate performer, more and more will bring less and less.

Rugby amateur J.P.R. Williams also played professional tennis. He said, 'I couldn't have played any harder. I played tennis for both appearance money and the prize money and it made no difference to me.' Billy Beaumont said that money would not be an incentive to play harder but added an interesting postscript: 'When I put 100 per cent in, I got more enjoyment out . . . but money would probably have made me a dirtier player!'

Money would certainly have made the task of preparation much easier for most amateurs, a view confirmed by Peter Snell. Pat O'Callaghan said that it would have allowed him more time for training. Herb Elliott said that it might have kept him in sport for longer. David Bryant said, 'When you've been doing a job of work all day, often you don't feel like practising, but it wasn't a chore, it was relaxation.'

Even with increased sponsorship, almost all of today's amateur sportsmen and women are out of pocket attempting to reach a level where they represent their country. The ideal of amateurism is laudable in many ways but the Western sports person or his or her family has the price to pay and that means that some are denied access. At least those who are major championship medal prospects from Britain are assisted through the Sports Aid Foundation. Nevertheless there is clear injustice when some moderately good sports professionals can become millionaires, and a comparable performer in many amateur sports is living hand to mouth. Carl Lewis has not done too badly out of his sport successes but still feels somewhat bitter. He said, 'It's unbelievable how amateur athletes are looked down on for accepting money . . . Stevie Wonder signs a $40 million recording contract and the world rejoices; I make a token of that and they say, "You dog!"'

Less than 10 per cent were not sure whether prize money would have improved their performance. Rod Laver made the significant observation that if money was riding on every shot in his early days, he might not have allowed himself or been allowed to continue experimenting. 'My game was allowed to grow. I'd be hitting a winner and then the next shot would be into the cheap seats. It finally gelled but maybe I'd never have taken those risks if thousands of dollars were riding on it. Maybe I wouldn't have gone for the shots and played conservatively, but ultimately I would not have developed the shots which were my trademark, hitting top spin or slice from any angle.' Rod was one of a group of four who for five years barn-stormed the United States in a mini-van, driving 500 miles, doing pre-promotion, getting the papers to write about it, playing and moving on, and thereby helping to get professional tennis off the ground. As with several others in this group, this story illustrates that if individuals have the courage to take the initiative, they can help to change the course of events.

Still on the subjects of money and personal endeavour, I have intentionally left two special cases until last because I wanted to highlight what I believe to be very unusual. I would love to think awareness of this might prompt others to do more. Many performers give their time and their names to charitable efforts. Nick Faldo also gives considerable financial support. I asked Nick what had initiated his giving. His reply was that it had been prompted by having a family. 'Once you have children you realize what would happen if you lost one – how you'd be devastated. So we thought, if a bit of money can help relieve somebody . . .' Just to name some of the causes Nick has supported: leukaemia research for children; Sports Aid hospital; cystic fibrosis; cot deaths; and a scanner. As most people earn more their 'sufficiency' level is lifted to match that income. It was great to meet someone giving back so generously.

Another story of generosity was unknown by most people until a few years ago. Kip Keino and his wife, who is a nurse, have been taking into their family abandoned and orphaned children from all over Kenya. When people asked whose were all the children, Kip would simply say, 'They're mine.' Out of his earnings from a couple of sport shops and a little help from missionary funds Kip has developed his farm where he currently has more than fifty children and from where more than that again have moved on. He supports them through to two years after their education is completed.

Summary of learning points:

- Competitiveness seems to be innate. Most top sport achievers have an inner drive for self-improvement and self-challenge.
- Competitiveness with others need not be destructive. Effort from one individual or team challenges the opposition and can draw more from both.
- Without challengers there would be no contest and no winners. And the better the challenge the higher the level all achieve, and the greater the potential for excitement and enjoyment for performers and spectators alike.
- A performer who doesn't mind losing is more likely to lose.
- Self-doubt is a crippler.
- Giving 100 per cent allows a performer to acknowledge that on that day, win or lose, they reached their own gold medal level.
- Criticism by outsiders of less than 100 per cent success is easy. Greater understanding and respect need to be given to those who have worked for months and years to produce their best effort.
- Winners can be defined as those who try their hardest to do their best. What is asked for is recognition of personal improvement.
- The 'winner takes all' attitude in sport misvalues and dehumanizes all involved.
- Don't dwell on losses.
- Learn from mistakes, technically and personally, what you will do differently next time to improve.
- A performer's greatest regret will be recognizing that they didn't give themselves 100 per cent to the attempt.

Competitiveness

- The responsibility for winning is taken by the performer.
- For top achievers, money is not the catalyst for greater effort. They could try no harder anyway.
- Top performers have a personal pride in performing well.
- Money makes preparation easier and will keep players in their sport longer.
- Almost all amateur performers and their coaches are out of pocket attempting to get to any reasonable representational level. This inevitably denies some the opportunity to try.
- If a young professional must win to survive, their creativity and experimentation will probably suffer.
- Most top performers give something back in time and endorsements; a few special ones are also giving back financially and in personal effort.

20
GETTING AN EDGE

Did you always have the self-confidence that you could produce your best effort when you asked that of yourself? On several occasions the achievers referred to having the 'confidence' in themselves and their abilities to take risks and perform up to expectations. Self-confidence means having a positive view of yourself and what you can do.

Even at this level, there were about 10 per cent who lacked some confidence in either themselves or their ability. Both Joan Benoit Samuelson and Lynn Davies were testing themselves right up to competition time, just to prove to themselves that they still did have the capability to perform well. Ron Pickering pointed out that Lynn went to do some weight-lifting on the morning of the Olympic long jump final, just to reassure himself that he still had his strength. Lynn said, 'I was never very confident. The whole process was seeking a feeling of mastery and the good sensation that confirmed that the good performance of a month ago was still going to be there in half an hour's time. The constant seeking of reaffirmation of one's abilities.' Joan was also constantly testing, even on the day before competition, taking a hard run just to reassure herself that she was ready and it was still there.

Herb Elliott saw self-doubt as an asset. 'I think one of my strengths has been my doubts of myself: if you're very aware of the weaknesses and are full of your own self-doubts, in a sense, that's quite a motivation.' Steve Ovett said, 'There's always a worry that I'd never live up to the expectations of my friends or whatever. If I have a failing, it's that that the confidence level in my own ability is very low really.' Seb Coe's opinion was similar. 'I never go into a race believing that I'm invincible.' The two exceptions he noted were the 1500m final in the Los Angeles Olympics and his first 800m in Oslo where he said that he felt something special was going to happen. In the latter, he broke the world record running 1 min 42 sec. Lucinda Green also said that she still lacked a bit of confidence.

In spite of these top achievers' admissions of self-doubts beforehand, during the competition they maintained the necessary self-control to perform their chosen sport superbly and with authority.

Although it could not really be attributed to a lack of confidence, Bobby Charlton said that he could never be sure whether or not his actions were going to be able to flow. He was not worried about his technical skills letting him down, just that there were days when he felt right and everything was fine and other days when it just wouldn't work. This would happen despite being prepared. Research on human bio-rhythms has shown a distinct probability that there are physical, emotional and intellectual cycles in each of us which can account for the up days and down days. On the 'critical zero' days, we are three to four times more prone to mistakes or accidents. Japanese bus drivers are taken off their routine on the days when these midpoints coincide, with the result that their accident rates have been cut.

Jackie Stewart took his lack of confidence out of the realm of competing and said that he was never going to be secure about having sufficient money. He was interested to hear Paul McCartney say the same thing in a radio interview.

However, the vast majority of these high achievers, 90 per cent, had a very high degree of self-confidence. In many cases this was attributed to their knowing that they were as well prepared as they could be. With a few, it developed over time. Chris Evert said that winning when young brought self-confidence, supporting the theory that those who win reasonably consistently from an early age see themselves as winners, and believe in most cases that they can and will win. It did not make much difference what the early competitive level was as long as they instilled in themselves the vision of being a winner. It behoves both the teachers and parents to attempt to create more situations in which early success can be achieved by more children. Perhaps it is a case of staging handicap races and balancing sides in games so that at different times various youngsters see themselves as capable of winning; likewise, in training sessions, allowing different individuals the opportunity to lead. Kip Keino was in the forefront of the Kenyans' distance running success. He said, 'We ran as a team and shared the lead on interval sessions. That helped the spirit and encouraged the less able. We worked as a team and encouraged others to do better.' Presumably the reverse is also likely to happen; if a child never experiences success then he or she will believe that success is beyond their grasp.

Some individuals have always had confidence. Daley Thompson said, 'I've always been confident of doing well. I know whether or not I'm going to win. I have doubts but come a week or ten days before the event, they're all gone. I've never gone into a competition with any doubts. I've always had confidence of putting 100 per cent in and at the end of the day, I think regardless of where you come, you can't do any more than try your best.' Daley's amazing winning streak came to an end when he was competing with an injury. His courage to finish all ten events knowing that he was going to lose and his genuine generosity of praise despite being clearly upset at the close gave viewers a fine example of sportsmanship.

Shane Innes said that she always had confidence in her ability and thought it might have come from her father 'brain-washing' her that she was capable of anything. 'He had a confidence in my ability in every aspect,' she said.

Geoff Hunt also said that he always had confidence in what he could do. 'I went on the court and felt that I could win the matches. Even when younger, I remember playing the top player in the state and I was only about number fifty, but I thought I had a good chance against him and I led him 7–1 in the first set. I'm sure I did that because I played to win. He went on to win it 3–0, but even though I knew winning was unlikely, I still gave myself a chance.'

Barry John pointed out that it was a willingness to accept responsibility for the outcome of one's actions, which brings up an illustration Billy Smith gave. 'Most of us in a tight basketball game with one shot left would hope that the ball didn't come our way, so that we would not be the ones to blow it! Yet Larry Bird is begging for the ball; baseball star Ted Williams was dying to be at the plate in the pressure situation.' Two things occurred to me. Firstly, these are the people who perform better under increased responsibility or pressure, and secondly, they want to have control of their own destiny. If they take the ball they are in control. They do not want to leave their destiny in someone else's hands. Some love being in the spotlight when the pressure is on. One such case is Al Oerter; he felt as though the discus circle in the Olympics was the same as being under a magnifying glass with the sun making the spot white hot. 'I love it there.' Steven Hendry said, 'I'm best under pressure.'

Billy Smith pointed out that Larry Bird, many times named as the most valuable player of the year in US pro basketball, was the one staying after everyone else had left, taking 100 to 150 foul shots then running laps around the balcony track, all the time – even during the play-offs at the end of the season. Bobby Charlton said that he always liked to take extra individual skill practice on his own after the team training sessions. Improved competence increased confidence. Mary Rand said that there was a mental discussion going on with one side of her saying, 'I could win' and the other side saying, 'Don't get too cocky.' 'The balance reached was thinking I've got a good chance here and I'm going to give it my best.'

Despite the differences in the aspects of confidence which each chose to mention, the belief was always the same. Torvill and Dean and Kip Keino said that a personal best was always their aim. Steve Davis had a similar view saying that he always had confidence that he would do his best and not panic under pressure. David Bryant said that he had complete confidence in the mechanics of his game. Steve Cram was confident that he could dig down and find what was needed – 'I can drag it out.' Ian Botham said that there were two things which gave him an edge. 'The belief in myself and the fact that I don't believe any situation is lost until it's actually gone. I believe you've always got a chance.'

Pat O'Callaghan said, 'I felt that whatever the opposition did, I'd do better. It was a state of mind from training.' Like the others, Pat had confidence in his ability and in his body's performance.

Despite Joan Benoit Samuelson testing herself up to the last minute, it is worth recounting a discussion which took place when Joan and I were coaching at Boston University and Julie White was a student who had high jumped for Canada at the Olympics. Joan had a marathon coming up and she expressed worries over having to make a pit stop during the course of the race. She had been having trouble with her stomach on some recent training runs. I reflected that my only concern in not being able to do my best, as a contact lens wearer, was that just as the gun sounded for the start of my race a gust of wind might blow some dust into my eyes and the pain would force me out. Julie made an astute observation that although we didn't dwell on them, we both feared things which were beyond our control. The reverse was unfortunately true for her; she would often be worried about things over which she did have control. Could that focus of anxiety be one of the factors which makes a difference between the elite and the good athletes? Acknowledge and dismiss the things over which you have no control and control the things you can. There is no place for worry over the aspects beyond your control. You simply have to execute the best you can on the day.

Did you do anything special to get an edge on others? Many people wonder whether there is any one thing which made these athletes into winners. Some reporters from a few years ago were so out of touch with what went into any great performance that they would ask questions like, 'What on earth did you have for breakfast on the morning of the competition?', as if there might have been some magic potion which created success.

As one will have already gathered, there are so many factors which contribute to the overall pursuit of excellence that there is no one miracle element. However, it is my experience to look back and say, for example, that for me sand-dune running was a significant training edge. It is so difficult to run fast up a long soft sand hill that it taught my mind as well as my body to hang on despite discomfort. I also felt that, for me, the hardest way was the best way because I would be mentally toughened and uplifted by having gone out and done a session while it was snowing. I would come back in and think to myself, 'I don't think my opponents would have gone out today; that puts me one step ahead or gives me a little bit of an edge.' Most of the performers believed that their training was doing something special and would make a difference to their performance. Naturally, most related that they placed an emphasis on physical fitness and for some, it was long before it became fashionable in their sport.

Arnold Palmer mentioned that he had learned discipline through having to cut the greens and fairways with his father. He also did physical exercises such as chin-ups with him to build himself up. Lester Piggott ran to gain extra fitness but said that his greatest edge was his good temperament for racing. 'It made a difference on the big occasions because nothing bothered me.' Clive Lloyd stressed fitness for his team but added that the other two things were playing other sports to relax and avoid staleness, and each season he tried to look for something new to do in order to make himself a better player. Chris Evert pointed out that she had done weight training before it was common practice, but for her an important edge was that she really enjoyed what she was doing. Heather McKay also said that her fitness level gave her the edge, but added that she thought it helped coming to the British tournament with a tan! Stefan Edberg, specifically referring to his legs, said 'the most important thing for me today is staying physically strong. I believe if you're physically strong it's easier for you mentally because you believe you're strong.' This view parallels the belief of Carl Lewis's coach, Tom Tellez, and my personal experience, that *confidence* comes from *being* and *believing* you're totally prepared. Apart from track training, weights, hurdling and exercises, Billy wrote to me in Mexico before the Olympics underlining the preparation to build my confidence, 'There are 1000 hills and sand dunes behind you and they don't have time to catch up!' Stephen Hendry said, 'Only a small percentage of snooker players put in a lot of practice – sort of six hours per day on your own grind. That gives me a lot of consistency. Having done the work gives me more confidence to play well all the time.'

Valeriy Borzov said that he was used to training on holidays and days off and that his training was more intense than the other athletes. He also had special training to stimulate the muscles. This is being introduced more now in the West, but with particular emphasis on rehabilitation from injury. If it is the same piece of equipment, the electrodes are simply placed at either end of a muscle group and the electrical impulse causes the muscle to contract. It can be very beneficial to either wasted or healthy tissue in building muscle condition and size. Both Jonah Barrington and Daley Thompson reiterated Valeriy's point and cited the hours which each of them put in as giving them their edge over others. Jonah referred to his six hours of training each day. Daley would play at sport for part of his day and be intense at other times, but training in one form or another took up all of his day. Billie Jean King referred to the intensity of her two-hours-a-day training involving two-against-one practice. She said that her training was longer, harder and more efficient than the others. 'I didn't think about it so much then. I knew that if I paid the price, I'd be a better athlete.'

Torvill and Dean mentioned that they felt as though they got an edge on their opponents by practising on Christmas Day when they knew that everyone else would have had a day off. Having mentioned this to Daley Thompson, he told me that the next Christmas he'd managed two training sessions, thus gaining a double advantage over his arch-rival Jürgen Hingsen!

Barry John said that his touch of playful arrogance was based on a strong sense of self-confidence, but he added that you have to be prepared to back it up. 'Although I wasn't the greatest trainer, I still went out on my own when I felt I needed sharpening up, even in the snow and ice on the field by the river. I'd clear a little path through the light snow, of about 100 yards, and I'd do twenty to twenty-five minutes to prepare my mind for the weekend game.'

In the cases of Joan Benoit Samuelson and Peter Snell, training was sacrosanct. Peter said, 'It was a sin to miss a day's training. A target would be set, like you've got to try to hit 100 miles a week.' Joan also said, 'I would never sacrifice training.'

An extreme example which reflects top achievers wanting to be stronger than their conditions is that of American football running back O.J. Simpson. He played for Buffalo which averages more snow than Anchorage, Alaska. In these winter conditions he would continue to wear his regular T-shirt, because he did not want to believe it was too cold to play well. He also refused to go near to the heaters while he was on the sidelines, so that he would not be thinking about getting back there, while on the field again. During his best season in successive weeks he gained over 200 yards, the first in a blizzard and the second with ice all over the field.

Seb Coe referred to his ten years of background work up on the Sheffield moors. 'When it was very, very bleak I would be the only one who would be likely to go out in that weather. Athletes tend to hang on to anything that they feel might give them that little bit of edge and the extra motivation – that feeling of satisfaction that you were out there when it would have been easier not to have been.'

Rod Laver cited an example of how well he pre-planned for tennis, although he confessed that the same did not hold true for the rest of his life. He said that in a tournament at the Spectrum in Philadelphia, matches were beginning at 8.30 a.m. He and Arthur Ashe were challenging for the number one position. Rod had breakfast at 6 a.m. and was on court by 7 a.m., so that he had an hour and a half's practice on the same surface before the tournament. He saw that as gaining a usable edge, especially as he knew Arthur wasn't doing likewise.

Ken Read also had some practical application of preparation which he felt gave him an edge. Apart from his dedication to physical training, he spoke of the times when he was in transit overnight; they might have arrived at noon and while the others shopped he ran. Also during the Christmas break he would spend some time with his family in Canada doing light training but then would move on to a routine which included readjusting to European time and getting himself ready, knowing that all the others were having a more generous break and would come back a bit off.

This aspect of doing more than the others is certainly a common theme. It was mentioned again by Nick Faldo: 'I always believed the more I worked on it, until I was totally satisfied, the more I was hopefully gaining an edge, because my opponent's not going to work as hard as me.' I asked if he was a perfectionist. 'Yes, but you can't have perfection, just keep fine tuning your game closer and closer to it.'

Ginny Leng saw it as covering every detail. 'Perhaps that's where I benefit. Perhaps they don't think of things enough.' Peter Scudamore had a similar response, 'I did everything possible. I'd make myself available to as many trainers as possible. I'd do the minimum weight so I had the broadest spectrum of horses. I may have sacrificed style for getting over and away from obstacles quickly; plus I concentrated on the finish. And when the ground is soft I'll walk the course.'

J.P.R. Williams, who lived very near to Merthyr Meyer sand-dunes, felt that the work there gave him more stamina than most other rugby players. Another edge was that he never missed a high ball and he said, 'I never had to practise catching the high ball because it was ingrained in me by my father. When I was young he used to pump the ball up in the air and I used to catch the ball wherever it went. The tackling was timing and I did practise that. I'd get two people to run at me in the space of ten yards and almost be able to make them pass the ball when I wanted. Normally if you get a two-on-one situation, the two would always get the ball past the one but if you get your angle and approach right, if he doesn't dummy you, you're going to get him and there are occasions when I have quite often taken two men out of the game either by psyching them out and making them pass too early or making them hang onto the ball by approaching as if I'm going for the other person. I think it's something that most people don't practise. I got the other full-backs doing it on the Lions tour and they found it a tremendous benefit.'

Viv Richards felt that he got an edge when he played shots which would take the heart out of a bowler, like hitting the ball for six no matter what the delivery. He said that his aim was to keep cool and calm because the longer you stay that way, the more runs you are going to score.

Lucinda Green felt that an edge was gained because she had some land to train on even when it snowed and others were prevented from training. She said that it was a very good morale boost in her favour.

Sean Kerly saw his edge as cracking the ball first time, in open play.

Not waiting to manoeuvre, thereby not allowing the defence to get set. Also, 'If I lost the ball I'd try to get it back quickly. If you don't react straight away you've had it.' In the US, players are judged by how fast they get up after they've been knocked down.

The special edge for Shane Innes was training with men. She felt as though that gave her a challenge which was not usual for other women at that time. For Wayne Gretzky it was that he was on skates from the age of two! Jackie Stewart said that his special lift came from him gaining the awareness that he was not competing against others but with himself. Ed Moses talked about how he fasted for up to a week and continued to train hard. He felt that his training was more efficient and that this proved one of his theories that people over-eat, even when training.

A summary of many of these responses would be that if you can realistically say to yourself that no one else has prepared as well as you have, and you believe that, it will provide a self-confidence that is stronger than your self-doubt and will carry you through the pressure times.

It must be noted that simply doing more work is certainly not the whole answer. Many performers have done too much and have injured themselves. Each person must carefully and gradually extend their mental and physical capacity.

How did you cope with thoughts of your opponent? Half of them said that they never gave their opponents much thought. Their focus was on themselves and what they were going to be doing. The other half wanted to find out all they could about their opponents, so that they would be more fully prepared. This latter group would be using this knowledge both in terms of assessing how they would compete against their opponents as well as coming to terms with any anxieties these opponents might cause. However, the thoughts given to the opponent would only be used as a tool for better personal preparation. Respect, apprehension, even some anxiety were possible by-products, but their thoughts were not dwelling on any possible negative outcome.

Steven Hendry said, 'You've got to think of every opponent and give them 100 per cent respect. It's not easy to do, if you think you can beat someone easily.'

Nick Faldo cautioned about the other end of the spectrum. 'Once you start thinking someone's got something over you, then they're going to win.' The warning here concerns negative thoughts. Peter Scudamore had an illustrative story about 'a very good rider having had a terrible run, not having ridden a winner for three weeks. Going into the last fence he had me well beat and I wondered what was going through his mind – the fact that his run's over; and as soon as he starts thinking that, there's going to be a hesitancy and whether it was a hunch or not, his horse made a mistake and jumped out, and I got up and beat him. I was aware he was having a bad run and it suddenly hit him. He tried too hard. You've got to be aware of bad runs and good runs and it's all got to be the same.' Negative thoughts can be replaced by an over-positive attitude – trying too hard – which is equally disruptive to smooth efficient performance.

Of those who wanted to deal mentally with their forthcoming opponents, several referred to the situation as one-on-one, even if they had to face several at once. Ed Moses spoke about one-on-one mental rehearsal which I had used and found very helpful in believing I could win if I ran up to my potential. He said that sometimes mentally, he would run races one-on-one but that he never worried about anyone but himself. He said, 'Purely for preparation, I might see what would happen if I found myself behind, but when I got on the track, I'd block that out by not allowing myself to be in that position and that's how I'd run. I just energize myself to eliminate that automatically. Whatever it takes to win that's what I do. I get the best out of myself by not expecting an easy race, giving the opponent a lot of respect. Take them seriously but don't dwell on them. It's easier when there's pressure. You don't have time to think, you get emotional and go out and perform.'

Jonah Barrington's coach would talk him through each player, discussing the reasons why Jonah was better than the other player, in all aspects of the game. Additionally, when it was clear that the opponent was better in certain areas, his coach, during the build-up, would take Jonah into the sort of game that would not play to that opponent's strengths.

Barry John used humour to defuse pressure concerning opponents. He said, 'When the Press said things like, "What about this giant you're playing tomorrow? What about sleeping tonight?" I'd say, "Sleep! Of course I'll sleep. All I know is that he's going to have to mark me and he's got to sleep tonight!" But once you've created that situation, you'd better back it up!'

Bobby Charlton said, 'Opponents never bothered me unless they were particularly close to me. I hated playing against my brother or close personal friends like Jimmy Armfield and George Cohen. Other than that I completely cut myself off. It didn't matter because I knew that they were trying to beat us just the same.'

Sean Kerly said that there would be a team meeting with a video of the upcoming opponents. The questions being asked were: 'How do we do our best? How do we exploit their weaknesses? How will we defend against their corner shots? What are they good at? What are they likely to do? How do we best respond? So we're *aware*. We're generally aware of how they play and what they're good and bad at and we agree on what we're going to do.'

Valeriy Borzov was interested in the opponents as people, but said that at the time of the competition, the only thought was on his own performance. This last aspect is true for all the performers, even those who had studied the opposition in as close detail as possible. Once it was settled in their minds that they could control what they did against their opponents, they were no longer involved in thoughts about them until the contest was over. The only time that would change was where their play demanded a constant reassessment, for example in cricket where a variety of bowling attacks might have to be employed against one good batsman, or if agreed tactics needed changing.

David Bryant said something which was alluded to by many but not said in so many words. 'You mustn't be dictated to by your opponents.' While many of his opponents were busy coming to terms with how they would control their own efforts and how to focus on their performance, he was stamping his own authority on the game. Not that it always resulted in a win, but at least he was attempting to determine his own fate rather than allowing others to dictate it for him. David said that he was not worried by opponents; his main focus was on how he was playing and if he felt that he was playing at his best, then he was going to win. This statement exudes the sort of self-confidence which made these individuals consistent winners.

My own experience of coping with thoughts of opponents altered according to the level of competition. The higher the level the greater the preparation. I liked to see the stadium before running there as it took away some of the unknown. Similarly, I liked at least to know what my competitors looked like and how they ran, so that I had clear images for my mental rehearsal one-on-one races with each of the probable con-tenders for the gold. If my mind started to run away, allowing my opponent to take too commanding a lead, I would start again until I was sure that, given an equal chance, I could successfully finish ahead of him. Certainly the main focus during competition must be on one's own performance. Coping effectively with thoughts of the opposition is helpful prior preparation. It can settle the mind, establishing confi-dence, commitment, and full concentration on what one must do at the time of the contest.

Summary of learning points:

- The few who lacked confidence before a major event still competed confidently and with authority.
- Predictably, the more complete the preparation, the greater the fitness, consistency and *confidence*.
- True physical fitness is one of the greatest contributors to confidence.
- There's no substitute for hard work.
- Bio-rhythms could account for the days when one is really flowing and other days when one is accident prone.
- Sufficient experiences, when young, of winning and feeling one can achieve could carry into adulthood the sense of self-confidence and the capacity to achieve greater things.
- Confident performers want to take responsibility for the outcome. They would rather hold their destiny in own their hands than allow others to dictate the result. Under pressure, they held the same or even greater dispassionate control than at any other time.
- Although they are not dwelt on, top performers recognize what they cannot control and confidently execute the things over which they do have control.
- Doing more training and working under more adverse conditions than opponents prompts performers to have greater mental toughness, and confidence that they are better prepared than their competitors. It also reduces their self-doubt.
- Simply doing more is not the whole answer – too much, too fast results in injury or sickness.
- Performers are judged by how fast they get up after they have been knocked down.

- Whether or not top performers prepare by thinking about the upcoming opponent, all in the end focus on themselves, what they can control, and how best they are going to perform.
- No matter what apprehension opponents produce in a performer, thoughts should never dwell on a negative outcome.
- Equally disruptive are over-positive thoughts, as trying too hard produces excessive tension.
- Thoughts, negative and positive, are frequently self-fulfilling.
- Personally successful one-on-one mental performances against the top competitors help to deal with self-doubt and unnecessary worry.
- Reviewing the 'What ifs', and knowing what your best responses will be, is an invaluable preparation. It can settle your mind, providing confidence, helping commitment, and enabling full concentration on what one must do at the time of the contest.

21
CONTROLLING YOUR DESTINY

Do you feel that you control your own destiny? The reason for this question was that many individuals simply let things happen. Achievers usually make things happen. The question was whether they considered that they had control of their lives. Some voiced the obvious qualification that certain things were outside their control, however they were in control of their direction. Ninety per cent said that they felt in control of their own destiny, most simply saying 'Yes'. Jackie Stewart, more forthright, said 'absolutely'. Wayne Gretzky said that he believed that you make your own fate but also believes that luck plays a part as to where you end up.

Destiny involves a question of who has the power and the choice. As achievers feel in control of their direction, clear goal setting has a large part to play. A very powerful illustration of the process is the story of John Naber, who was US national high school swimming champion in the backstroke. In his first year at UCLA he watched Mark Spitz on his gold medal bonanza in the 1972 Olympics. John immediately set his target on winning gold in the 100m backstroke in the 1976 Games. He then set a personal performance goal to break the world record in that event, to put himself in with the best chance of winning. The difference between his personal record and the time needed to break the world record was five seconds, which in 100m is an enormous chunk of time. To make this highly positive and challenging goal realistic, he divided the five seconds by the number of hours he would be training in that four years. It worked out that he only had to improve by one twelve-hundreth of a second for every hour he spent training. And that he equated to one-fifth of an eye blink. He reasoned that if he worked intelligently, as well as hard, he was sure he could improve by one-fifth of an eye blink for every hour spent training. He advanced so well that he was selected to captain the US swimming team and won the 100m backstroke gold in a new world record and the 200m in an Olympic record. The long-term vision was changed into attainable, measurable steps.

The idea that you can either take control of your destiny or just let things happen was taken up by Peter Snell. He was referring to his own achievement and said, 'I felt that there were lots of people around that could have done it but they didn't know they could, and so I felt I was lucky that I was able to get involved and discover that I could do it. My coach Arthur Lydiard obviously played a part, but there were a lot of other factors as well.'

Lester Piggott and Kip Keino made it sound very simple. Lester said, 'You have to really because it's us doing it.' Kip said, 'I do whatever I want to do.' Valeriy Borzov said that he was in control of his own destiny. Running fulfilled his personal desire and he also saw it as something which helped his country.

Half of those who said yes gave qualifications. Most said things such as 'to an extent', or 'generally' or 'up to a point'. Billy Beaumont pointed out that his fate lay to an extent in the hands of the selectors. But Bill also said, 'On the field you control your own destiny.' A similar response came from Sean Kerly: 'You do and you don't. If you get the chance you make your opportunities but the selectors make their judgements.'

On the more cautious side of the fence, Gareth Edwards, Duncan Goodhew and Rodney Pattisson thought that they could not control their fate but that they could influence it. Duncan referred to his belief in deterministic fatalism. He described it as follows. 'It's basically like a tree; you start at the bottom, you climb up and you choose the various options. I also believe that if you have talent, it's sacrilege not to make the most of it.'

The five performers who said no to this question answered as follows: Bryan Robson said, 'No, you could be injured tomorrow.' Peter Scudamore said, 'You can try hard, have a fall and the horses gallop over one and not another. What's that?' Both Jayne Torvill and Christopher Dean said that they believed in predetermination. Al Oerter referred to himself as a fatalist. He said that several people had tried to imply there was a Messiah-like destiny in his career which he rejected.

Ian Botham said that he felt that he controlled his destiny as a player but not in the rest of his life. He related an interesting coincidence, one of several premonitions which have subsequently come true. He dreamt that his hundredth Test wicket victim would be the Indian captain, Sunil Gavaskar. Ian was amazed to read in the Press, after it happened, that Sunil said he had also dreamt that he would be Ian's hundredth victim!

Are you superstitious? More than half of these achievers said they definitely were not. Sean Kerly pointed out that he wore number 13.

John Whitmore was warned not to become superstitious. 'Before my first race, Alan Stacey warned me not to become superstitious. He said, "Do not get attached to the shirt you wear in your first race, because you'll wear it for the first half-dozen races, then you'll lose that shirt. You won't have it and your anxiety will grow and that will make you perform badly and that will confirm your worst expectations." So I was very conscious not to allow anything superstitious to creep in.'

A quarter of these performers said that they were a little bit superstitious, some putting it down mostly to routine. Nick Faldo said, 'A little bit. However I sometimes try to make a conscious effort to do it differently if I start getting superstitious. But you like certain colours and you play well in certain colours. Some golfers won't use a number three ball as that could mean a three putt. Mostly it's just rituals.' Stefan Edberg also admitted, 'Yes, a little bit. I'll keep the same habits. If I take one place in the locker room, I'll keep it for the week. If I go in one shower, I'll go in the same one. Those things are sort of routine and those things make you comfortable.' It is said that man is a creature of habit.

One could see that a fixed and successful routine might become a superstition, and it might be bad luck to change it. Two immediate reasons to stay with a routine are, firstly, why change a successful preparation, especially before an important competition? And secondly, the fact that a routine is known and familiar provides a more settled environment within which to work on calm, clear, positive thoughts of a forthcoming contest.

Some in this group cited small quirks. Billie Jean King said that she had her own peculiar routine to which she adhered. Barry John said that he always put his right shoe on first. Heather McKay said she was not really superstitious but did carry around a four-leaf clover with her for the last twenty years, having replaced it many times!

Joan Benoit, while not feeling that she was superstitious, did have two recurring dreams which happened before major marathon races; usually she found that was a good sign. 'If I don't have one of those recurring dreams before a big race then I kind of wonder if I'm going to perform well. One dream is a race that's held in a small European village or in a department store. In the store, I'm running up and down escalators and stairs, hallways and corridors, and I get lost and the race is going on and I can't find the rest of the course. The same thing happens in the village: I can't find the path. The other dream is where I'm running very fluidly and all of a sudden I can't run and I start to walk and from a walk I go to a crawl, from a crawl I go to trying to move myself on my belly and then at the last minute, I'm hanging off a cliff, trying to hold on for dear life . . . those dreams usually signal a good race.' The anxiety level is obviously high in both dreams. As a stable and easy-going person, Joan has experience of controlling her emotions before a big race. Dream analysts would no doubt have much to say about how personally important the coming race was to Joan. It certainly indicates that her arousal level was working subconsciously to prepare Joan for a good performance if she could maintain her personal control. She obviously did!

Approximately 20 per cent said that they were superstitious, some mentioning certain aspects. Rodney Pattisson said that he and most sailors would not have green on their boat. Bryan Robson spoke of his shirt having to be number 7. Arnold Palmer said that he always had a new pair of shoes for a big competition. J.P.R. Williams did not like the warm-up practice to go too well. 'It'll be all right on the night, you don't need all your best plays before the game starts.'

Lucinda Green spoke first of her superstitions and then of her view of being lucky, making that work for her by working hard on everything. 'I'm very superstitious. The same old shirt, same old socks, same old T-shirt, for the last seven years, and the number 7 – although I don't really have an unlucky one because I'm a lucky person. I believe strongly that you get as much as you give and if you've just been a bit slack along the line, you won't get what you want. You put into it and often you don't get what you want out of it, and you keep putting into it and you win in the end; and that is the thing I've learnt most, that when it seems that all the effort is to no avail, you are just being tested for that bit longer than you thought was possible.'

Do you consider yourself lucky to have been in the right place at the right time? Nearly 90 per cent of this group agreed that they were, saying that they felt they had been very lucky to find their right sport and the people to help them. Some thought that they were in the right era, Stephen Hendry saying it was just when the boom in his sport started. Kip speaks for most of us saying, 'I'm happy with my time.' Some said that it had been a fortunate coincidence of timing.

Stefan Edberg's thoughts of his good fortune came when things weren't going too well; acknowledging and appreciating how lucky he really is. 'I think so, very lucky. Sometimes you have to think about it, because sometimes when you play tennis you sort of live in your own world – wanting to win, wanting to do that. And you'd better say to yourself, "Hey, you're healthy. You've got a great job. You're out there doing a job that many people would love to do instead of yourself. You've got a lot of friends. What more can you ask?" Those sorts of things come to your mind when everything's going against you.'

Most of the performers realized that they had been very fortunate but they also knew that they had contributed to their own good fortune. The proverb that God helps those who help themselves was in evidence. Billy Beaumont said, 'You make things happen for yourself.' Wayne Gretzky said, 'You make your own fate.' Rodney Pattisson similarly said, 'You make your own luck.'

Duncan Goodhew has a view that each individual has talent and the lucky ones are those who find it. 'I think probability would show that almost everyone is good at something or has the possibility to be. I think you are lucky to discover it and are extremely lucky and maybe shrewd to recognize it at the time and then the rest is the follow-through.' Herb Elliott knew that it was particularly lucky for him when he met his coach Percy Cerutty, but he also knew that there were many different routes to the top and that maybe it could have been done another way.

One who did not think that she was necessarily in the right place at the right time was Billie Jean King, saying that she wished that she was starting today. She equated herself with Arnold Palmer as pioneers in their sports, and in spite of their years of playing, they have earned nowhere near the money of the stars of today. She also thought that she would have thrived on the tour set-up of today.

For some, luck plays no real part and their belief could be summed up in Gary Player's now famous remark: 'It's funny, you know, the more I practise, the luckier I become!'

A couple of aspects stand out from these replies. There is a general recognition that success relies on proper timing and opportunity. Also it is necessary to consider how you can influence your own future fortunes by taking personal responsibility for appreciating the good things we have, including health, and the opportunity of life itself.

Summary of learning points:

- Quote: 'It's funny you know, the more I practise, the luckier I become!' God helps those who help themselves.
- Probability would show that almost everyone is, or has the possibility to be, good at something.
- Success relies on proper timing and opportunity. We can take responsibility for helping ourselves here, but it should also be appreciated how important it is to provide opportunities for aspiring youngsters.

22
GAMESMANSHIP

Sport is a microcosm of life. We see in sport all the social problems we have off the field – social and performance enhancing drugs; verbal abuse and physical intimidation of officials and other performers; racism; sexism; financial exploitation of performers and performers' exploitation of their situation. We also have expression of the best of human traits – cooperation, mutual trust, balance, a striving for excellence in mind, body and spirit, Olympic idealism. At every level we have opportunity to make choices and to learn from action in those choices. What better place for youngsters to learn and practise values than in the sports arena? Like life, we should enjoy it and do the best we can with the talents and opportunities we're given. The sports arena is the perfect scene to check ourselves. It is an agreed area where we can leave our baggage outside. We can't hide. Every play shows us how committed we are and what we're thinking and doing or not doing. Parents, teachers, administrators, coaches and participants have a responsibility to see sport for the opportunity it provides. Learning to play within the written rules and the spirit of a game may well be a more important lesson for life than any of us first realize.

From a behaviour research viewpoint, sport has been described as a walking laboratory without dials. Much can be learnt from the level of behaviour which we find acceptable in sport. This is because it holds an unusual separateness from the outside world. The rules of sport do not change across social, economic, political or religious differences between people. With the option to participate open to almost all, there is the possibility for a study of behaviour and ethics. Violence erupts only where there is over-intensity of emotion. Drug-taking to enhance performance only takes place through an over-intense desire to be competitive. Sport provides a testing environment, and the test is whether the participants can learn to control their emotions and their competitiveness – to channel them into enhanced performance rather than the debasement of the individual.

Did you ever employ gamesmanship, and if so where would you draw the line? Moral principles are often not clear-cut. Where does a competitor draw the line in trying to win or gain an advantage? Is the 'professional foul' really professional? For example, holding a faster player's shirt when marking them, or intentionally bringing down a player who has made a breakaway and will probably score. In 1990 the English Football Association brought in tighter rules, asking referees to dismiss players from the game for blatant intentional fouling when it impedes a player who would otherwise almost certainly score.

Twenty years ago a survey by Professor Heinila of Finland showed that 70 per cent of English professional footballers accepted behaviour such as handling the ball when the referee had not seen it, or gaining a penalty kick for their team by acting as if they had been badly fouled. I would like to see a follow-up study because my impression is that change is happening. Gary Lineker, exemplifying fair play, was made captain of England, and in the previous summer's 1990 World Cup England received the 'fair play' award and, sign of a growing awareness of the problem, there was considerable commentary on the unfairness of fouls and play-acting injury. Diego Maradona, to name one culprit, demonstrated the best and the worst of football. At one moment he was displaying dazzling skill which inspires emulation and within seconds he was feigning serious injury after taking a dive! Television is helping to 'spot the cheats'.

In my study of high achievers, the cross-section of sports and the high calibre of performers combined to produce a very different percentage. More than 60 per cent said that they would not employ gamesmanship at all. And the figure for those who would not intentionally foul or cheat is over 80 per cent. With such a wide variety of sports, several types of illustrations and reasons were given as to why performers would and would not use such tactics, and where they would draw the line.

Gamesmanship has been defined as talk or conduct to put one's opponent off. As stated in the statistics above, the majority of these highest achievers simply said no, they would not intentionally employ any gamesmanship. Ed Moses said, 'I never got involved in that.' Billy Jean King said, 'You've got to get your own act together, to be great.' Ginny Leng added, 'Please someone tell me if I am!' Stefan Edberg said, 'I've had a few sportsmanship awards. Cheating hasn't been any part of my life. I like fair play. In tennis some people will stall for more time. I wouldn't feel good doing things like that.'

Both Faldo and Scudamore raised the issue of karma, the fact that

what you give is what you get; everything balances out in the end. Nick said, 'I've never tried to employ it at all because I've always believed it will have its come-uppance on you. It will get you back. I've had it done to me occasionally and I think if it ever comes out that it's been done deliberately, it's just devalued the other person who's done it to you.'
Peter referred to the fact that in his sport there is no draw for positions at the start. 'Within reason you want to get to the inside. Basically you want the clearest run you can get over the shortest possible route. And you can be going down the inside sometimes and there can be someone in trouble behind you, running away or hanging, asking, as we say, for a bit of light. And very often I'll give it, and let the person up the inside, because if you find yourself saying, "Sod it, I'm not going to let them pass", something happens to you. You have to be as hard as you can, but it's those little decisions you make.'

Billie Beaumont said that he was prepared to do everything within the laws, then added, 'I might bend them slightly but I'd draw the line at cheating. If I can hurt a player with a fair tackle that's okay but if he had his back to me, I'd never kick him in the back of the head or hit him because that doesn't appeal to me – it's a question of the ethics of the game really.'

From this survey it would appear that team games provide more opportunity and temptation to have a go at the opponents than do individual sports.

Des Drummond said that his form of gamesmanship had been to appear to be tired, puffing heavily or acting uninterested and catching the opposition off guard, so that when the ball came to him, he was gone. He did not like the dirty play after a tackle where mud was rubbed in his face or a rabbit punch given, just to get him angry enough to concentrate on getting back the other fellow. 'If you're concentrating on getting the other player back, the centre is running past you on the inside. I don't like the kicking and stamping on hands and legs, trying to put a player out of the game. I've had fights because you can only take so much but I wouldn't initiate the violence. I was suspended for five weeks for defending myself in 1983. A fellow was trying to scratch my face and had his fingers in my mouth, so my instinctive reaction was to bite his finger. A punch-up followed and I was suspended for five matches and he got three! . . . The crowds come to watch a good game – but they also like a good fight.'

Barry John said that he saw gamesmanship in terms of faking the other player, such as pretending to pass and not doing so, which was part of the game, but he did not consider this extended to faking or conning the referee. He gave an example which was also mentioned by Gareth Edwards and J.P.R. Williams, so the feelings of injustice obviously ran deep. An incident happened during the 1978 rugby match with the New Zealand All Blacks. The game was close and with two minutes remaining, Wales led 10–9. Then during a line out, as the ball was being put into play, Andy Hayden and Frank Oliver, two of the New Zealand players, ejected themselves from the line, each acting as if he had been shoved or hit when in fact, film replay showed that no body contact had been made. However, a penalty kick was awarded and because of it, New Zealand won the game 12–10. Gareth Edwards felt aggrieved to discover that the incident had been a premeditated plan to cheat. 'It might be splitting hairs because it might still be cheating, but I would say that if someone takes it on themselves to do a "Hollywood" in the heat of the moment, I can understand that, but I was really disappointed to read in Graham Mourie's book *Captain*, that he said it had been decided that if things were going badly for them, this was a tactic they would employ. It was preconceived and as much as I liked the man and admired him as a player, he'd gone down in my estimation for saying that. Now I might be naive but I never remember being on a team where anything like that was discussed. We would always talk about what we'd be trying to do on ability alone.'

Gareth was one of those who said that he did occasionally employ his own forms of gamesmanship. He said it was never premeditated but that at international level, rather than sit back, he met fire with fire including conning the referee. He said in the cold light of day it may be called cheating, but he would collude in a con of the opposition in an attempt to cause his opponent to commit a penalty offence. He would tell his scrum hooker to wait for the ball and he would make a gesture, slapping the ball as if it was being put into play and cause the opponent to lift his foot early and thereby receive a penalty. Gareth added, 'You don't necessarily have to do it to succeed but you have to be very much aware of it.'

In athletics where contact is rare, Steve Ovett said that he saw a race like a game of chess. 'Gamesmanship, if it's in the mind, is beautiful in the sense that you can use your mind and body in conjunction. You are using them in the same way as you can imagine chess – your body is the piece and your mind the player; if you can use that when you're under par or in a difficult situation, then all the better. I think I draw the line when it comes to physically damaging someone else in a sport.'

Those in favour of intimidation tactics aim to upset the confidence and concentration of the opponent. The form can be verbal, visual, physical or psychological intimidation. Sean Kerly said, 'The game is policed by umpires. You do what you can get away with. The game [of hockey] is supposed to have no physical contact but there's a lot of pushing and shoving. People hit me and you can get wound up.' Sean went on to recall a personal lesson from the start of his international career. 'The first time I played for England an Australian full-back hit me in the face. I was so shocked that I had to come off. The next time, I got angry with him. At the end of the game I was so angry and wound up by the whole thing I called him names. He went for me saying, "Sean you've got to learn to win as well as how to lose." Basically he was saying, whatever happens on the pitch happens on the pitch and is part of the game. I've never forgotten that. He was trying to sort me out and I've never done it again. I'm a good winner and a good loser.' From this story Sean illustrates his rapid learning of self-control as well the importance of not holding a grudge. Nevertheless I feel sympathy with Sean's feelings of injustice. Is unprovoked aggression acceptable in this game or in society? Certainly players should normally leave policing to the referee and not take the law into their own hands; however, that in no way reduces each individual's responsibility to police themselves.

In cricket one form of gamesmanship is the bouncer, which is definitely aimed to intimidate. Ian Botham accepted that he used both verbal and eye contact to attempt to intimidate and also just an aggressive, threatening demeanour directed towards the opposition. 'I'll give as good as I take and at times I'll instigate it verbally. I'm a great believer in when in Rome do as the Romans. For instance, if I play against the West Indies, there's no gamesmanship because that's the way they play, whereas against Australia, gamesmanship is important. You can also do it by appearing aggressive or showing your aggression, just letting it flow through – the odd stare doesn't hurt, things of that order. The Australians are past masters at it and I can say that I'm one of the few Englishmen that have hardly ever been slagged off on the cricket field by an Australian because they have a love–hate relationship with me. They know that it will fire me up; it's not going to detract from my performance, it's only going to improve it and that can also rub off on the rest of the team. Where I would draw the line is that I would never blatantly cheat. Oh, I'll go after an lbw appeal that I think is close enough for a shout and I'll have a jolly good shout . . . When I say I would never cheat, that's not true because when the Australians play this game they have this great belief that if you nick the ball, you stand and let the umpire make the decision and I think if that's good enough for them, that's good enough for me; but if you do that, you've got to be prepared to take the bad decisions with the good . . . I think there's no point in cheating and then complaining when you get a bad decision against you, so I think you've got to take the rough with the smooth.'

Duncan Goodhew said that for him the gamesmanship line was drawn when the whistle was blown. 'If someone tried to intimidate me after the whistle blew, I became nasty. I mean, in America, when you're under starter's orders and they'd try to break your concentration by coming to shake hands and wish you good luck, I'd swear at them. It was something I would never have said in any other situation – they were cheating and I told them where to get off.' About his own form of intimidation Duncan said, 'There was a chap called Graham Smith who was the most aggressive person I ever met. Nobody went close to him before a race, he used to break chairs and beat things. When I tried to mimic that, I found that it didn't work for me but I did find that it had an effect on other people. So what I started doing was ignoring people, making a conscious effort to ignore people and act as if I was getting aggressive and it became a kind of routine, ritual almost, and I found it was really affecting people because they'd start looking at me and not at themselves. I think that's one of the reasons I won the Olympics because I intimidated the Russians even before I got there. I'd swum so fast throughout the year they saw that I didn't have a weak spot. They tightened the thumbscrews by saying that I was the only guy who was going to win the 100m breaststroke, hoping that the pressure would get to me but it all seemed to work for me – they were totally intimidated by being ignored.'

Jonah Barrington used to eye his opponent. 'When I went to serve after a particularly long rally, I would give him what is known as "the stare", which in itself would probably reduce some people to a moan but did put quite a few people at a disadvantage. They were aware that I was dominating them and in a clinical fashion assessing how well they were coping at that point. I would definitely draw the line at cheating. If I knew that the ball bounced twice I would never, ever, play on because I considered that was cheating. I also feel that in a game where the interpretation of the rules is so difficult, there is a terrific responsibility on each player to play fairly. For example, it's in the rules that a player must make every effort to keep the game flowing and these days a growing number of players make no effort and in a premeditated fashion bring the game to a grinding halt.' Jonah cited the tactics used on him. He had based his game on ultra fitness and usually wore his opponents down. He said that his opponents intentionally broke the rule which says that play must be continuous. In order to get inside his head, they would obstruct him continually and give themselves a breather.

Geoff Hunt said, 'It was very rare that I'd ever talk on court. Just occasionally, if my opponent hit the tin and he was winning at the time, I'd say, "Right, that'll cost you the game" and then I'd change the tactics and try really hard for a few rallies. The fact that I won a couple of those rallies was because I'd changed my tactics and applied myself.'

John Newcombe used the element of surprise to intimidate the opponent on an important second serve. 'If you do it all the time, it loses its psychological force. I had a very strong forehand. Say we've been playing for two hours and on a big point the guy misses his first serve, goes back to serve the second, looks up and sees me standing in the alley [tramlines]. He knows I'm going to hit a forehand and that he can't reach my backhand. I'd call that gamesmanship. It's subtle because you've actually chosen the moment to use that tactic. I never consciously went on to the court wondering how I'd psyche the guy out there.'

J.P.R. Williams said that he would drop the odd comment when changing ends in tennis, such as, 'You're going to serve a few doubles soon.' He added, 'I always looked on that as fair psychological warfare. In rugby there's a lot of talk that goes on on the field, but I think that's an acceptable part of the game really. I think I draw the line with physical intimidation. There's a very fine line in rugby. I think it's fair comment to hit somebody as hard as possible and try to hurt them when they are coming towards you; but if they haven't got the ball, then it's not fair play. So it's playing as flat out as you can, both physically and mentally, but within the rules.'

Peter Snell recalled his coach inviting Tom O'Hara, one of his main Olympic 1500m opponents, to run in an 800m time trial. Peter ran 1 min

47.8 sec and believed it psychologically shattered Tom. 'He didn't even make the final. He ran about 1 min 52 sec which is okay for a time trial.'

Torvill and Dean's form of intimidation was that each time they practised at the competition site, they skated right through their programme, as if they were in competition giving an exhibition. They were not going to stop and start, publicly repeating any fragmented image or giving any impression that it was anything short of complete, but skate as close to perfection as was humanly possible. Chris said, 'In the week prior to competition, all the judges are there and other competitors can go in and watch. Our gamesmanship would involve going onto the ice very well dressed, as if it was the actual competition rather than just a practice session. Psychologically, the other competitors would see that and think, "Gosh, they're well prepared."'

Only two top achievers, Wayne Gretzky and Bryan Robson, said they would employ the 'professional foul'. Wayne Gretzky said, 'Usually I'm the one being held; it's part of the game, it goes with the territory I guess, but when I was younger I didn't like it at all. Now I believe you do anything to win. If you have to grab a guy from behind to stop him from scoring, you've got to do it; but I'd never try to injure somebody.' Bryan Robson held the same view. He has openly and obviously gone against the rules in dire situations, but he also said that he would not intentionally injure anybody or cheat behind the referee's back. 'In open play I don't think I'd use gamesmanship, but if someone went through with just the goal-keeper to beat and I could catch him by bringing him down, I'd bring him down. If I didn't, I'd feel I'd let my team-mates and my fans down . . . I've never been a player who, when the ref's back's turned would kick somebody or elbow somebody because they were getting an advantage on me. I'd never do that.' The football refereeing changes, mentioned at the start of this chapter, will undoubtedly have effect on this action.

There are, in my view, four levels of gamesmanship. The first level includes those who could not, under any definition, be considered breaking any rules of the game: e.g. a boxer after a painful punch, or a rugby player following a severe tackle, or a cricketer hit by a bouncer not showing that they've been hurt. The second level includes all those who were willing, to a certain extent, to indulge in conning the referee and who condoned that action by others if it was done in the heat of the moment. Gareth Edwards used the illustration of the All Blacks game to denote where he drew the line. There is an understandable difference between a player's action in the heat of the moment and the premeditated cheating referred to before. However, in the eyes of the law, the only difference would be in the degree of wrongdoing. The rules exist to make the game as fair and equal as possible. Any rule infringement lessens the status of the individual and the game. The third level is in the open field, as referred to by Wayne Gretsky and Bryan Robson, and involves the 'professional foul'. Both of these men are a credit to their sport and play more cleanly than the average professional in their respective sports. However, both said that if they could, they would bring down a player who had made a breakaway and only had the goal-keeper to beat. My personal belief is that if you can't win fairly, you don't deserve to win. Once the rules have been broken, even by only a small margin, the game has been changed. The line has to be drawn somewhere. If the rules are wrong, have them changed for everyone, but while they exist they make the game all that it is. If it became known that a politician cheated on his taxes, then the average man in the street would feel more justified in doing the same. It is my belief that the performers who are right at the top of their sport have to set the best example possible because it is absolutely certain that the youngsters of tomorrow will be following and copying every move their high achieving role models make today. The fourth level, I am pleased to say, did not include any of this study's achievers. I refer to those performers who foul with the intent of ending another player's career. It serves no purpose to give gruesome illustrations of the injuries which have ended great performers' careers. The people who indulge in that type of intentional, premeditated action should not be allowed to return to the competitive sports field. Their actions are criminal and have no place in sport.

Where should the line be drawn in gamesmanship? Some performers spend a lot of time and energy pushing at the line and testing the rule enforcement. Some spend more time focusing on playing the rules than playing the game. We see a parallel in life with individuals searching for loop-holes in laws which are intended for the greater good of the whole. In sport, if most of your mental effort goes into how you can get away with something or cheat somebody else, little attention is being given to what you could be improving.

Peter Sterling said that he had changed his views. 'In my early days, I used to try to put my opponents off their game, saying things like, "I didn't know you were still on" or "Look at the score" – something silly, but as I came into contact with better coaches, it was explained to me by a person I knew and respected that it was also putting me off my game because my mind wasn't where it should have been.'

David Bryant pointed out that intent was an important issue. For example, was the intent to bring yourself on or to put your opponent off? 'You have to be honest with yourself in order to make it to the top. I want what's mine. I don't want what's not mine and my good name is worth more to me than any result. In my opinion it comes down to having confidence in your own ability and not having to stoop to games-manship.' A similar sentiment was expressed by Rod Laver who was direct in his approach. 'I wanted to beat them at their best and I let my racket do the talking.' As stated at the start, nearly two-thirds of these high achievers were against any form of gamesmanship.

Carl Lewis was only too aware of the gamesmanship which was employed on him. In most books it would simply be called bad sportsmanship or cheating, because time and again he would find that the other high school competitors had moved the marker from where he would start his long jump approach. His own approach was not to get involved with that, but he added a very mature philosophical approach to competitive sport. 'Winning is not the aim, only a part of the whole. You have talent, you work within that talent and that's it. We're not out here to win, we're out here just to do our best and winning is a part of it, so let them do their best.'

It was the opinion of several performers that because of their ability they didn't have to indulge in cheating. They thought that the ones who most indulged in cheating to get an edge were those who doubted their own abilities.

Apart from not believing in the use of gamesmanship, Lynn Davies said, 'I just don't believe that at the highest level, the kind of guys you're competing against are susceptible to gamesmanship. I think the main gamesmanship is trying to convince yourself that you can do it.' An added point here is the reaction Ian Botham mentioned. If you goad a top performer in some way he or she is just as likely to move up a gear rather than be deflated.

Bobby Charlton said that he would not personally employ games-manship but could understand it in some cases. 'I never accepted anyone pulling my shirt. If you run past a defender and beat them fairly for pace and they just stand in front of you and catch you, that I can't forgive, but if I'd beaten a lad for pace and he tried to chase me and realized he couldn't do it and he'd maybe pulled me down, I could half forgive that because he could have stopped me unfairly in the first place and it was a last resort. Everyone's in the game to make a living and I don't think it's unforgivable. Nobody is perfect. Personally, I wouldn't do it but it's not in my make-up. My philosophy is live and let live, but I was not a defender or a hard tackler and I think the game needs them just the same.'

Clive Lloyd spoke of his opposition to intimidation. He was against the use of gamesmanship and said that he thought that players had over-used it. His concern was the name calling by opponents to get their team psyched up. 'Comments like, "Come on, let's get this black bastard" are just plain abuse. I'm not saying that I can't take it but it's been over-used. I don't think being abusive to other players is right.'

Summary of learning points:

- Sport is a microcosm of life, holding the potential for the best and the worst. As such it has enormous potential as a learning environment.
- Learning to play within the written rules and the spirit of a game can be a valuable lesson for life.
- Gamesmanship can take many forms – from not showing hurt or the performers exuding confidence to criminal intent to injure.
- Karma is a fact of life. You will get back what you give. Everything balances out in the end.
- Cheating can backfire: e.g. putting someone else off distracts attention from getting the best from yourself. Also trying to get at an opponent may inspire them to rise to a higher level.
- Learning self-control and not holding grudges are invaluable lessons.
- Everyone must learn to take responsibility for themselves and their actions.
- If you choose to play only by the officials' rulings (e.g. not acknowledging a ball that is out, or a goal when you know that it was and the official is unsure or unsighted) then you must accept the unjust calls against you, without complaint. You can't expect to have it both ways.
- Breaking the rules even by the smallest margin is still crossing the line. If the rules are wrong, work to have them changed.

- Those who play the rules rather than the game will not be getting the most from themselves in the long run.
- You have to be honest with yourself to make it to the top.
- Keeping a good name is worth more than any result.
- Winning is only part of the whole.
- Thoughts of cheating show that you doubt your abilities.

23
DRUGS

The problem of drug-taking, to artificially improve sport performance, has been receiving increasing attention. International governing bodies of sport keep extending the list of substances which performers are not permitted to take. There are two problems: one is the grey area, the other the performer's overpowering desire to win. The grey area is, what constitutes drug-taking? Some banned substances originate in the human body and the excess is what is deemed illegal.

Many substances we ingest without even thinking that they contain ingredients which affect our moods, emotions and metabolism. Alcohol, coffee, tea and chocolate are just a few. We are all familiar with items such as decongestants, pain relievers and stomach settlers, all of which have performance-altering ingredients. Society today accepts as normal a certain level of drug-taking.

The medical profession makes a decision as to which drugs can be sold without prescription. The ones deemed to be potentially harmful, unless carefully monitored, are only available on prescription. Medical advisors also ally with the law in coming to terms with the social and hard drug scene. Statistics are frightening and public concern is increasing over the use and availability of all types of drugs to junior school age children and upwards.

If the sports world does provide a microcosm of society, should we be surprised to find drug-taking in its midst? In the United States, steps have been taken to monitor and reduce the spread of hard drugs in professional sport. The administrators realize that the image which these individuals project can be a strong role model for the young. They also realize that a tarnished image is going to be bad for business.

Medical advisors have to make difficult judgements: what is considered to be beyond the norm for health purposes? And what is excess? The British Olympic Association's medical advisor on drugs mentioned that one performance-enhancing drug is produced within our bodies, in excess, during our first hour of sleep, obviously producing an impossible rule-making situation. Also, just like the police being a step behind the criminal, those monitoring the use of artificial performance-enhancing drugs are one step behind the chemists researching their effects on humans.

What are your thoughts on the current drug scene in sport, specifically the use of performance-enhancing drugs? Have you ever experimented or been encouraged to experiment with them? Obviously current performers are not readily going to admit breaking the rules which could ban them from future participation in their sport. Nevertheless, the additional supportive evidence tended to lead one to believe that in almost all cases their answers were honest. There was virtually universal condemnation of drug usage. A few performers expressed understanding of the pressures and temptations and felt that the decision whether or not to get involved had to be left to an individual's morality. All saw the potential which drug-taking had for wrecking their sport, let alone their futures, if they were used. All but one denied ever having experimented with performance-enhancing drugs. In many sports the use of performance-enhancing drugs is virtually unknown – cricket, rugby union, motor racing, yachting, ice skating and squash are just a few. The performers who were competing before the mid-1950s would rarely have heard of drugs in sport. The advent of anabolic steroids came about through their use during the Second World War when patients were given these steroids to speed up the process of rehabilitation. Where the patient was weak, the drug would assist their body in putting on weight and generally stimulate the recuperative powers of the human system. The follow-on thoughts of some were, if it could do this for the sick, how much might it assist the healthy to perform enhanced feats. In about 20 per cent of cases, the side effects produced serious damage to the organs which were excreting the substance from the system, for example the liver, kidneys and urinary tract. The latest evidence identifies that in males, the prostate is the most lastingly affected area.

In the 1960s, the heavyweight activities were the most common areas of use: weightlifting, throwing events in athletics, and American football to name but a few. The premise was that whatever muscles were used they would be developed at a faster rate than normal, the key being that more work could be done because the steroid was assisting the recovery rate, and the water retention assisted their quest for more mass. In those early days, little emphasis was placed on the amount being taken, and as testosterone is produced in the male reproductive system, ingesting large quantities from outside the system supplanted the function of the body producing its own and as a result many males became impotent. This and other noticeable side effects apparently disappeared a short time after the users came off the drug. By the early 1970s, the pressure of competition moved the usage of this drug into the explosive running and jumping events as well as the endurance ones. In the 1980s, one advance, if it can possibly be referred to as that, was the development of a human growth hormone. This is a stimulant to the pituitary gland which promotes growth and is therefore irreversible. In 1990 it became public knowledge that EPO enhanced the oxygen-carrying supply for endurance events. Some cyclists died from its use. Some of the performers interviewed said that they understood the temptation facing today's top achievers. The ambition to win and in some cases the potential for substantial financial gain blinds them to either the potential physical damage or the moral issues of cheating or genetic interference.

Lynn Davies was the British athletics team manager during the 1980s. Although he was competing before the advent of widespread drug-taking in the sport, he expressed his understanding of the motivation to take drugs. 'I was competing in the early 1960s and we didn't experience drugs. We didn't even talk about them . . . I'm sympathetic to some extent to the whole approach to them because they are perceived to be a highly significant factor in winning in present day sport, not just in athletics. I think it's far more widespread than people think. I was never pressurized to take drugs and never wanted to take them because they just weren't part of the scene then, but what one gleans from conversations now with athletes and others is the pressures they feel if they are not taking them, the need to explore the possibility. To some extent, I think British athletes have felt second-class in terms of support services. This was most marked at the World Championships in Helsinki, this feeling of helplessness in terms of medical support and scientific monitoring of performance.' Having said that, Lynn added, 'I would like to see it wiped out.'

Al Oerter talked openly about his experimentations with the anabolic steroid testosterone before it became a banned substance. He recalled the problems which he experienced and illustrated the dangers of the human growth hormone. 'I found that with anabolic steroids I retained so much body weight, water weight primarily, that my blood pressure went through the ceiling. I thought I'd get off that before I killed myself. I also found no real difference in performance. It's a drug that increases your aggression. It almost levelled everything off for me because in competition I was always fairly aggressive, but when I became equally aggressive in my daily life, I found that very uncomfortable. It just wasn't me. I had to be able to relax and enjoy the 99.9 per cent of my life when I wasn't in the discus ring in competition.' Oerter continued, 'The nature of the performer today is quite different. It's instant gratification which is required today and if it's their belief that a drug can help them gain immediate recognition they're going to take those drugs. The rewards are there. Previously, the reward was strictly recognition, and came out of long periods of work rather than short bursts of high chemicals. I still think that virtually the same level is attainable naturally but it takes a longer period of time to reach it.' Al expressed particular concern about the human growth hormone. 'Those drugs are so damn dangerous. They began by using an extract from the rhesus monkey and some athletes began to develop the properties of the monkey, protruding forehead, expanding jaw and problems such as a perfectly functioning ball and socket joint which would somehow get out of shape and create a long-term arthritic condition. Now they're taking it out of human cadavers [corpses], so those particular problems are gone, but the doctors I've talked to say that the performers who are on these things are still experiencing tremendous growth. Even with mature people the bones start growing again. The first problem that they're seeing is that the performer's heart is expanding. I don't know whether the heart muscle will go back later on. I suspect that they're going to have long-term difficulties with it . . . they're really messing around with nature. Male hormones or something like that might make you more aggressive, but once you are off them, you return to your normal personality and size, but with human growth hormone the long-term effects are absurd. Your body just doesn't return to where it was. The performers are looking at this risk/reward ratio much more, much differently than they did in the past. They are saying, in effect, forget the risk because the rewards are there.'

The exposure of Ben Johnson as an anabolic steroid taker at the 1988 Olympics prompted a swift response calling for greater random testing worldwide. It is moving in the right direction but it has certainly not scared off the search or usage. Many internationals from various countries have been caught since. One of the saddest by-products is the question marks left over every great achiever. As Peter Scudamore said, that creates a real problem because then all real achievements become suspect. 'Any great achiever is automatically accused. Martin Pipe's horses achieved so much, he started to be accused by people saying, "They must be using something." So they were dope-tested and cleared, so then they say, "Oh they must be on something which can't be detected", which leaves a nasty taste in my mouth because it takes something away from the achievement.' Peter continued by expressing his own values and beliefs. 'Being a horse person you have to be green-minded, nature-minded, because you have to be close to the horse. And to improve a horse's performance by the use of drugs takes away the whole nature of the game, I think. By being involved with a horse you're trying to go back to nature not go to the laboratory!'

There is no doubt that some of the top performers have been taking drugs to assist the amount of training they can undertake; however, it is also the case that many others are not. It is interesting to see the athletes' performances in relation to the important games where they will be drug-tested. It was quite common to see performances in certain events substantially drop off. Athletes must get off their detectable drugs some weeks prior to the tests in order for these drugs not to show up. In that time some of the anabolic steroid effects will have reduced and the performances slip.

It is good to be able to cite a well-known exception. Perhaps the athlete most likely to take ergogenic aids would be the decathlete; he is, after all, cited as the man who has the greatest all-round ability and must master ten events. Daley Thompson won two consecutive Olympic titles and the World Championships in that event, each time producing personal best performances. He is known to be against taking even an aspirin, and was an early crusader against the use of drugs, volunteering himself as an athlete willing to undergo unannounced drug testing. He expressed his feelings as follows: 'I think it's terrible. It's bad for the sport in general. It's bad for the kids coming into the sport because they feel that the only way they can get on is by taking all the drugs that they suppose most of the people are taking, especially here in the US [where Daley spends time training]. I must admit I understand why people take the stuff. They want to win almost as badly as I do, so I mean, I can understand. That's why I'm glad I don't have to do anything like that. I don't need to. You see, most of those things enable you to work harder – I don't want to work any harder. I can understand that if I wasn't as good, I might, but I have no need to, so it never occurs to me. I feel sorry for those who have to go that far . . . most of those taking it are not quite good enough – they're fifth or sixth or tenth in their country or the world.'

That statement has turned out to be an underestimate. Occasional world record holders have been caught since 1988 and with the dissolution of the East German sports institutes exposure has come of drugs being issued to their world-beating athletes.

Apart from Daley, several other achievers referred to their dislike of any form of drugs, right down to aspirin. This clean approach was expressed by Wayne Gretzky. Wayne said that he refused to allow DMSO (dimethyl sulphur oxide, a liquid which is rapidly absorbed into the body's tissue and is claimed to have assisted in numerous medical cases from soft tissue injury to rheumatism) to be administered to the shoulder injury which kept him out of action for three weeks, because the Canadian Medical Association were not yet sure whether there were any side effects.

J.P.R. Williams is a medical doctor and gave his medical, as well as personal, opinion. 'Talking as a doctor now, we should let the athletes know what are the side effects and potential consequences of anabolic steroids and leave it to the performers themselves to decide whether they are going to take them. The interesting thing is that most of them will still take the chances. You know how single-minded athletes are in particular; they don't care about the future if they can get a gold medal. I don't know what the answer is because I don't believe in drugs but on the other hand I don't believe in hypocrisy. The anabolic steroids have not been proved to increase strength but what they do is to allow you to train more times a day and harder. In other words you are enhancing your ability to train harder . . . I don't agree with them. I would never take them myself because I know the potential problems. A lot of them at the moment are thought to be reversible, like high blood pressure and liver problems. It's very frightening . . . I'll never prescribe them to anyone but you know this is going on.'

Three of the points made by J.P.R. Williams were brought out by top athletes. Firstly, the dangers are there and should be heeded. A second point made by J.P.R. was that these drugs simply allow one to train harder. Many athletes pointed out that they achieved their success without drugs simply by working hard over a long period of time. Ed Moses and Steve Ovett both referred to the time factor. Ed said, 'I hung in long enough to reach this level. At Moorehouse State, we barely had a set of weights. No one ever offered steroids to me until I came to California [after his 1976 Olympic victory]. I'm all against it. I know that hard work has got me to where I am and I will never consider it, never have considered it and never had any urge to experiment or try it or anything. I know it's dangerous from what the doctors say . . . I have high school students asking me what they should do. People are trying to get them to take them. I just tell them that I've never tried it; that it's dangerous, you never know what's going to happen, and if you're thinking about a scholarship to an educational institution and they are approaching you now, just think what will happen when you get there and you don't want to do it.' Steve Ovett referred to the third point made by J.P.R.: that it is up to each individual to decide. Steve said, 'It's solely and purely up to the individual. I don't think you can enforce rulings on drug-taking, it's been done outside sport in narcotics and the results are disastrous. I believe that if an individual feels he needs to take a drug to succeed then that individual is the one who has to live with it at the end of the day. If he walks off at the end of the day with three gold medals round his neck and he knows he's got them because of X, Y and Z drugs, then he's the one that's got to live with that. It's never really interested me and I've never been encouraged to try them because I've been successful without things like that.'

Carl Lewis was another who was of the opinion that it was up to each individual's conscience but that there should be a constructive programme to try to rid sport of it. 'People are taking drugs. We know that. It's more prevalent now than it was but I don't think as many people take it as everyone thinks. You don't really necessarily have to take them to be the best; Edwin's [Moses] not, I'm not. But who am I to tell somebody that they can't take drugs to be the best they can be? If they're doing what they think is right to be the best, then that's right because it comes from within inside. But of course, there are rules so you can't do it . . . I shouldn't be running around saying you shouldn't take steroids; what I'm trying to do is help support the programmes that are against it and that's the only way we're going to fight the problem. We're not going to fight it finger pointing. We've got to say, let's start a programme against steroids and start making appearances, start being tested, so we can show the kids in particular that you don't have to take them to be a great athlete. I don't take them. And I'd test everyone. I've always said I think everyone who sets a world record or national record should be tested the day they set the record. We need to get people involved.' This suggestion has since been taken up.

Ken Read felt strongly about drugs and saw it as an issue of cheating. 'An element that gets forgotten is that it's cheating. It's not a question of physical enhancement. It's unhealthy and it's against the rules. It's totally unacceptable.' Kip Keino had similar feelings. 'I think it's bad. You are not competing as one human being against another. You have something else to compete against with the drugs. And it doesn't show that that's human achievement, it's drug achievement and you may be also ruining your future life. You have to consider the longer period. You never know in the future, it might be damaging anything in your body. You will not be running and playing other sports at that level all your life. It's a very short period and why do you ruin your body? It is your life and life is very important. One day for a few minutes and it's all over; even if you break the world record today, tomorrow someone else will break it. It's not going to stay up there permanently.' At this point I said to Kip, 'Some would say that the one time world record could set you up for life.' Kip replied, 'Well, you may not enjoy that life! You may have the money, because of what you've taken [chemically]. It's easy to take, but cure is the problem! It may damage so don't risk it. The somebody giving it to you, he might not be using it. He may want to give you money, but you might spend more later, trying to get better!' I was certainly another who could not have lived comfortably with myself if I had won by cheating, through drugs or any other means.

Steve Cram was indignant that not enough was being done to put a stop to drug-taking. 'Until they start giving out life bans that are real life bans then it will continue. It's a ridiculous situation to have. The problem is, as certain people are allowed to do it, then the pressure on everyone else is for them to do it. I've purposely never been involved.' In athletics, the International Federation has allowed banned drug offenders back into the sport within two years of their offence. My own view is that a ban for less than four years is not a real punishment for an Olympic performer, as they will be permitted to return for the next Games.

Duncan Goodhew also saw the need for wider testing and harsher rule enforcement. 'My current feeling is, I think we're going to have to take drug testing to small meets, unexpectedly, and try and clobber as many people as possible. "Banned for life" should be totally irrevocable. To have somebody back who has been on steroids is a disgrace. No. In swimming, when I was competing, I took the attitude of "let others take it"; it's a weakness and if you feel you have to take drugs, you are at a psychological disadvantage.'

Peter Sterling said that the Australian sporting public were aware of steroids but that he had never seen anybody in his club take drugs. 'I would never do it. I'd be disappointed in myself if I ever had to resort to that. It's probably a sign that you haven't got much further to go.'

Jonah Barrington was personally against it but realized the dilemma for coaches with gifted young athletes. 'I think it's dreadful. I'm appalled by it. A journalist once asked me, "If I had a drug you could take which would win you another British Open Championship, would you take it?" I said, "No, because I would know that I had cheated." It's not a goody-goody thing. What I did was sheer hard work – blindly at times but increasingly systematic; hard work without having needles stuck into me or taking pills. It would be very difficult for me as a coach to know whether I would continue with someone who I felt had the ability to get to very near the top, but wasn't actually going to make it unless they took drugs.'

A non-drug medical issue greatly concerned Jonah. He said that young Tour de France cyclists were being pushed exceptionally hard while still in their teens and at a crucial stage in bone development. This and other stress-related concerns are being addressed by medical practitioners. Other endurance activities such as ultra long-distance running; intensity and impact activities, such as weightlifting; and hyper-extension activity, such as back extension in gymnastics, all are cited as having caused serious and permanent injuries. Awareness of the implications of health and injury prevention can be acquired through the British National Coaching Foundation.

A further drug concern has been the puberty-retarding drugs, reported to have been used on some Eastern European competitors. Since the time of Olga Korbut, the image required to win in gymnastics has changed to one of pre-pubescence. With the crumbling of the Eastern bloc one hopes that with it will end such practice. Even if it does, world-wide genetic engineering research continues outside of sport. I fear that it will not be long before science will offer us children of our choice, including such excesses as ranges of aggression and size. The responsibility of what we do with our scientific capabilities is best faced today, with our comparatively simple drug use issues.

It is pleasing to hear from these high achievers their belief that drug-taking is not wanted, and that the mind, will and dedication of the performer play just as large, if not a larger, part than purely physical talent. That is certainly my belief and experience. Drugs do work but I believe that our minds can be used to produce even greater results. Perhaps the best illustration is the emergency situation when a small woman saw her child run over. Many witnessed her, single-handedly, lift the side of the car so that the child could be pulled free from underneath. She suffered compression damage to her back, but the point is that even if she had taken performance-enhancing drugs, gone into training, and then was tested to measure what she could lift, the difference between the car and the weights would have been huge. This illustrates the potential of the aligned integration of single, clear goal focus (mind), desperate feelings (emotion) and total commitment (will) in action. Power flowed through her. Drugs were not needed.

It is to be hoped that a combination of education and sensible rule enforcement will allow sport to play the role it can in the future. Sport must retain elements of enjoyment, learning and human dignity. Drug-taking and other forms of cheating could so easily ruin sport, causing individuals and organizations to self-destruct. It can be hoped that each individual will use their conscience to guide their choice. Sport, at its best, is a visible demonstration of the exciting potential of the human mind, body and spirit.

Summary of learning points:

- Drugs in various forms are a part of our daily lives, in food and drink as well as medication.
- The variety of performance-enhancing drugs extends almost daily.
- All the top achievers wanted to see performance-enhancing drugs having no part in sport.
- Performers who take such drugs are running serious health risks, with unknown long-term effects.

Drugs

- Sport life is short; why run the risk of ruining your body for the rest of your life, and possibly losing your life?
- Although in several sports such drug-taking is unknown, in others it is unfortunately widespread.
- The desire to win was understood. The cost was questioned.
- Some saw it simply as cheating.
- The penalty for those caught was considered too lenient. Minimum bans of from four years to life were recommended.
- Ultimately, each of us must take responsibility for what we do. Let your conscience be your guide.
- Will you be able to truly appreciate your win if you know you cheated?
- A sad side effect created by the drug-takers is the question mark put over great 'clean' achievements.
- The top can be reached without drugs, it just takes longer.
- Mind, emotion and will aligned in action, on a single target, are capable of extraordinary feats.

24
RELIGIOUS AND MORAL
STANDARDS

It is clear from the statements in the last two chapters that the standards and values of these top achievers were generally high. Perhaps the teachings of their parents did have some effect; almost all had stressed fair play and keeping within the rules. Most codes of ethics have some basis in religious instruction, although many countries in the Western world pay only lip service to formal religion.

Did religious values, either through going to church, prayer, meditation or other non-formal religious aspects, ever have any influence on your sporting life? Although phrased broadly I believe many performers were off put by the words 'formal religion', and quickly said no. I wanted to touch on any spiritual perspective they might hold. The door was open for comment across the spectrum of what might or might not hold religious connotations.

Of these achievers, approximately 60 per cent did not think that religion, in any form, affected their sporting life. Several individuals in this group held some form of personal religious beliefs but felt that their sport was in no way mixed with that belief. Others were quite forcefully opposed to the mixing of sport and religion and a few were opposed to religion in general. In the 40 per cent who did find some assisting influence from religious belief, there was also a spectrum from those who referred to being on the right path for their life, to one or two others who were begging for assistance in a time of need! Many sports followers will have seen the film *Chariots of Fire* and some, myself included, will have identified with the belief of Eric Liddell that God-given talent is there to be developed to the best of our abilities.

Duncan Goodhew was one who strongly objected to those who prayed for divine intervention to help them to win. 'To me competing to win is the ultimate self-interest, although I believe it is sacrilege not to do it if you're good because that's an insult to your talent. But to pray to God for success or to say when you lose, "Well, God didn't mean me to win this time . . ." It makes me cringe because it's you praying to somebody for victory. That means you are praying to beat somebody, asking for divine intervention and to me that's wrong.' Al Oerter was very much of the same thinking. 'I find it difficult with some performers, boxers in particular, if they win the match, a microphone is stuck under their nose and the first thing they say is, "I want to thank God Almighty for helping me to beat my opponent." If there is a God, why would he or she or whatever not treat everyone equally? Why would the Deity help somebody to beat up on some other creature on earth? I find it difficult to understand . . . I know there is a God. I know there is something out there guiding me because every once in a while I feel that I've been nudged in a direction, but I don't have an appreciation of my religious life.'

Pat O'Callaghan felt that religion in sport was just a crutch: 'You're missing something within yourself.'

Bobby Charlton was another who did not think the two areas mixed but said that although he did not go to church regularly, he had attended church when he was younger and knew what religion meant. 'Whether you believe in God or not, the Ten Commandments are good rules to stand by.' Steve Cram referred to the indirect application of one's values. He had a reasonably strict moral code – basically Christian principles and values without going to church.

Daley Thompson and Torvill and Dean said that they believed in God, but neither asked for help nor thought that it had any influence on them.

Where do you think your values were taken from? This question was asked of top performers whose response to the first question was that values had not been taken from religion into their sport. In most cases, it was from the home. Steve Ovett referred to working-class values, Heather McKay spoke of home and Ken Read referred to the family.

Religious values were certainly not the criteria on which to judge standards of fair play. Geoff Hunt, for example, said that he had strictly scientific beliefs and was cited by Jonah Barrington as having the highest ethical standards of any player he knew. 'Just because the referee and marker had not called the ball down, he [Geoff] was so fair that at 7–7 in the fifth set he would call his ball down if he thought it was down.' Geoff said, 'My philosophy was, "I want to win and win fairly on the court." No one would even know, probably, that I won within myself and I didn't cheat on the court and I didn't give myself second bounces, even though my opponent may have done. I'd have more satisfaction in coming off the court having won. I'd get a bit cross at times when I saw them do it but it made me more determined to win and say, "Right, you couldn't even beat me with your cheating." That's the way I used to tackle it anyway.'

Rod Laver was not sure where the thought came from. He said he didn't think it was religious but he said, 'When I was down by two sets to one and by four games to one against Emerson at Wimbledon in 1962, the thought came to me that I was going to win the match! How does that get into your head? I don't necessarily put that down to religion. I put it down to your attitude of accepting where you are and if destiny says you should win the Grand Slam in 1962, then, given the chance, it will happen – as long as you want to work hard. You're not fated to it and you're not going to do it without an effort, but given all those combinations together, you can do it.'

Valeriy Borzov said that for him the State had the higher purpose. At the time of the Olympic final, his first thought was of himself, but later his feelings were for his country, for their training and support. Although this was predictable, national patriotism was by no means limited to the communist 'State' performers. As with Borzov, it was usually a secondary thought after self-fulfilment.

Almost all of the individuals interviewed who felt that they did gain benefit from their religious beliefs saw it giving them a more complete perspective on life and themselves. They were not usually asking for direct intervention, so objected to those who saw it as a crutch or sacrilege. John Whitmore said, 'During the period between my two racing careers, first I had a psychological, then a spiritual awakening. Not in a fanatical sense at all; I feel that a spiritual practice and spiritual values are just a part of my everyday living. It's not a separate thing. I don't see it as going to church on Sunday. It's integrated. I'd say my relationship with the bigger whole, the Universe as a unity, played an important role in my sense of confidence and security.' Clive Lloyd felt that his faith had a calming influence on him. 'My personal belief in Christ helped me quite a lot – as a human being, you tend not to get too annoyed. You can weigh up situations . . . and as they say, engage brain before putting mouth in motion.' Carl Lewis said that it gave him a perspective on life. 'It keeps me pretty level-headed because I realize that this is a God-given talent, like everybody else has, I believe that's what I have.'

In earlier discussions on personal sacrifice, reference was made by Herb Elliott to the connection he felt to striving for a higher cause. 'There was a certain connection with the mystics and Jesus and people who suffered as a result of their religion. I guess it was a way in which you could relate your suffering to a higher cause than just winning races . . . I did feel some sort of association with the Almighty God through my running. I felt in contact there. I think it helped. It gave a sort of total sense, a justification for what I was doing.'

Joan Benoit Samuelson also referred to her feeling of being closer to God while running. 'I consider myself to be a religious person. I have a great deal of faith in God. I don't spout it off or try to push my religion or faith in God on anyone. I have respect for anybody regardless of their religious preferences. I feel that God has been very good to me and my family and I think prayer and things like that have certainly helped. I go to church every Sunday but I think I've been closer to God in races and on training runs than I have in church. Prior to a race, my prayer is just to be at peace with myself and make myself happy and satisfied and those who are expecting good things of me. It's not to win, nor to set a record, it's just to run as well as I possibly can at that time and try to keep calm, tranquil and peaceful.'

Lucinda Green never prays to win, just to do her best and not hurt her horse. 'It's one of those things which keeps me on an even keel. I wouldn't go round preaching but it's one thing I have got to hang on to and say "Help".' Similarly Kip Keino said, 'I prayed to do my best and that helped my self-confidence.'

Gareth Edwards said that at times the prayers did become appeals. 'Please God help us to win this one and we won't ask for any more – hoping he was Welsh or British! It was really asking to be given a break, not making a deal. Give us the opportunity to show what we're made of.' He added that his religious beliefs did give him an inner strength. He also said that for five minutes before the start of the British Lions matches, the captain, Willie John McBride, would tell them, 'Now go and make peace with yourselves' and there would be five minutes of quiet in which everyone settled themselves. Psychologically, as well as spiritually, centring oneself before competition is very sound as it will enable greater calmness, focus, control and sense of purpose.

Billie Jean King had a good deal of religious involvement as a child and also in her teens, although that is not a part of her life now. She said that a significant influence on her had been a passage from the Bible about the need for faith to be combined with hard work in order to succeed.

Jackie Stewart spoke of the religious experience which took place at the time that he decided to end his motor-racing career. Part of his religious understanding came at the time of the violent and tragic death of his team-mate, François Cevert. 'When I made my decision to retire I didn't tell anybody. I made it in April but agreed to race through to October. My wife Helen had become very religious. I had never seen the value, never seen the results, if you like, of that strength. About a month after I'd made the decision to retire, I suddenly wondered if I could handle everything. I started to become very nervous about it – I'd been cocooned by the sport so completely, literally smothered with generosity. It was then that I ran into a situation where religion came to me. An Anglican priest in Indianapolis asked me if I'd ever been confirmed. I said, "No", and he said, "Would you like to be because maybe you can be helped?" I knelt on the floor of the motel room and he confirmed me and it was like somebody had saved me from drowning. I felt myself pulling out of it and I just knew categorically then that I was going to retire, that I was going to be happy, that I was going to get through . . . I felt totally comfortable. It didn't give me a recklessness but I had a very calm knowledge. On the day before my final race, the US Grand Prix, which was my hundredth, my team-mate was killed in practice. We were fastest and second fastest qualifying. It couldn't have hurt me in a more profound way had it been a member of my own family. He was killed right in front of me and I had to stop and go to him. It said to me, "Hey, never take anything for granted." Still nobody knew that I was retiring – it was the week after that I announced it. The whole thing – understanding of life, a comprehension of energy and power, a being there – was unaccountable. It was part of a basis of religious understanding or belief that hadn't made itself evident to me previously. I've really felt that communication exists.'

There is an unwritten rule that in polite conversation one does not mention politics or religion. I had wondered whether it was inappropriate to include an enquiry into religious and spiritual beliefs influencing these performers' sporting lives. I decided that I should because I felt that it had been helpful for me. I had been brought up in a family who valued the teachings of Jesus. Over the years I have continued reading, discussing and reflecting on religious philosophy, attempting to integrate my spiritual perspective with practical physical reality. Each individual will have his or her own understanding of what God, a life force, an intelligent energy and soul source, means to them, but I have valued the feelings of connection, particularly in difficult times, praying for guidance. I believe that there are right paths for everyone's life. We may stray from that path but we will soon have the choice to move onto a new right path. We can learn from each experience in life. It appears to me that similar testing situations keep repeating until we *get* the personal learning point. At every moment we have choices as to our direction and actions and in those decisions, we can choose to go off at a tangent, or move directly away or we can choose the best inner growth and development route for our lives. Every next decision repeats the options, infinitely giving us the choice for change.

Abraham Maslow said that individuals feel happiest while working to fulfil their potential and most frustrated and unhappy when not on that quest. He did not overtly put religion or spiritual aspects into his hierarchy of human needs, but he did refer to the development of each individual with the central theme being one of *transcendence*. This, I believe, is the evolutionary thrust of the human soul. The hierarchy of human needs moves from physical through social into psychological aspects and culminates with the open-ended fourth stage, referring to the development of the ideals in human values. These include items such as justice, honesty, being alive, integration, wholeness, uniqueness, simplicity, effortlessness, playfulness, self-sufficiency and many others. The most logical extension, in my perspective, is that the spiritual overview is the ultimate step in the sequence. The 'need drives' are constantly drawing each individual's soul through experiences by which it evolves. The body is the vehicle; the mind the active link between the two. I am not a body with a soul. I am a soul with a body.

At the Mexico Olympics, I felt very much on the right path for my life at that time. I was not praying that I be allowed to win but I prayed that I be enabled to do my best, and that I be in tune with my higher purpose in life, whatever that was to be in the future. I was feeling a great deal of self-imposed pressure and found that this sort of prayer gave me a sense of connection with some ultimate life force, which was very settling. It gave me a sense of peace and an almost tangible inner strength. For that time I was also very clear about my purpose. Having had this experience I did not want to omit this subject from my enquiry. For me it would be impossible to separate life in general from the development of talent and personal growth through my sport experiences. And with self-awareness and personal responsibility sport is a brilliant learning environment.

Summary of learning points:

- For some, religion provides a code to live by.
- Top performers have had to be honest with themselves in training and competition; there is no hiding place on the sports field. Perhaps this has assisted their general level of honesty and integrity.
- Some object strongly to performers seeking divine bias in their personal desire to win.
- Those who see religious belief assisting them, largely see it helping to give a larger life perspective into which sport is integrated.
- Some of these see their lives fitting into a bigger unified whole.
- Centring oneself before competition will assist personal calming, focus, control and sense of purpose. 'Go and make peace with yourself.'
- Being on a 'right path' for mind, body and spirit can provide a powerful feeling of being with the flow, rather than fighting against it.
- Those whom prayer or meditation has assisted have received feelings of calmness, confidence, security, connectedness with a higher purpose, control, peace, a more even keel, understanding, inner strength, clarity and comprehending.
- We can learn from all experiences; sport provides a special opportunity.
- Our human path is *transcendence*.
- We will be most happy while working to fulfil our potential.
- Life can be seen as a journey of the soul; the body is the vehicle of the soul and the mind links the two.

CONCLUSION

Throughout this book I have drawn out learning points or miniconclusions. I would not do justice to the subjects if I summarized the summaries. Instead I would like to pick out a few features which I find important, and make a few reflections and challenges.

To me it is obvious that throughout this survey we have been looking at human endeavour, something which transcends the outcome of any contest and is not limited to sport. I believe that if any of these individuals had put their thoughts, enthusiasm and energies into another area in which they had a reasonably good amount of talent, they could have become high achievers in that area. Interestingly, they are all very 'normal' people. They are not freaks of nature.

On the physical side, the performers asked emphatically that youngsters do not start specializing and pushing themselves whilst too young. Again a word to parents: let *them* choose when they want to push themselves and try something new. As parents we have the role of providing opportunity and support.

Once growth is completed and the body and mind are ready for intense work, that is what is required. Sorry folks! in the pursuit of excellence, there is no substitute for hard work, in sport or any other area of endeavour. The process may be intense at times, but a consistent, step-by-step approach is what's needed. Needless to say, self-discipline is required.

Socially, support and encouragement are valuable to all performers; 'pushy' coaching turns people off.

A balanced life includes personal time, social or family time, recreation time (which might not be sport) and work time (which might be sport!). Too often, the last of these takes over the high achiever's life. Here is a special reminder. There's nothing wrong with striving for achievement, but at some point it will feel empty unless you hold it in conjunction with an understanding of a bigger whole picture. For me that was a belief that we are souls on a learning journey, finding and experiencing balance between the physical body and the spiritual eternal part of ourselves. My striving was to prove myself, and to fulfil my talent;

and the bigger context was that if I touched Olympic excellence I could share my experiences and beliefs with the next generation.

No one could have failed to recognize my belief that our conscious mind is the key to achievement. Our thoughts, whether conscious or unconscious, determine our action. So if our thoughts, emotions and will affect our actions, how do we harness them for achievement? A key element of thought is awareness – knowing what's going on, what's happening (now); knowing where and who we are (identity); knowing where we're going and what we really want (goal). If we can get a goal that interests and positively enthuses us, that emotion will enhance our performance towards that goal. How great is your enthusiasm for your goal? If it's not very high, you need to review your goal. Are there things getting in the way? What options do you have?

Finally you need to involve your will in choosing what to do, what you're willing to commit yourselves to doing. If man can achieve any-thing within the scope of his imagination *and* we are co-creators in life, then we all have awesome potential. We simply don't often dare to dream what we might achieve in our lives. Doubt is our greatest crippler. Do you dare to set yourself a challenge of personal excellence? Did you ask yourself that question just then or did you gloss over it? What limits do you *really* have, and what elements *are* under your control? What is your true potential? What do you really want to achieve? If you could wave a magic wand, what would you want to do or want to achieve? Are you willing to put more thought into that? The more you can sense what it would be like and the more clearly you can see the steps to your target, the more probable it will become. Can you commit yourself to going for excellence? If not you, who then? Why not you?

PERFORMERS'
MINI-BIOGRAPHICAL DETAILS

JONAH BARRINGTON (Squash)
1941   Born 29 April, Morwenstow, Cornwall
         Specialized: 23 years old
1966–68   British Amateur champion
1966, 1967   British Open winner
1969   Turned professional
1969–1972   British Open/World champion

BILLY BEAUMONT (Rugby Union – Lock forward)
1952   Born 9 March, Preston, Lancashire
         Specialized: 17 years old
1975–82   34 caps. Captained England 22 times
1980   Triple Crown, International Championship and Grand Slam win

VALERIY BORZOV (Athletics – Sprinter)
1949   Born 20 October, Lvov, Ukraine, USSR
         Specialized: 12 years old
1968   European Junior champion 100m & 200m
1969   European champion 100m
1971   European champion 100m & 200m
1972   Olympic champion 100m (10.14) & 200m (20.00)

IAN BOTHAM (Cricket – All-rounder)
1955   Born 24 November, Heswall, Cheshire
         Specialized: Never
1974   Started with Somerset (captain 1985)
1977   Began international career including 85 consecutive games for
         England up to 1984
1978   Best bowling figures 8–34 v Pakistan at Lord's
1980   Highest first-class innings 228 for Somerset v Gloucestershire

Record 1000 runs and 100 wickets in 21 Tests; 2000 runs and 200
    wickets in 42 Tests
1986 Reached 350 Test wickets

DAVID BRYANT (Bowls)
1931 Born 27 October, Bristol, Gloucestershire
    Specialized: 16 years old
1960–90 More than 20 British singles indoor and outdoor titles
1962 Started the first of his 6(!) winning Commonwealth Games
    appearances
1966 & 1980 Outdoor World champion
1978–85 5 International Masters titles
1979–81 Indoor World champion

BOBBY CHARLTON (Soccer – Inside forward)
1937 Born 11 October, Ashington, Northumberland
    Specialized: 15 years old
1956–75, 206 goals in 644 League appearances, 49 goals in 106 inter-
    nationals
1956–57, 1957–58 & 1966–67 League Championship with Manchester
    United
1963 FA Cup
1966 World Cup – British and European Footballer of the Year
1968 European Cup

SEBASTIAN COE (Athletics – Middle-distance)
1956 Born 29 September, London
    Specialized: 14 years old
1978 European 800m bronze
1980 Olympics 1500m champion & 800m silver
1982 European 800m silver
1984 Olympic 1500m champion & 800m silver
1986 European 800m champion
World records: 800m twice (best 1.41.72); 1000m (2.12.18); 1500m (3.32.1);
    mile three times (best 3.47.33)

STEVE CRAM (Athletics – Middle-distance)
1960 Born 14 October, Gateshead, Northumberland
      Specialized: 13 years old
1982 Commonwealth Games and European Championships, 1500m champion
1983 World 1500m champion
1984 Olympic 1500m silver
1986 Commonwealth games 800m & 1500m champion
1986 European 1500m champion & 800m silver
World records: 1500m (3.29.67); mile (3.46.31); 2000m (4.51.39)

LYNN DAVIES (Athletics – Long jump)
1942 Born 20 May, Nantymoel, Glamorgan
      Specialized: 18 years old
1964 Olympic champion
1966 Commonwealth Games and European champion
1970 Commonwealth Games champion
Jumped over 26ft (7.88m) on 67 occasions and improved UK record by nearly 2ft to 27ft (8.23m)

STEVE DAVIS (Snooker)
1957 Born 22 August, Plumstead, London
      Specialized: 16 years old
1980–90 6 times UK champion, 4 times World Singles champion, 5 times World Doubles champion and numerous Masters and other world-wide tournaments

DES DRUMMOND (Rugby League – Wing)
1958 Born 17 June, Westmorland, Jamaica
      Specialized: 16 years old
1976 Signed for Leigh
1980 International debut
1980 Scored two tries in the historic win (10–2) in New Zealand
1980–81, 1981–82 Truman's Young Player of the Year
1984–85 Touring team Australia, New Zealand, Papua New Guinea
1988 24th international cap, v France

STEFAN EDBERG (Tennis)

1966 Born 19 January, Dastervik, Sweden
   Specialized: 8 or 9 but has always done other sports as well.
1983 Won Junior Grand Slam
1986 Masters Doubles champion
1987 Australian Open Singles champion, Australian and US Open Doubles champion
1988 Wimbledon champion
1989 Masters champion
1990 Wimbledon champion; during year ranked number one in world

GARETH EDWARDS (Rugby Union – Scrum-half)

1947 Born 12 July, Gwaen-cae-Gurwen, Wales
   Specialized: 18 years old
1967 International debut
1969 Named captain of Wales
1969–72, 1975, 1976 & 1978 International Championship
1969, 1971 & 1976–78 Triple Crown
1976, 1978 Grand Slam
10 Test appearances for the British Lions
53 international appearances for Wales scoring 20 tries
   (a Welsh record)

HERB ELLIOT (Athletics – Middle-distance)

1938 Born 25 February, Perth, Western Australia
   Specialized: 18 years old
1954–1960 Unbeaten in 44 races over 1500m and mile
1958 Commonwealth Games 880yds and mile champion
   World records: 1500m (3.36.0); mile (3.54.5)
1960 Olympic Games champion in new world record of 3.35.6

CHRIS EVERT (Tennis)

1954 Born 21 December, Fort Lauderdale, Florida, USA
   Specialized: 9 years old
1974, 1976 & 1981 Wimbledon champion
1974, 1975 & 1980–82 Italian champion
1974, 1975, 1979, 1980, 1983, 1985 & 1986 French champion
1975–78, 1980 & 1982 US champion

1982 & 1984 Australian champion
Ranked world number one 1974–78, 1980 & 1981
A.P. Female Athlete of the Year 1974, 1975, 1977 & 1980

NICK FALDO (Golf)
1957 Born 18 July, Welwyn Garden City, Herts
      Specialized: 16 years old
1976 Turned pro
1977–90 Won 24 major titles
1977–Present Ryder Cup team (1985 & 1987 winner)
1978–Present Hennessy Cup team (1984 captain and winner)
1983 European Order of Merit – first
1985–Present Dunhill Cup team (1986 captain, 1987 winner)
1987 Spanish Open champion
1987, 1990 British Open champion
1988 US Open runner-up
1988, 1989 French Open champion
1989, 1990 US Masters champion
1989 BBC Sports Personality of Year; Sportswriters' Sportsman of the
      Year

DUNCAN GOODHEW (Swimming – 100m breaststroke)
1957 Born 27 May, London
      Specialized: 17 years old but diversified later
1976 Olympic Games 7th; New Olympic record in heats (65.00)
1978–80 British swimming team captain
1980 Olympic Games champion, World Invitational Masters
      champion; world best 110yds
1981 European Championships two-man bobsleigh team
1982 World Masters; five gold medals

LUCINDA GREEN (née Prior-Palmer) (Equestrian – Three-day
      eventing)
1953 Born 7 November, London
      Specialized: 18 years old
1971 European Junior Team champion
1973, 1976, 1977, 1979, 1983 & 1984 Badminton winner (each time on a
      different horse!); also runner-up in 1978 and 1980
1975 European Individual champion and Team silver

1977 European Individual and Team champion
1982 World Individual and Team champion
1984 Olympic team captain, Team silver

WAYNE GRETZKY (Ice hockey – Centre)
1961 Born 26 January, Brantford, Ontario, Canada
      Specialized: 14 years old
1978 Signed professional contract aged 17, joining Edmonton Oilers
1981–90 Selected for the All-Star first team
1981–82 National Hockey League record 92 goals in one season
1982–83 NHL record scoring in 51 consecutive games
1983, 1984 & 1988 Won the Stanley Cup with the Edmonton Oilers
1990 Became the only man in NHL history to score 2000 points
1991 Scored his 700th goal in less than 900 games
18th player in NHL history to reach 1000 points – achieved in five and a
      half years, average time of the others sixteen and a half years

DAVID HEMERY (Athletics – Hurdler)
1944 Born 18 July, Cirencester, Gloucestershire
      Specialized: 20 years old
1966 Commonwealth Games high hurdles champion
1968 US National Collegiate 400m hurdles champion
      Olympic 400m hurdles champion; world record (48.12)
      BBC and Sportswriters' Sportsman of the Year
1969 European Championships high hurdles silver
1970 Commonwealth Games and World Student Games high hurdles
      champion
1972 Olympic bronze 400m hurdles, 4×400m silver
      World best 300m hurdles (34.6)
1973, 1976 British Superstars winner
1983 Past Masters Superstars winner

STEPHEN HENDRY (Snooker)
1969 Born 13 January, Edinburgh
      Specialized: 13 years old
1984, 1985 Scottish Amateur champion
1986, 1987 & 1988 Scottish Professional champion
1986 World Doubles runner-up with Mike Hallett

1987 World Doubles champion with Mike Hallett
Australian Masters champion
1987, 1990 Rothman's Grand Prix champion
1988 British Open champion
New Zealand Masters champion
UK Championships runner-up
1989, 1990 UK champion and twelve other world ranking points championships
1990 European Open runner-up
World champion (youngest ever)
1990–91 Record 31 (as at 31.12.90) consecutive world ranking points match wins

GEOFF HUNT (Squash)
1947 Born 11 March, Melbourne, Victoria, Australia
Specialized: 12 years old
1967, 1968 & 1969 World Amateur champion
1976, 1977, 1979 & 1980 World Open champion
1981 Won his record 8th British Open title

SHANE INNES (née Gould) (Swimming – Freestyle)
1956 Born 25 October, Sydney, New South Wales, Australia
Specialized: 13 years old
1971 Shortly after 15th birthday Shane held every freestyle world record: 100m, 200m, 400m, 800m & 1500m
1972 Olympics 200m, 400m & 200m individual medley champion – setting new world records in each; 800m silver & 100m bronze

BARRY JOHN (Rugby Union – Fly-half)
1945 Born 6 January, Cefneithen, Glamorgan
Specialized: Never
1968 Two Lions tours of South Africa
1969, 1971 Triple Crown with Wales
1969–72 International Championship
1971 Tour to New Zealand – where he scored a record 180 points
25 international appearances for Wales, scoring 90 points

KIP KEINO (Athletics – Middle-distance)
1940 Born 17 January, Kipsamo, Kenya
Specialized: 16 years old
1962 Commonwealth Games 11th in 3 miles
1964 Olympic Games 5th in 5000m
1965 World record 3000m (7.39.6)
African champion
1966 Commonwealth Games 1 mile and 3 mile champion
1968 Olympic 1500m champion (Olympic record of 3.34.9)
1970 Commonwealth Games 1500m champion
1972 Olympic champion 3000m steeplechase

SEAN KERLY (Hockey – Centre-forward)
1960 Born 29 January, Tankerton, Kent
Specialized: 18 years old
1976 Schoolboy international U-16
1979 First Junior international U-21
1981 First England international v Poland
1983 First GB international v Spain
1984 Olympic Games bronze
1986 World Cup silver
1987 European silver
1988 Olympic Games gold
Scored 15 goals in the 14 Olympic matches in 1984 and 1988

BILLY JEAN KING (née Moffitt) (Tennis)
1943 Born 22 November, Long Beach, California, USA
Specialized: 11 years old
1966–73, 1975 Wimbledon Singles champion
1966, 1967 & 1969 South African champion
1967, 1971, 1972 & 1974 US champion
1968 Australian champion
1970 Italian champion
1971 German champion
1972 French champion
Record 20 Wimbledon singles and doubles titles

ROD LAVER (Tennis)
1938 Born 9 August, Langdale, Queensland, Australia
       Specialized: 16 years old
1956 US Junior champion
1960, 1962 & 1969 Australian Singles champion
1961, 1962, 1968 & 1969 Wimbledon Singles champion
1962, 1969 French Singles champion
1962, 1969 US Singles champion
1962–68 Played National Tennis League, helping to force tennis 'open'
       Only player to have twice won the Grand Slam – Wimbledon,
       Australian, French and US championships, all in the same year

GINNY (HOLGATE) LENG (Equestrian – Three-day eventing)
1955 Born 1 February, Malta
       Specialized: 16 years old
1973 European Junior Individual and Team champion
1975 Canadian Mini-Olympic champion
1981 European Team champion
1982 World Team champion
1983, 1984, 1985 & 1987 Burghley winner
1985, 1989 Badminton winner
1986 World Individual and Team champion
1987 European Individual and Team champion
1988 Olympic Games Individual bronze, Team silver
1989 European Individual and Team champion, Burghley
1990 World Team silver

CARL LEWIS (Athletics – Sprints and long jump)
1961 Born 1 July, Selma, Alabama, USA
       Specialized: 16 years old
1980 Pan Am Junior champion 100m & 200m
       Olympic place; US did not send team
1981–90 14 US TAC sprint & long jump championships titles
1981 20 indoor and outdoor sprint and long jump wins
1983 World champion 100m, long jump & 4×100m relay
1984 Olympic champion 100m, 200m, long jump & 4×100m relay
1987 Pan Am long jump champion

1988 Olympic champion long jump & 100m (after Ben Johnson was disqualified for taking anabolic steroids); 200m silver
1989 4×200m world record
Has been unbeaten in the long jump for over ten years in 64 major competitions. He has 52 jumps over 28ft (8.53m) and the world best sea level jump at 8.79m
World record 100m (9.92)

CLIVE LLOYD (Cricket – Batsman)
1944 Born 31 August, Georgetown, Guyana
Specialized: 13 years old
1963 International debut for Guyana
1968 Began career with Lancashire
1969 County cap
1969–85 Captained West Indies in 69 Tests
1974–75 Highest Test score, 242, for West Indies v India in Bombay
1975, 1979 World Cup winner
1977 Benefit year
1981–83 & 1986 Captained Lancashire

HEATHER MCKAY (née Blundell) (Squash, racketball and hockey)
1941 Born 31 July, Queanbeyan, New South Wales, Australia
Specialized: 18 years old
1960–73 Australian Squash champion
1961–73 New South Wales Squash champion
1962–77 British Open/World champion
1967 Named to All-Australian women's hockey team! ABC Sport Person of the Year
1976, 1979 World champion (separate tournamant established in 1976)
1979 US Amateur Racketball champion
1980, 1981 & 1984 US/World Professional Racketball champion
Between 1959 and 1979 she lost only twice at squash, once in 1960 and once in 1962!

EDWIN MOSES (Athletics – 400m hurdles)
1955 Born 31 August, Dayton, Ohio, USA
Specialized: 15 years old
1976 Olympic champion; new world record (47.64)

1977 World champion; world record 47.45 then 47.13
1979 World Cup winner
1980 Olympic team (US did not compete); world record 47.02
1981 World Cup winner
1983 World champion
1984 Olympic champion
1987 World champion
1988 Olympic bronze
Between August 1977 and June 1987, Ed went undefeated in 122 races,
    107 finals

JOHN NEWCOMBE (Tennis)
1944 Born 23 May, Sydney, New South Wales, Australia
    Specialized: 11 years old
1965, 1966, 1968–70 & 1974 Wimbledon Doubles champion
1965, 1967, 1971, 1973 & 1976 Australian Doubles champion
1967, 1969 & 1973 French Doubles champion
1967, 1970 & 1971 Wimbledon Singles champion
1967, 1971 & 1973 US Doubles champion
1968 German Singles champion
1969, 1973 US Singles champion
1969 Italian Singles champion
1973, 1975 Australian Singles champion

DR PAT O'CALLAGHAN (Athletics – Hammer)
1906 Born 24 January, Kanturk, County Cork, Ireland
    Specialized: 26 years old
1928 Olympic champion (51.39m)
1931 European record (56.06m)
1932 Olympic champion (53.92m)
1933 European record (56.95m)
1934 British AAA champion (51.44)
1937 World record (59.56m)

AL OERTER (Athletics – Discus)
1936 Born 19 September, Astoria, New York, USA
    Specialized: 16 years old
1954 Set an American high school record (56.14m)

1956   Olympic champion (56.36)
1957, 1959, 1960, 1962, 1964 & 1966   US National champion
1960   Olympic champion (59.18m)
1964   Olympic champion (61.00m)
1968   Olympic champion (64.78m)
1980   Aged 43, set a personal best 69.46m
Improved world record four times from 61.10m in 1962 to 62.94m in 1964

STEVE OVETT (Athletics – Middle-distance)
1955   Born 9 October, Brighton, Sussex
         Specialized: 16 years old
1971   English Schools Championships 400m bronze
1972   English Schools Championships 800m champion
1973   European Junior 800m champion
1974   European Championships 800m silver
1975   World Cup 800m champion
1977   World Cup 1500m champion
1978   European 1500m champion, 800m silver
1978   World record 2 miles (8.13.5)
1980   Olympic 800m champion, 1500m bronze
1980   World Cup winner 1500m
World records: 1500m three times (best 3.30.77); mile twice (best 3.48.40)

ARNOLD PALMER (Golf)
1929   Born 10 September, Latrobe, Pennsylvania, USA
         Specialized: 17 years old
1954   First major title – US Amateur
1955   Turned professional and won first tournament – Canadian Open
1955–73   61 US Tour wins
1958, 1960, 1962 & 1964   US Masters champion
1960   US Open champion
1961, 1962   British Open winner
1967   Individual World Cup winner
1970   Won the American Athlete of the Decade Award for his 7 'big
         four' wins, 19 overseas tour wins and 32 Ryder Cup matches
1980   Joined the Senior Tour; won Canadian PGA
1980, 1981   US PGA winner

RODNEY PATTISSON (Yachting)

1943 Born 5 August, Cambelltown, Scotland
    Specialized: 13 years old
1960 International Cadet champion
1968 Olympic champion and European champion (Flying Dutchman)
1969 World champion (Quarter-Ton and Flying Dutchman)
1970 European champion (Flying Dutchman)
1970 World champion (Soling and Flying Dutchman)
1971 World champion (Flying Dutchman)
1972 Olympic champion and European champion (Flying Dutchman)
1975 European champion (Flying Dutchman)
1976 World champion (Quarter-Ton); Olympic silver (Flying Dutchman)
1983 British America's Cup Challenge; co-skipper
1985 World champion (One-Ton)

LESTOR PIGGOTT (Jockey – Flat-racing)

1935 Born 5 November, Wantage, Berkshire
    Specialized: 12 years old
    Record 29 English Classic victories
1954, 1957, 1960, 1968, 1970, 1972, 1976, 1977 & 1983 Derby winner
1957, 1959, 1966, 1975, 1981 & 1984 Oaks winner
1957, 1968, 1970 & 1985 2000 Guineas winner
1960, 1961, 1967, 1968, 1970, 1971, 1972 & 1984 St Leger winner
1960, 1964–71, 1981 & 1982 Champion jockey
1970, 1981 1000 Guineas winner
1948–85 Rode an incredible 4349 winners
1990 Comeback aged 54 and the winning total extends!

MARY RAND (née Bignal) (Athletics – Long jump, hurdles and pentathlon)

1940 Born 10 February, Wells, Somerset
    Specialized: 17 years old
1957 National pentathlon champion
1958 Commonwealth Games, long jump silver
1960 Olympic Games 80m hurdles, 4th
1962 European Championships, long jump bronze (4 months after daughter born)

1963 World record 4×110yds relay
1964 Olympic champion, long jump – new world record (6.76m); pentathlon silver; 4×100m bronze
1966 Commonwealth Games champion

KEN READ (Skiing – Downhill)
1955 Born 6 November, Ann Arbor, Michigan, USA (but Canadian nationality)
     Specialized: 11 years old
1974–83 Represented Canada on World Cup tour
1975–80 Won 5 Canadian titles
1975 World Cup winner, Val d'Isère, France
1978 World Cup winner, Chamonix, France and Schladming, Austria
     Canadian combined champion – slalom, giant slalom and downhill
1980 World Cup winner, Kitzbuhel, Austria and Wengen, Switzerland

VIV RICHARDS (Cricket – Batsman)
1952 Born 7 March, St Johns, Antigua
     Specialized: 17 years old
1976 Most runs in a Test series, 829 (an average of 118.42) for West Indies v England
1976 Highest Test innings 291
1977 Cricketer of the Year
1985 In match for Somerset v Warwickshire, scored 322 in 294 minutes off 258 balls and just 133 scoring strokes, including 42 fours and 8 sixes
1985 Named captain of West Indies
1986 Passed 6000 runs in Test cricket
1986 Fastest ever Test century, off just 56 balls v England in West Indies
By the close of 1990 Viv had amassed a staggering total of 6501 runs and 118 wickets in Test cricket

BRYAN ROBSON (Soccer – midfield)
1957 Born 11 January, Chester-le-Street, Tyne and Wear
     Specialized: 15 years old
1975 Signed professionally for West Bromich Albion
1977 Third broken leg in 12-month period

1981   Record fee transfer (£1.5m) to Manchester United
1983, 1985 Captain of FA Cup winning side
1986   Led England team in World Cup finals in Mexico
1989   Won 75th cap for England
1990   Although injured and unable to play, again captained England's
       World Cup Squad

JOAN BENOIT SAMUELSON (Athletics – Marathon and
       long-distance)
1957   Born 16 May, Cape Elizabeth, Maine, USA
       Specialized: 17 years old
1983   Pan American Games champion 3000m
1984   Olympic champion, marathon
1985   Chicago marathon winner (personal record 2.21.21)
World best times on the roads: 10km – 31.37; 10 miles – 51.38; 25km – 1.25;
       half-marathon 1.08.23

PETER SCUDAMORE (Jockey – National Hunt)
1958   Born 13 June, Hereford
       Specialized: 12/13 years old (continued other sports)
1979   Rode first winner
1981–90 Six times champion jockey
1988–89 Record fastest 100 winners in a season
       Record fastest 200 winners in a season
       Record 221 winners in the season
       Became only 3rd jockey to ride 1000 winners
1989–90 Fastest 50 winners (15 days faster than 1988–89 record)

PETER SNELL (Athletics – Middle-distance)
1938   Born 17 December, Okunake, New Zealand
       Specialized: 19 years old
1960   Olympic champion 800m
1962   Commonwealth Games champion, 880yds and mile
1962   World records: 800m – 1.44.3; 880yds – 1.45.1; mile – 3.54.5
1964   Olympic champion 800m and 1500m

PETER STERLING (Rugby League – Scrum-half)

1960 Born 16 June, Toowoomba, Queensland, Australia
     Specialized: 17 years old
1978–91 Played for Parramatta Club
1981–83 Rugby League Grand Final champion
1982–88 Australian national side, considered one of world's best scrum-halves
1983–85 Played for Hull
1985 Silk Cut Challenge Cup final
1986 Vice-captain of Australian touring team

JACKIE STEWART (Motor-racing)

1939 Born 11 June, Dumbarton, Scotland
     Specialized: 23 years old
1965 Italian Grand Prix winner
1966 Monaco Grand Prix winner
1968 Dutch, German and US Grand Prix winner; runner-up World Driving Championship
1969 British, Dutch, French, Italian, Spanish and South African Grand Prix winner; World Driving champion
1970 Spanish Grand Prix winner
1971 British, Canadian, French, German, Monaco and Spanish Grand Prix winner; World Driving champion
1972 Argentinian, Canadian, French and US Grand Prix winner
1973 Belgian, Dutch, German, Monaco and South African Grand Prix winner; World Driving champion

DALEY THOMPSON (Athletics – Decathlon)

1958 Born 30 July, London
     Specialized: 16 years old
1977 European Junior champion – 8190 pts
1978 Commonwealth Games champion – 8467 pts
     European silver – 8289 pts
1980 Olympic champion – 8495 pts
     New world record – 8622 pts
1982 Commonwealth Games champion – 8410 pts
     New world record – 8702 pts
     European champion and new world record – 8743 pts

1983 World champion – 8666 pts
1984 Olympic champion and new world record – 8797 pts
1986 Commonwealth Games champion
1986 European champion

JAYNE TORVILL AND CHRISTOPHER DEAN (Skating – Ice dancing)

1957 Jayne born 7 October, Nottingham
1958 Chris born 27 July, Nottingham
      Specialized: 18 years old
1971 Torvill, British Pairs champion (with Mike Hutchinson)
1974 Dean, British Ice Dance champion (with Sandra Elson)
1976 Torvill and Dean, British Northern Ice Dance champions
1978–84 British Ice Dance champions
1981 World and European champions
1982 World and European champions
1983 World champions
1984 Olympic, World and European champions
1985 Embarked on professional career
1985–90 World Professional Ice Dance champions, 1984, 1985 and 1990

SIR JOHN WHITMORE (Motor-racing)

1937 Born 16 October, Orsett, Essex
      Specialized: 20 years old
1958 Started career with RAC International Rally
1959 Won more than half the races he entered
      Second in class at 24 hour Le Mans partnering future world champion Jim Clark
1961 Won British Saloon Car Championship
      Won a wide variety of sports car and racing car races
1963 Drove for the enormously successful Ford Works Team
1965 Won the European Saloon Car Racing Championships for Ford
      Ford Shelby Cobra Team won World GT championships
1966 Ford Team 7 litre GT 40's Le Mans 1st, 2nd and 3rd places
      Retired
1987–90 Comeback aged 50 – raced Ford Saloon and 8.4 litre CanAm McLaren sports cars with equal success. In the 12 races before retiring July 1990 he won 8, with 2 seconds, a third and one retirement

J.P.R. WILLIAMS (Rugby Union – Full-back; and tennis)

1949 Born 2 March, Cardiff, South Glamorgan
      Specialized: Never
1967 Junior Wimbledon champion
1969–81 Played international rugby for Wales
1969, 1971 & 1976–79 Triple Crown winners
1969–72, 1975, 1976, 1978 & 1979 International Championship winners
1971 British Lions tour of New Zealand, winners
1974 British Lions tour of South Africa, winners
1976 & 1978 Grand Slam winners
1978 & 1979 Captain Welsh side

PERFORMANCE COACHING FOR MANAGEMENT

Fitness in sport was seen as the paramount, if not the only, pre-condition for success. Technique could be learned and skill was assumed to be something that was God-given and simply enhanced. It is now generally accepted that the mind is important and thus on the agenda of sport.

Mental rehearsal and attitude training are now a norm at the top levels of most sports. Acts of mental preparation, seen as ridiculous a generation ago, have been given labels. They have been systematized and are being taught. It now seems that the world of business is waking up to the potential of mental training methods, with ever wider accept-ance on both sides of the Atlantic.

David Hemery's study of top performers resulted in a practical distillation of important factors that influence sporting performance. The results of these studies have been encapsulated in the concept now known as Performance Coaching which provides a coaching/management model of awareness development with a distinct edge over sole concentration on skill improvement.

If sport is a metaphor for life, then business can be viewed as the daily activity platform where most sport is undertaken. That is not to suggest that business is not serious, simply that all aspects of our ability to be personally successful and satisfied in our performance are a game ruled substantially by our ability to let our mind have more control over our own destiny.

The central messages of excellence in sport are focused around five key issues:
- Ownership of or responsibility for a goal.
- The level of self-awareness that can be achieved.
- The ability for concentration and focused attention one can bring to bear.
- Your own internal motivation to achieve goals.
- Your ability to be relaxed and minimize the stress.

The coach or, indeed, the manager's role is to create the best quality of relationship with performer or staff. This recognizes that coaches and managers as coaches should do less telling and more asking. Because we cannot be on the field of play or with each member of staff at all times during the events of sport or business, the responsibility is always in their hands.

The intellectual and practical union between David Hemery and his colleagues in sports coaching and The Grass Roots Group's approach to people improvement has resulted in an approach to management education which exhibits an enlightenment in important relationships. From boss and subordinate to coach, manager and performer may seem a giant leap. In truth the awareness of the potential is rapidly accepted by those put through the course work. Managers, most of whom have played some sport, can see the relevance of the metaphor and, more importantly, how much more effective they can be and thus more satisfied with their performance.

Performance Coaching, whether for sporting coach or a manager who should be a coach, helps solve problems, helps plan performance, helps review activity and goal progress but, most importantly, helps the total development of the individual's assets involved.

The Grass Roots Group's sponsorship extends to paying the sports coaches' room and board costs on the National Coaching Foundation monthly course 'A Question of Style' at Bisham Abbey as well as the luncheon and ceremonies for the regional and national sport 'Coach of the Year Awards'.

For further information on Performance Coaching, management training, consultancy, and motivational programmes offered by The Grass Roots Group, please contact the Training Division at 281 Glossop Road, Sheffield S10 2HB, (0742) 700321; FAX: (0742) 725123; or Head Office at Pennyroyal Court, Station Road, Tring, Herts HP23 5QZ, (0442) 891125; FAX: (044282) 5660.

INDEX

Index